D1616241

Juana Briones
OF NINETEENTH-CENTURY
CALIFORNIA

Juana Briones
OF NINETEENTH-CENTURY CALIFORNIA

Jeanne Farr McDonnell

THE UNIVERSITY OF ARIZONA PRESS
TUCSON

The University of Arizona Press
© 2008 The Arizona Board of Regents

www.uapress.arizona.edu

LIBRARY OF CONGRESS CATALOGING-IN-PUBLICATION DATA
McDonnell, Jeanne Farr, 1931–
  Juana Briones of nineteenth-century California /
Jeanne Farr McDonnell.
    p. cm.
  Includes bibliographical references and index.
  ISBN 978-0-8165-2586-7 (hardcover : alk. paper) —
  ISBN 978-0-8165-2587-4 (pbk. : alk. paper)
    1. Briones, Juana, 1802–1889. 2. Women pioneers—
California—Biography. 3. Pioneers—California—
Biography. 4. Hispanic American women—California—
Biography. 5. Hispanic Americans—California—
Biography. 6. Frontier and pioneer life—California.
7. California—Biography. 8. Santa Clara County
(Calif.)—Biography. 9. California—History—19th
century. I. Title.
F864.B76M38 2008
979.4′04092—dc22   [B]   2008018869

Publication of this book is made possible in part by
the proceeds of a permanent endowment created with
the assistance of a Challenge Grant from the National
Endowment for the Humanities, a federal agency.

Manufactured in the United States of America on acid-
free, archival-quality paper containing a minimum of 30%
post-consumer waste and processed chlorine free.

13 12 11 10 09 08   6 5 4 3 2 1

To my husband, Eugene Edward McDonnell

Contents

Illustrations

Acknowledgments

So many people have helped in so many ways over the twenty-plus years I have been connected to the Juana Briones story that I fear I will neglect to mention someone or will inadequately thank important people.

My interest in Juana Briones started with a newspaper article about Susan Berthiaume, now Susan Kirk, and how much she cared about the Juana Briones house, where she had lived for many years and which I had never heard of before that time. Later I would come to know Tom Hunt, who also had lived in, esteemed, and cherished the house.

I investigated the situation with the help of volunteers, a group that expanded in personnel and goals over the years to include Clark Akatiff, Kathy Akatiff, Suzanne Beaver, Diana Berghausen, Ralph Britton, Tony Cisneros, Penny Colman, Elizabeth Colton, Wilma Espinoza, Margaret Feuer, Mary Hansen, Corri Jimenez, Bob Knapp, Muriel Knapp, Ooga Loya, Edith Mayo, Rosemary Meyerott, Don Nielson, Freyda Ravitz, Gail Ravitz, Greg Smestad, Sally Wiatrolik, Gail Woolley, and others. Some were deeply involved, and some less so, but this crew managed in different ways to research the topic and teach others about it; arrange for tours of the house; promote its preservation; publicize, raise funds for, and obtain state recognition of Juana Briones and her house; and plan public functions. That Juana's house originally introduced all of us to her and subsequently to each other substantiates the case that preservationists make for retaining physical reminders of the past.

Archives always amaze me. If one category of person exists whom I almost certainly admire, it would be librarians and archivists. I will not list all those people and institutions from whom I received help because they know who they are, and there are few I missed in the entire San Francisco Bay Area. If a little town or a big one or a church or presidio is mentioned in this book, rest assured that I went to them or their representatives—such as Jeffrey Burns at the Archives of the Archdiocese of San Francisco in Menlo Park or Steve Staiger, in charge of the Palo Alto Historical Association's archives and a true activist in town history.

About ten years after my early forays into getting word out about the California of Juana's time and about Juana herself, the idea came to me to attempt to write her biography, but I doubted if an illiterate woman could have left behind enough information for a full-scale study of her life. At this time, I noticed Jacob Molyneux's class "Writing with a Sense of Place" at Stanford University's Continuing Education Department and decided that it might offer a potential approach because Juana lived in such fascinating places. She really knew how to pick out a piece of real estate.

After I wrote for that class, the project seemed worth trying, but at the time I had no idea that I would invest ten years in the research and writing. Without the Institute for Historical Study, I would have been lost. It is way too lonely to be an independent scholar without other independent scholars to provide companionship. The institute's biography writing group, all of whom share their own work and critique each others', made that sense of community even more immediate for me.

If I had one mentor who meant the most, that person would be Frances Richardson Keller, long a professor of history at San Francisco State University and now deceased. One mention seems incapable of explaining how much her friendship and belief in my work has meant. Frances served with me on the board of the Women's Heritage Museum and introduced me to the Institute for Historical Study. Her dedication to history strengthened mine. Another friend, Barbara Voss, understands the Briones family, generously shared her insights with me, and gave me more confidence because her approach, although archaeological in essence, agreed very much with my interpretation from a historical perspective. Stanford Professor Al Camarillo's belief in Juana's importance to history and his support for making her better known reinforced my own determination to fill in the gaps in the story of her life and times.

Los Californianos and especially Boyd de Larios gave me living proof of the continuity of history and the urgency of making sure that details of the past in which Juana starred harmonize with the society that owes much to her and her people. The members of the now-disbanded Juana Briones Heritage Foundation board of directors—among them Ruben Abrica, Melanie Cross, Tony Tucher, Halimah Van Tyle, and the now deceased Hans Wolf—have had a huge impact on me and the community with their commitment to making known the importance of the house Juana built in order to explain her life and the region.

I am especially indebted to Alan Kelsey Brown, whose wisdom about time and place in Santa Clara County and about the earliest explorers in the area is monumental; to Randy Milliken, who has gone where none went before to analyze Indian mission records of the Bay Area; to Palo Alto Stanford Heritage, an organization of Palo Alto preservationists; to the Western Association of Women Historians; to members of the history committee of the Palo Alto Women's Club; and to the California Historical Society for its long attention to preservation and education.

With an artist's eye and knowledge, Shannon Abbey negotiated the technical side of locating, gathering, and transmitting the illustrations herein in the best form possible. Her enthusiasm and interest enabled her to go far beyond the ordinary.

And then there is my supportive family and on a daily basis for years, in every way, my husband, Eugene McDonnell.

Juana Briones

OF NINETEENTH-CENTURY
CALIFORNIA

INTRODUCTION

History circles in recent years have taken issue with a version of U.S. history that puts California and the western coastal states in the appendix. Some are reminding themselves and others that European-style governments and the social network to back them up were in process in California right when people three thousand miles to the east were getting notions about their own prosperity and lifestyle. They are saying that the United States without the West Coast would be quite a different place and that it is time to examine more carefully what flowed from west to east, instead of the other way around.

Santa Clara County in northern California, where Juana Briones spent the second half of her life, has a larger population than Maine or New Hampshire, and county inhabitants are awakening to the subject of how they and the place where they live got to be the way they are. Several historians have mentioned that Juan Bautista de Anza should be high on the list of readily recognized people of national importance, along with men such as Lewis and Clark or Paul Revere.

Stanford University now has the Bill Lane Center for the Study of the North American West. Santa Clara University calls its vibrant research and publishing program the California Studies Initiative. Several newspapers run weekly history columns about people, places, and things in local towns and counties. In 2007, Santa Clara County moved its original records into a spacious building where researchers can finally examine paper accounts instead of microfilm. In the Palo Alto that did not yet exist as a town during Juana's lifetime, parts of her ranch house remain intact despite efforts to put the land to other use.

This atmosphere and other little-heralded moments of research—

finding a little book in a small-town library or history center or used book-store—have contributed threads to the whole fabric of this book.

A distant influence on my method of composition was a class about early Greek philosophers that I took as an undergraduate at Ohio State University. Our professor often brought in current-event articles from the daily press that significantly illuminated our study's relevance to modern times. That lesson—what the present tells us of the past—has stayed with me. I use it in several ways, but especially in my chapter sequence. I begin and end in the same place, the place where Juana Briones died. Those first and last chapters show that "now" and "then" are less separate than we often believe and that current remnants give immediacy to long ago events. On founding expeditions, Juana's ancestors passed through the place where she died, connecting a time before she was born with her last years.

When my biography was two-thirds or so completed, I read another biography that felt to me like an encouraging pat on the back. Stephen Greenblatt, author of *Will in the World,* although admitting that little actual, archival information exists about Shakespeare, uses events in the plays and poetry as a magnifying glass that strengthens other hints from records about the lives of Shakespeare and his people. I felt I had Green-blatt's approval for amplifying small clues to Juana's life with the deep knowledge I had gained about her personality from her achievements, surrounding conditions, and other lives connected to hers, such as that of her father. That he, who died when she was in her midforties, was one of a small number of soldiers recognized for bringing perfectionism to their careers, reinforces clues that Juana either learned or inherited from him the propensity to let no detail escape careful attention in the pursuit of one's occupation.

Juana's environment of people, terrain, and custom gave me handles to elaborate on her experience. For example, I have no letters or journals about Juana's actual journey after her mother died and her father moved the family from Santa Cruz to San Francisco. I do know the difficulties at the time, the resources available to them, and some details of a similar trip by another girl who was about Juana's age when she traveled even farther with her father to the same place. Juana and this young woman, Mariana Martínez de Richardson, became neighbors for many years. I enjoy visual-izing their laughing together about the number of times they fell from their horses or the near impossibility of getting across a particular stream and then staying wet for days, or their recalling the story of the time when the Murphys snatched to safety their infant who had fallen into the Yuba River.

I was well into the writing before I realized that two related topics needed to be explained separate from a chronological sequence: the native peoples and medicine. Indians were the majority population in California during the first half of Juana's life. She learned much of her medical skill from them and bought her ranch from them, both defining features of her life. She lived for forty years on the ranch, and her occupation and fame as a healer lasted throughout her mature years.

I deviated from chronology by inserting two chapters on these subjects in a period of disconnect for Juana. For about half her life, she lived in a town environment, close to her church and her people. In the second half of her life, she was a rancher, a landowner, and, within a short time, a citizen of the United States instead of Mexico. She and her compatriots had to operate within a new system, a new language, and a new social hierarchy.

The legal profession also entered this world, a profession that her people had previously barely conceptualized. Lawyers rather rapidly became pivotal, involving themselves in situations where one might either gain and enjoy wealth or learn the meaning of destitution. Globalization similarly entered Juana's world, not as the word that had not been invented yet, but in daily reality. People pouring in from nearly every place in the world ripped up small-town familiarity and left it in tatters.

I trust it is not too much to say that hardly anything is shallow for historians. I look out my window as I work and think about streets made of asphalt and about English ivy growing under imported trees in a place where Indians once harvested food that grew naturally. I marvel at living one block away from a high school that resembles a college campus and another block away from one of the world's great universities. I find connections between them and the person with little or no formal education who has become my friend, Juana Briones.

People have described Juana as "astute." I find her culturally compatible with my life, surrounded as I am by places of learning. She learned to play the hand she was dealt and even subtly to change the prevailing rules, or at least to bend them slightly. I found her life worth knowing.

Part One

SPAIN, 1769

One

STROLLING THROUGH MAYFIELD

Reminders of the First Pioneers

By looking around Mayfield, California, the place where Juana de la Trinidad Briones y Tapia de Miranda lived her last years and died, one can assemble a framework for her life story. Reminders persist about her, her parents, her children, her grandchildren, and the unique circumstances of her era in the region.

Unlike most women of her time, Juana has received frequent mention in early scholarly books, journals, memoirs, reminiscences, oral histories, legal documents, and newspaper articles, although never in Mayfield's press, which was published only briefly before and after she lived there. Reporters found her descendants newsworthy, though, in part because of her and in part because they were interesting in their own right, having inherited her pragmatic dignity and persistence.[1]

Juana still makes her way prominently into print, exhibitions, place-names, dedicatory plaques, public educational programs, and controversy because of her many achievements, her 160-year-old ranch house in Palo Alto, the various fine lands she owned in the San Francisco Bay Area, and her deep connections to her contemporaries, to issues past and present, and to history.

Juana learned hardiness from her parents, for whom luxury sometimes meant having needle and thread to repair their ragged clothing and enough food to stay alive. Her children helped her prosper by participating in family enterprises, and they benefited in myriad ways from her wisdom and good sense. She negotiated with acuity the drastic changes of people and environment that occurred from her birth in 1802 on the western, ocean side of the coast range to her death in 1889 on the eastern, bay side. In today's geographic terminology, she was born in Santa Cruz and died in Palo Alto.

Explaining Juana's full name fills in some of her background and that of her people in eighteenth- and nineteenth-century California. Juana's maternal grandfather was Felipe (Phelipe) Santiago Tapia, and her mother was Ysadora (Ysidora, Isadora, Isidora) Tapia, so "y Tapia" was included in Juana's name. Her first name may have been given to her in honor of Ysadora's mother and stepmother. Juana Filomena Hernández, Felipe's first wife and Ysadora's mother, died in New Spain (Mexico) before he journeyed to California. He then married Juana Cárdenas, who came to California with him and his nine children. Felipe and Juana Cárdenas increased the family by five more children after they moved to San José, the first California pueblo, along with its other founders.[2]

In Juana's name, "de la Trinidad" refers to the trinity in Catholic theology—the Father, the Son, and the Holy Ghost. Religion formed a firm, enduring stanchion for Juana's people. Saints or points of dogma underlay both place-names and the names that appear in the thousands of baptism, marriage, and death records that the Catholic Church has respectfully preserved.

In the custom of her people, Juana always called herself by her father's family name, Briones, passed down by Vicente Briones, her paternal grandfather, and Marcos Briones, her father. One Spanish listing for Vicente gives his last name as "Vriones," a mix-up that occasionally happened because B and V sounded similar. Anglos also often spelled "Briones" as their English-attuned ears heard it. One memoirist refers to Juana as "Madam Barona," and in a land grant case the name was spelled "Bryones," which at least came closer to the actual pronunciation.[3]

Juana married Apolinario Miranda, so "de Miranda" was added to her name in accordance with Hispanic custom. Their children were officially named "Miranda y Briones," but were seldom called anything but "Miranda." Under U.S. law, which prevailed after 1850, Juana was sometimes called "Juana Miranda," as in some census records, and the name "Miranda Ranch" identified her land in several legal documents. In Hispanic usage, however, she was always "Juana Briones."

Juana's father, Marcos, and his father, Vicente, participated in the very first move by Spain into California through New Spain. None of Juana's relatives held top positions in the military, church, or government. California expedition leaders' names tend to stand in for all: Gaspar de Portolá for the first expedition, 1769–70, and Juan Bautista de Anza for the 1774–76 group of settlers he led into California. These two men connect in deeply significant ways to Juana's parents. Several current visual reference points to Portolá and Anza can be seen in Palo Alto, the town that now incorporates Mayfield, where Juana lived her last few years and where some of her descendants remained for several generations.

Portolá commanded the first brigade of Europeans to invade upper California, although the terms *brigade* and *invade* may make the expedition seem like an exclusively military venture. Most of the Portolá expeditionaries were indeed soldiers, with aides such as muleteers and packers. Spain's military investment in California in 1769 hinged on its competition with its European neighbors and on the perceived need to prevent Russia from extending its reach southward from Alaska. The Spanish government's sponsorship, however, mingled with religious goals. Franciscan priests aimed to convert California Indians into good and responsible Spanish Catholic subjects, and for the government's purposes they would thus peacefully extend the empire.

Franciscans' writings show that they saw this move into unexploited territory as a momentous opportunity to extend knowledge of the truth as they saw it and to save Indians' souls. Spain intended to conquer intellectually, spiritually, and economically, not by force of arms, but the Spanish colonists would nonetheless protect themselves, their belongings, and, as it turned out, the land they put to use on their own account. The overall policy succeeded only partially.[4]

The colonial project included creating a port on the west coast of mainland New Spain at San Blas to transport supplies and personnel to the capital of Baja (Lower) California, which partially outfitted the overland expedition headed by Governor Portolá. As the troops traveled north, they also requisitioned materials from the Jesuit missions of Baja California along the way. More supply ships departed from San Blas to meet the party at the two planned destinations, land adjoining San Diego and Monterey Bays. Before he returned to his home base at Loreto in Baja California, Portolá's objective was to set up a mission and a fort at each of those places in Alta (Upper) California. The mission would educate the Indians. The fort would protect the mission and warn other powers, especially the English and French, to stay away from Spanish territory.[5]

Not much of the region's geography was known at that time, but the name "California" had already been commonly used in the Cabrillo journals from 1542. Much of Spain's knowledge of the coast rested, somewhat incredibly, on favorable descriptions of harbors by the two prominent maritime explorers Juan Rodríguez Cabrillo at San Diego and Sebastian Vizcaino at Monterey sixty years later. Regular but distant sightings by sailors on the annual Manila galleons and the curiosity of such priests as Eusebio Francisco Kino, a Jesuit cartographer famous in Europe for his maps, were the basis of much of Spain's knowledge of and curiosity about the area.[6]

With this sketchy information to guide them, the Portolá party reached San Diego Bay, left a contingent there to found a church, and proceeded on to Monterey. When they failed to recognize the bay they sought, they continued north along the coast until sheer cliffs like a wall cut them off from that route. They then crossed over the mountains, viewed a large body of water that later came to be known as San Francisco Bay, and turned south on flatter land. When they came to San Francisquito Creek, now the northern boundary of Palo Alto, they rested for a time under a double-trunked redwood.

The chief diarist of Portolá's journey, Padre Juan Crespi, created names for hundreds of places along the way, usually honoring the saint commemorated by the date they camped at one spot or another. However, other than leaders, he did not record the names of his traveling companions, probably assuming that to be the task of the military or the government.[7] Experts thus differ on whether Vicente and Marcos Briones actually came with the overland party or followed by boat as part of the total operation. Vicente's death record of May 1813 at the Carmel Mission states, "Uno de los primeros conquistadores de esta Tierra desde el año de 1770" (One of the first conquerors of this land, here since the year 1770). His participation in the original endeavor is therefore certain, but in which of its segments is unclear. He may have come overland on the first or second trip with Portolá from San Diego to Monterey and stayed behind when Portolá returned to Baja California, or he may have been on the ship that soon transported Padre Junipero Serra and others to Monterey, where Serra became father-president of the California missions.[8]

From the time of his arrival in California to the end of his life, Vicente lived at missions, first as a corporal with mission guards, then as manager of the Carmel Mission ranch. Marcos and Guadalupe, his two children by Antonia Padrón, his first wife, appear in the San Luis Obispo Mission records of 1774, but there is no information about when or how they arrived because Indian attacks destroyed previous records of that mission.[9]

Many in the Portolá expedition stayed at San Diego, while others headed by sea toward Monterey Bay. Scurvy among the first arrivals by sea at San Diego had debilitated them so that they were unable to put down boats to row ashore, but other supply ships arrived, and by the time Serra set out by ship for Monterey from San Diego the prospects

El Palo Alto in 1875. This tree sheltered Portolá and his crew in 1769, Rivera in 1774, and in 1776 the Anza settlers as they traveled to found San Francisco Mission and Presidio.

had improved somewhat. It was at Monterey that Marcos Briones's life intersected with his future wife's and where he was stationed when the Anza party arrived, six years after the first Hispanic people put up the church and fort there.

For the first group that went ahead by land, success at one point appeared so dim that Portolá took a written vote of his officers on whether to proceed. Their incorrect calculations of latitude had caused them to fail to recognize Monterey. Engineer Miguel Costanso wrote in his journal that if they all died, they would nevertheless "have fulfilled [their] duty to God and man." Some later surmised that God had blinded them to the existence of Monterey Bay so that they would continue north, climb a hill on the peninsula, and be the first to record having seen San Francisco Bay.[10]

Portolá returned to San Diego—a supply ship did finally come there that essentially saved many lives—and he arranged for a smaller, faster group to make the trip again, correctly convinced that they had in fact reached Monterey and could do it again. On this second attempt, he left some personnel behind, including the first military governor of California Pedro Fages, at the first capital, Monterey.

The next phase of the founding of California moved in settlers, led by Juan Bautista de Anza. Their stated goal was to create another church and fort at the land adjacent to the entry to San Francisco Bay. The new governor, Fernando Rivera (1774–76), had checked out that land area later named "San Francisco," but believed the place to be unsuitable for occupation and himself to be too short of personnel and supplies. Anza, however, in his impatience and unwillingness to accept Rivera's view, went there himself and marked one place for the fort and another for the mission. Marcos Briones was one of the soldiers who accompanied Anza from Monterey to San Francisco. Instead of simply returning to Monterey, Anza and his escort extended their journey into the land east of San Francisco Bay, a daring exploration for Anza, who had shortly before been in such pain that he could barely walk. Perhaps being accompanied by young, curious men such as the nineteen-year-old Marcos energized him.[11]

Anza, a Spanish soldier of Basque ancestry, born in New Spain and stationed at Tubac in southern Arizona, had dreamed of establishing a land route to the five-year-old California province. Families signed on to go with him, lured by the possibility of improving their lives even by trekking to a potentially inhospitable and dangerous land. Some who took up his offer may have been persuaded because a devastating flood had left innumerable people homeless in Sinaloa, New Spain, where Anza recruited.

The promised recompense made the venture sound like a paying job: free transportation and expenses, rations for five years, and wages.[12]

Estimates of the number of participants in the party vary from 195 to 240. In the course of the trip from Tubac, one woman died giving birth to a healthy infant. Four other mothers lived, along with their newborn babes. Children twelve and younger composed more than half the company, a demographic that must have created a cheerful air of vulnerability as they crossed Indian lands. The Yuma—especially the women, described as excellent swimmers—carried supplies on their heads to assist the party in crossing the Colorado River. They would have extended this help graciously because a caravan swarming with children would have alarmed the local populace less than later groups that relied more on well-armed soldiers. After Yumas murdered Rivera and several of his soldiers at the crossing in 1781, the trail closed down until Anglo trappers began filtering across half a century later.[13]

The trials of the Anza settlers' journey were many and severe. The women and children suffered especially from the cold due to their thin clothing. One place in the Santa Clara Valley was called the Hills of Tears because the children cried from hunger there. Getting the people through alive was an achievement much to Anza's credit. He had made the trip in advance to study the trail before risking his company's lives in so dangerous and arduous an effort. But the penetrating cold, the lack of blankets and warm clothing, and the frequent lack of firewood must occasionally have inspired conversation among the pioneers about whether it was too late to turn back.[14] Historian Patricia Limerick writes that Anza should be, but is not, one of the heroes of American history because instead of bragging like Fremont and Custer, he had "an excess of good sense" and occupied himself more in succeeding in virtually all of his endeavors than in self-promotion.[15]

Both Juana's mother and her husband's mother, María de los Santos Gutiérrez, came as children with the Anza party, a distinction comparable to arriving on the *Mayflower*. Although Anza, with some of his soldiers and assistants, returned to Tubac, Arizona, those who stayed in California more than doubled the total Hispanic population there. Of the new arrivals, an estimated 197 traveled to the tip of the peninsula to found the place that developed into the Presidio of San Francisco and today's city. Descendants of Anza party members gather to honor that heritage every year on June 27 at the presidio.[16]

Juana Briones died more than a century after her mother and mother-in-law traversed the area with the Anza party on its way to settle San Francisco and after her husband's father arrived in the area by boat. Conditions in her time had improved so much that illness and death from starvation no longer figured into the region's problems.

On El Camino Real, roughly the north–south trail used in Spanish times, there are two National Park Service signs that designate the road as the Juan Bautista de Anza Trail. They are a short block away from the redwood tree, El Palo Alto, where Portolá is believed to have camped and rested before his party made their way south again toward San Diego. Leland Stanford named Palo Alto after that tree, the place where the faculty of his new university would live. Another tree across town reminds us of Juana more directly, however. In 1976, an ancient oak on Miranda Avenue, the street named for Juana and her children's ranch, became Palo Alto's Bicentennial Tree.[17] That the redwood, a very tall, thirsty tree, shares a habitat with the California live oak, a short, drought-tolerant tree, inspires thoughts of ecological symbolism about the wide range of peoples known to have inhabited the region for an estimated ten centuries.

Juana was living under the democratic U.S. government when she built her Mayfield house in 1884 about two blocks from El Camino Real. She may have been only vaguely aware of the road's geographic connection to her family. During her years there, people referred to what we now call El Camino as the San Francisco–San José Road or the County Road or Main Street in Mayfield. Even Palo Alto had not been founded by the time Juana died in 1889. Mayfield had the stores, the train station, and the community, and though that area has now been absorbed into Palo Alto, it retains something of its old personality, a congenial business street with small shops and housing nearby. Juana would not recognize it, though, even without the cars and the pavement.

Before moving into the bustling town of Mayfield, Juana had never lived far from cows, horses, chickens, pigs, sheep, a vegetable plot, a trellis for drying herbs and chilis, and an orchard near her kitchen. It was said of her that she loved ranching.

In the Mayfield of the 1880s, the sound of rumbling steam trains, clanging bells on oxen pulling timber to the mill, and clattering horse-drawn coaches on their twice-daily run between San Francisco and San José had replaced the neighing of horses, the barking of dogs, and the cawing of crows, although residents still had miniature farms around their houses, and they still got around on horseback or in horse-drawn buggies.[18]

The first travelers to the area had slept under the stars. Travelers during Juana's youth and young womanhood would get a night's lodging and a meal at ranches if they were lucky enough to find them along the route and someone was home. Juana's move to Mayfield put her down the street from James Otterson's stage stop, first constructed in 1856. Such accommodations protected travelers from the rain and bears, but did not specialize in comfort. One visitor said that Otterson's gave privacy to the eye but none to the ear.[19]

If Juana could walk in Mayfield now, she would notice the courthouse and imagine how convenient that institution would have been in handling her land dealings. On California Avenue, which was Lincoln Avenue in her day, she would marvel at how handy the fountain would be for doing laundry. Her eldest sibling, José Antonio, had probably told her about the beautiful, wondrous fountain in Santa Barbara, where he lived for a time. Lucky women did their washing there in sparkling fresh water that issued from a stone carving of a bear's head and spilled from one stone basin into the next. It would have been worth riding a horse for a week to see it, but Juana probably would not have abandoned her commitments to travel that far. She would have been satisfied with the pleasure of hearing the fountain described.[20]

Juana flourished in a time when oral communication predominated, when telling and listening passed on knowledge, taught about change and continuity, and helped attentive students of their surroundings to determine how to solve problems. She hired people to do her writing for her. Like her ancestors, she survived and even flourished without book learning.

Two

LIMITED CHOICES

Soldiers and Settlers at the Missions, Presidios, and Pueblos

When Spain ruled California, a political environment that endured until Juana was a young married woman, Hispanic people there had effectively three potential places to live, by choice or by assignment: a mission, a fort, or a small town where they could own a house and its lot and have tentative ownership of a farming plot and access to shared grazing land. None of the three provided ease or what we today would call comfort. The few ranches in southern California that resembled a large farm were theoretically owned by the king of Spain.

If hardship builds character, there must have been plenty of character to go around in Juana's family. Her parents and three of her grandparents simply went where none like them had gone before, and they created a habitat familiar enough for them to call it home. From virtually his first arrival in California, Juana's grandfather, Vicente Briones, lived at missions on assignment from his headquarters, the Monterey Presidio. He worked for ten years at Mission San Luis Obispo and several years at Mission San Antonio, both early, isolated links in what would become a chain of Spanish missions between San Francisco and San Diego. Anza described the isolation when he wrote that at San Luis "our reception was commensurate with the joy felt by people who spend years without seeing [any] other faces than the twelve or thirteen priests and soldiers of the mission . . . during their long and difficult exile from the world." Anza added that at the time they feared an Indian attack like the recent one at Mission San Diego. After years at such outposts, Vicente continued his mission service at Mission San Carlos Borromeo, commonly known as Carmel Mission, his last home and workplace. He worked as steward of the mission farm there for more than twenty years.[1]

In the founding decade, soldiers protected priests, maintained order, guarded mission and presidio premises and assets, and carried mission and presidio mail. They also helped build a life-maintenance system. With little help other than from occasional visiting workers and a few local Indians, soldiers had to put up primitive structures for churches, housing, and granaries, and fences for gardens, cattle, and horses. They built irrigation troughs, took care of the livestock, and planted fruit trees, vegetable gardens, and fields of beans, barley, and wheat. Soldiers and priests made up the original workforce. Women show up very early in mission records of those founding years, but with little information about how or when they came or in what capacity they participated in mission management.

The Indians who constructed fine churches, many still standing, gradually joined missions for various reasons, one of them being to acquire job skills. Historian Lisbeth Haas describes the way that Indians would learn the jobs and then take over in virtually every phase of the production of saddles, boots, shoes, cloth, and wine, as well as of farming, from shepherding to tending the orchards. But the Hispanic people trained them and for a time were overseers, so both the overseers and the Indians had ample opportunity to gain experience in a range of work that helped Juana and her family thereafter.

Juana's father, Marcos, lived at missions for at least twenty-five years, from his youth until he retired, with his longest assignments at Missions San Luis Obispo and San Antonio. Juana's eldest siblings, Vicente and Diego María, were born at San Luis Obispo and died in early childhood. One daughter was born at Soledad Mission and another at Mission San José, but among all his assignments, Marcos and his wife, Ysadora Tapia, lived longest at Mission San Antonio.

Ysadora gave birth to five of their children at Mission San Antonio. Besides their own growing family, other relatives at various times made up part of their community there, such as Marcos's sister, Guadalupe, a noted *curandera*, or healer; his father; and Ysadora's sister Antonia Tapia de Buelna.

Junípero Serra performed the wedding ceremony for Antonia Tapia and José Antonio Buelna. He had been recruited in 1774 in Sinaloa, New Spain, by Captain Fernando Rivera y Moncada for service in Monterey. Antonia had arrived with Anza. At age thirteen, she stayed in Monterey to marry Buelna instead of going on with other members of her family

Mission San Antonio de Padua southeast of Monterey, ca. 1884. Decay and the appropriation of materials caused the mission to deteriorate. It has since been restored.

to found the San Francisco presidio and mission. Generations of Buelnas would long live near Juana's family, such as Antonia's descendant Antonio Buelna, who owned a ranch a short distance from the one Juana purchased five years after he died in 1839. His ranch became the basis of Stanford University's land holdings, which were eventually contiguous with Juana's. George Gordon, a wealthy San Franciscan, bought the ranch from the Buelnas in 1863. The Stanfords bought it from Gordon's estate in 1870, the first acquisition of the eventual university property.[2]

Marcos, like many others of his countrymen, looked after and stayed near family. Many hints remain that Marcos was a responsible father and husband and a good soldier, traits that a mission environment would have encouraged. Two aspects of his surroundings must have left an imprint on his personality: idealistic priests who lived what they believed and the wisdom and ways of the Indians, the majority population.

At first, Indian assistance came in the form of the exchange of gifts

*An Indian grinding stone used for preparing food or
medicine at San Antonio Mission in 2002.*

instead of labor, so the personnel of the earliest contingent sponsored by Spain in California engaged in a staggering amount of work. Military governor Pedro Fages took over the secular side of the endeavor as soon as Portolá departed. He saw to the construction of a rudimentary presidio at Monterey, and Father Junipero Serra began modest structures for the nearby Carmel Mission.

While work was still in the early stages at Carmel Mission, Serra gave two missionaries a few supplies and his blessing, said good-bye, and went back over the hills, leaving them in 1771 to create San Antonio de Padua, the third California mission. The following year, Serra repeated this performance, heading for the Valley of the Bears, to situate what they called Mission San Luis Obispo de Tolosa. He took Padre José Cavaller there, who stayed until his death seventeen years later.

In addition to sharing membership in the Franciscan Order, many of the priests who came to staff the California missions shared a variant of Castilian Spanish as their native tongue. Serra and the two padres at Mission San Antonio, Miguel Pieras and Buenaventura Sitjar, were born on the island of Majorca and spoke Catalan, as did the founding padres of San Luis Obispo, José Cavaller and Domingo Juncosa.[3]

As corporal of the first guard at San Luis Obispo, Vicente Briones had the honor of becoming the godparent of its first Indian baptized, an infant. There were no Hispanic women to serve as godmothers for the earliest baptisms. María Antonia Padrón de Briones is always named in church records as Vicente's wife and the mother of his first two children, but the lack of any other mention of her suggests that she died either before he came to California or soon after.

Whatever benefits of the simple life close to nature—beautiful star-lit skies, rampant wildflowers—that can be imagined at San Luis Obispo, danger and difficulty also waited in the wings. At first, all the structures had roofs made of reeds. Three times in the first three years, Indians shot flaming arrows into them. Safety finally made it necessary to make roofs of tile, requiring a large workforce to manufacture them and sturdy walls to hold them up.

Concave tiles became standard at missions throughout California. Sixty years later, vandals often stole them from deserted missions. Because both San Antonio and San Luis Obispo missions have been credited with being first to utilize that building improvement, the Briones father and son must have had some hand in the decision to use them and perhaps in their production. A further achievement at San Antonio Mission, an elaborate system for irrigation that included twenty miles of paved trenches to carry river water, required complicated construction knowledge and diligent maintenance, and Marcos was certainly part of that effort.[4]

When Marcos was fourteen and his sister ten, Vicente married Mariana, an Indian, at San Luis Obispo. Only twenty-four colonists married Indian women in the first three decades of the invasion. Both children of that marriage died at the mission, one in infancy, the other at age eleven. While they lived, Marcos thus had two half-brothers born of his Indian stepmother.[5] Indian culture deeply imprinted the lives of Juana, her parents, and all the non-Indian people of her childhood and youth. Historical perspective sometimes pastes the label "Hispanic" on California of 1784. One day it would be, but that year when Marcos and Ysadora married and Father Serra died, an estimated 300,000 Indians lived in the area that we now call California and only about 970 persons from Spain and New Spain, an astonishing ratio, given the subsequent reversal. The U.S. census of 1900 put the total Indian population of California at 15,377 and non-Indian at 1,485,053, an embarrassing legacy for Anglo and Hispanic people, whatever the explanations for such a reversal might be.

Disease played a very significant role in the decline of the Indian population, but historian David Weber suggests an intriguing idea, that the disparity between Spanish and Indian capabilities in oceanic travel caused the cultural confrontation to occur on Indian soil, on the very space that provided their food, shelter, and a base for rearing children and participating in family and community life.[6]

That neither Vicente nor Marcos ever attempted to own land legally connects them to some aspects of Indian lifestyles. The pre-Contact economic system of coastal California Indians used no written documents to validate land claims. Indians based their geography on usage, family relationships, custom, trading partnerships, and ecology. Traditional understandings between tribes allowed for reciprocity in resource access, trade, safe passage across territory, marriage, joint gatherings, ceremonies, and legal settlements. James Sandos writes that in general the Indians of California regarded themselves less as individuals and more as part of the larger scheme of life. One can see an echo of the habit of sharing resources in some Hispanic ranchers' hospitable welcomes, which were so far beyond the ordinary that many Anglo visitors recorded details of the custom in their reminiscences.[7]

Reading and writing, though helpful, did not necessarily equate with mental acuity. Marcos signed with a cross, but the man considered the most learned Californio of Juana's generation, Mariano Vallejo, wrote that Marcos was "a very intelligent old man and founder."[8] Hispanics' rather loose definition of boundaries and frequent reliance on oral agreements mirrored Indian customs by which a rock or a tree marked a place that needed to be remembered. Indian boundaries defined communal, not personal land, although individuals in some tribes claimed plots within the tribal territory. Some Hispanic people's habit of throwing grass to the four winds to demarcate a border may have derived from Indian practice. Martina Castro's son-in-law, Thomas Fallon, said that Martina often repeated, eyes closed, in a rhythmic chant: "I walked on the land, pulled up grass, threw handfulls of earth, broke off branches, and cast stones to the four winds." Her right to a sizable land grant was owing to her being a descendant of one of the six retired soldiers who were founding citizens of Branciforte, including Juana's father.[9]

Indian children's education included information about tribal boundaries and their region's geology. Entire communities preserved and transmitted knowledge of admired and expected behavior, medicine, spiritual beliefs, facts, and skills. Teaching methods incorporated rhymes, lyrics, songs, stories, and performances. A certain oddly shaped rock might be featured in a story so that the child would never forget the limit of the tribe's land or a sacred site.[10]

The Salinan Indians of the region in which Mission San Antonio was located taught their children mutual dependency. For example, boys who showed aptitude for hunting learned that eating of their kill before sharing it with others would diminish their strength. This practice encouraged restraint and self-denial, fostered an ascetic strain that sustained them during periods of scarcity and attack, and reinforced the societal underpinning that group welfare took precedence over personal.[11]

Under Spain's mission-government collaboration, King Carlos III (1759–88) and his emissaries expected the land to return to Indian ownership once the Indians mastered the missionaries' teachings, a concept that W. W. Robinson describes as "one of the most idealistic adventures in colonization ever attempted." Spanish leaders never doubted the superiority of European civilization or the truths of the Catholic faith, but their benevolence failed in practice. Mainly because of discomfort with European law and custom, Indians generally never owned or managed for long on their own behalf the few parcels of mission land granted them.[12]

Before the Spanish invasion, Indians of the region harvested only what food they needed for a year and acquired little more than necessary personal items. An overabundance of belongings would encumber them when the settlement picked up and moved to another site, as they did depending on seasonal harvesting. Mission agricultural practices disrupted such customs. Missions stored crops in large granaries. Indians stored acorns, seeds, dried fish and meat, and herbs for medicine in or near their households, usually in baskets or other containers made by women. Many retained this same lifestyle even into the nineteenth century. Where Juana lived, Indians periodically burned their homes to destroy pests such as fleas, rebuilding them with the labor of a day or two or, some said, of hours. Collecting plant food, storing and preparing it, building houses, and caring for the children were women's jobs. Tenya, an Indian leader of the Yosemite Valley, said in 1851, when told that his people had to move: "My people do not want anything from the Great Father you tell me about. The Great Spirit is our father, and he has always supplied us with all we need. We do not want anything from white men. Our women are able to do our work. Go, then, let us remain in the mountains where we were born, where the ashes of our fathers have been given to the winds."[13]

Sweathouses and ceremonial buildings, an important feature of Indian life in the coastal region and San Francisco Bay Area, were bigger than residences. Every Franciscan had studied medicine, but Spanish medical practice did not include sweathouses. Some missionaries discouraged their use, but San Antonio Mission priests thought they promoted good health. At least in one location, women recovered from menstruation in sweathouses.[14]

The temperate climate made minimal housing and clothing sufficient. The Spaniards who first met the coastal Indians wrote that women wore skirts and the men went naked, but they did not wonder why there was this difference. The padres quickly introduced the concept of modesty, which they considered essential. A drawing made in 1806 portrayed male Indians in dance regalia and body paint wearing something resembling diapers. Many Indians welcomed cloth, but more for warmth than for reasons of shame. Plastering the body with mud to keep warm must have been unpleasant at best. In 1790, the military paid a blanket for one month of a male Indian's labor. When the Spaniards attempted to set up their first mission at San Diego, the Indians stole clothing and anything else made of cloth, considering their loot as payment for Spanish appropriation of resources.[15]

The workload at missions included weaving and sewing. At San Gabriel, Eulalia Pérez de Guillen cut out the clothes that Indian women sewed at a time when four thousand Indians were associated with that mission. San Juan Capistrano had forty weavers. At the present Vallejo Adobe at the state historic park in Petaluma, visitors can see looms where Indian women worked. Making cloth and garments was a challenging occupation, especially when so much else of daily life depended on local labor and production.[16]

Juana's parents came from very different childhood environments. At the same time that her father's family worked at missions, her mother's family worked with others to originate settlements, first the San Francisco presidio and mission and then the Pueblo of San José. Other settlers came early on, a few here and there, but the Anza recruits made up the largest single contingent of settlers. Others joined soldiers already in California or came as artisans with five-year contracts, or they came with Captain Fernando Rivera y Moncado in 1781, or, like Apolinario's father, they remained behind when their supply ship left California and returned to New Spain.

Spain's main goal, to keep other countries from colonizing the region, could have been thwarted. Four hundred men spread out over five hundred miles and based in the four presidios that were eventually established—San Diego, Santa Barbara, Monterey, and San Francisco—would have been hard-pressed to stave off an invasion. Contributing most fortunately to Spain's success in Alta California was the perception that more women and children would be needed to keep the enterprise going.[17]

In order to assess the need to protect San Francisco Bay, the brig *San*

Carlos with a crew of thirty under Spanish navy captain Juan Manuel de Ayala entered the bay with orders to chart, make soundings, investigate landing sites, test the Indians' attitudes, and advise whether the port lived up to the description of the scouting parties that first saw the bay from land. Ayala's survey advanced prospects for the proposed settlement and demonstrated that the bay under investigation was not the much lesser bay the Spanish knew of to the north that we now call Drake's Bay.[18]

Alejo Feliciano Miranda, the father of Juana's future husband, Apolinario, is thought to have been aboard the *San Carlos* when it arrived the second time, in 1776, to aid in creating the church, fort, and settlement by Padre Francisco Palou, José Joaquin Moraga, and Anza pioneers. In the brief period of California Hispanic settlement to that time, ships had been grotesquely unreliable, such as one that left New Spain for San Diego and was never heard of again. The winds drove the *San Carlos* so far south of Monterey on this particular trip for supplying and assisting the San Francisco settlers that the relatively minor journey took them two and a half months. The settlers must have greeted the ship and crew as their saviors, with joy and thanksgiving to God for the food, clothing, and the building and farming equipment that saved their lives.[19]

San Francisco eventually developed as the main port, but when the Anza settlers first arrived, the land itself appeared to be inhospitable. Spain believed it was necessary to guard the entrance to the bay, but as a potential place to live it probably dismayed the Anza settlers, who had suffered so long to find a new home. Sand made growing food problematic, fog chilled people ill clad for any weather, and steep hills discouraged foot traffic and planting. The settlers had little choice but to set to work doing their best, but some of them must have lain awake at night wondering what they had gotten themselves into.

One can sense the officials' near desperation at the time in their selection of place-names, which are virtually a prayer, begging saints and angels and God in heaven to protect and sustain the people. Church and government officials named the military installation the Presidio of San Francisco, the newly founded church nearby Mission San Francisco de Asís, commonly known as Mission Dolores, and the harbor San Francisco Bay. Franciscan fathers considered these tributes an appeal to their patron saint to bless this crucial endeavor.[20]

Spanish military engineers located presidios for strategic purposes, not comfort. Sites for towns and missions took the presence and proximity of water, wood, arable land, and pasture land into account, but the government expected soldiers to endure inconvenience and discomfort so their guns could be properly emplaced. Because soldiers' families had to be housed, the company rejected Anza's choice of site for the presidio and chose to place the military installation where it would be less subject to cold fog and closer to freshwater. Mission Dolores's hilly district inhibited the fog and wind somewhat, and the nearby stream, named Dolores for Our Lady of Sorrows, provided a water source, but the lack of wood and good farm land meant that this mission never ranked among the more prosperous.[21] All this preparation and construction put in place the infrastructure for a community where Juana would one day live for more than thirty years and be remembered to this day as a leading citizen, perhaps even the first citizen of the pueblo.

That Marcos with other soldiers escorted Anza from Monterey to the tip of the San Francisco Peninsula to identify mission and presidio sites meant that he was on duty in Monterey when the Anza party arrived and would have become acquainted with his future wife's family. Men who heretofore had few marriage prospects would have talked excitedly together about the potential brides they noticed among a group that more than doubled the Hispanic population of California.[22]

Juana's mother's earliest memories connected her to this place with few amenities, much adventure, and a situation in which the word *settler* was somewhat inappropriate. Even after their journey appeared to end at the San Francisco Presidio, the Tapia family moved on because Governor Felipe de Neve (1777–82) recognized the hazards of attempting to feed a growing population that could not feed itself.

The lack of money in California in this period diminished incentives to grow more than one needed. Government commissaries set their own prices, and the soldiers in the early days received meager pay, but regardless of human discomfort, Spain discouraged trade with other nations. Neve decided that civilians needed to live where they could grow their own food as well as extra to sell to the military for reasonable compensation. Sporadic supplies from New Spain often arrived in contemptible condition, infested with worms and rats.

The year after the Anza party's arrival, Neve moved to establish the San José Pueblo, California's first, founded November 29, 1777, because of its superior agricultural potential. Juana's maternal grandfather, Felipe Tapia, assisted the San Francisco Presidio *comandante*, José Joaquin Moraga, in measuring and assigning house lots and larger planting plots nearby for San José. Sixty-six persons came, the Tapia family among them, as evidenced by baptisms of their children at Mission Santa Clara and by the San José census of 1778, which lists Felipe Tapia, "mulatto"; his

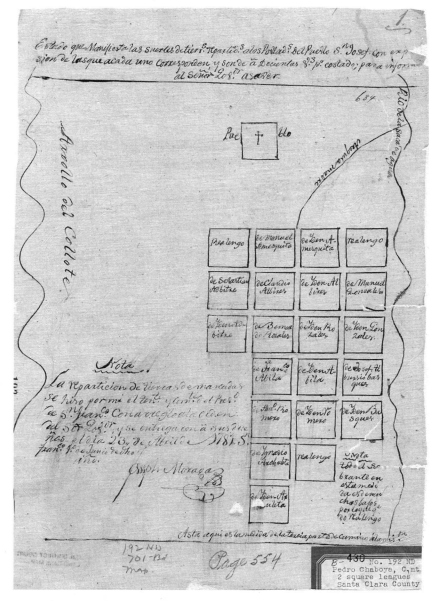

The Pueblo of San Jose had fields nearby called suertes. *Lieutenant José Moraga, assisted by Felipe Tapia, Juana's grandfather-to-be, allocated these farm plots in 1781, four years after the Pueblo was founded.*

wife, Juana Cárdenas, "mestizo;" and their nine children, including Juana's future mother, Ysadora (spelled Ygnasia in the census), age seven. If the census gives Ysadora's correct age, then it can be deduced that she married Marcos when she was thirteen.

The early history of the first pueblo is murky at best, and its precise location has never been exactly pinpointed. Juana's mother grew up knowing what it was like to go to a new place with others and to take the necessary steps to organize a community, build houses, and grow food, with the sanction of and some help from the government. The original settlers received animals, implements, and seed, which they would pay for eventually by delivering food to military warehouses.[23] Subsistence, not luxury, encouraged people to resettle. They expected dirt floors and improvised furniture. A story told as part of a practical joke indicates the primitive conditions in San José a generation after the Tapias moved there: a woman invited Governor Pablo Vicente de Sola (1814–22) to chat with her, offering him a whale bone as a chair because she had no other.[24]

When Ysadora married Marcos, she experienced life at a mission for the first time. San Antonio in particular had many ideal characteristics for a family, and Ysadora's whole life had entailed adapting to new environments. That quiet, little-populated place may have given a fine patina to a couple's life together, but Ysadora may well have found the isolation lonely after her life in the pueblo.

The San Antonio Mission locale has been called a "power spot." The wall-like mountains surrounding the mission's landscape direct the eye upward toward thoughts of the universe. At a distance from the present church, a huge white cross stands on the highest peak, named Santa Lucia by the Catholics, Sta Yokale by the Indians. The padres held the local Indians in high regard and set special store by Sta Yokale because an Indian shaman invoked its name in a medicine ceremony that effected a notable cure.[25]

One author attributes the success of this mission to Padre Buenaventura Sitjar's thirty-seven years there. He compiled one of the few Indian dictionaries and noted that the Salinan Indian language had thirty-four terms to describe various permutations of family relationships.[26]

Several of Juana's elder siblings were born at Mission San Antonio: José Antonio, Felipe Santiago, and María de Guadalupe. Two other sisters born there became part of the southern California branch of the family, Agatha Josefa and Agreda (Agueda). The unusual name "Agreda" was derived from Sister María de Agreda (1602–65), a nun and a close advisor of King Philip IV. Some California missions had a copy of her book

The Mystical City of God, which was published in several languages. After Agreda's death, her confessor revealed that she had several times described to him her out-of-body experience in being transported to New Mexico, where she had the great privilege of teaching the natives. When Father Miguel Pieras learned enough of the Hokan language group spoken by the Salinan Indians, he understood why the first Indian who presented herself for conversion did so. Her father and grandfather had told her that during their childhoods people who dressed like the Franciscans and taught like them had flown of their own power to her people. The rugged terrain and the wall of mountains that drop precipitously to the sea west of the plain where most of the Salinan Indians lived could have made it seem as if the first European arrivals had indeed flown there.

The assumption elated and invigorated the friars, who thought it entirely possible and even likely that Agreda had been transported not to New Mexico, but to their own spiritually sensitive place in California. It would have inspired the Briones-Tapia family as well to pray that their newborn daughter might respect and consequently receive the blessing of so wondrous a woman as her namesake.[27]

Besides its topographical separation from the rest of the world, another feature of the San Antonio Mission made it an enclave among enclaves for the Hispanic soldiers, their families, and the priests—the presence of people there with origins in Catalonia or the nearby island of Majorca. Spanish invaders of California were less homogeneous than they are often depicted. Besides their mingling with Indians and Africans in New Spain, the original invaders were a mixture of Basque, Visigoth, Roman, Greek, Jewish, and Moorish ancestry. Spanish was a second language for Basques and Catalans within Spain itself. Three Basques held prominent positions in California—Padre Fermín Francisco de Lasuen, the second president of the missions, and two Spanish governors, both of whom were recognized as notable administrators, Diego de Borica and Pablo Vicente de Sola. Another feature of Basque culture, that women had property rights unusual in Spain, had an impact on the California culture.

Padre Lasuen admitted to being hampered in his work by imperfections in his command of Spanish. At Mission San Juan Bautista, in the Monterey region, the Catalan priest Arroyo de la Cuesta said that his poor command of Spanish made it difficult for him to teach it to the Indians.[28] Historian Alan K. Brown notes the centrality of Catalans to the first exploration and early settlement of California. Portolá himself, Pedro Fages, who became better known later as the governor of Alta California (1770-74, 1782-91), and engineer-cartographer Miguel Costanso (Constanco) were

Catalans connected with either the overland or the oceanic segment of the Portolá expedition. Catalans also later planned and settled Branciforte, where Juana was born.[29]

According to Spanish law, top leaders in all endeavors were supposed to have been born in Spain, a requirement that became more difficult to meet over the years. In the early days of the occupation, soldiers tended to come from Catalonia on the mainland, and priests came from Majorca, the largest of the Balearic Islands. The Franciscans had been recruited among the farmers, the main occupation of that island, giving them a background of knowledge and experience that contributed to the spectacular agricultural success of some of the California missions. On Majorca, farmers spoke Catalan; wealthier islanders spoke Castilian.[30]

Basque was the first language of Governor Borica, who was central to the founding of Branciforte. He has been described as progressive, agreeable, and happy with his appointment to California, unlike many other governors over the years who felt themselves to have been exiled to a lowly, countrified settlement with too provincial a social life. The Basque Fermín de Lasuen became father-president of the missions the year Juana's parents married, replacing with a gentler, more courteous manner Serra's sometimes contentious attitude toward government officials and decrees.[31]

Juana's career as a successful farmer at San Francisco may have had a foundation in a childhood opportunity to become familiar with native languages, Spanish, Catalan, and possibly even Basque—a linguistic versatility that probably aided her in picking up English later on. And however much spoken language divided, the beautiful language of music unified. Indians came to missions because they were curious, saw an opportunity, or were adapting to change, but the gorgeous music of the churches also enticed them. Franciscans received music education as part of their training. Serra was said to have "come singing down the road of life . . . sacred song was one of his favorite ways of calming and cheering the hearts of others and his own." Some of the California missionaries excelled at music by any standards. Indians' musical aptitude fostered the belief that they all had natural ability.[32]

Indians had access to teachers and instruments at the missions. Among the instruments in use were three types of organs; string instruments including violins, guitars, violas, and bass; wind instruments such as piccolos, flutes, oboes, clarinets, trumpets, and horns; and for percussion, snare and bass drums and triangles. The Indians also made some of their own instruments, one of which, a two-hundred-year-old violin, was recently stolen from the San Antonio Mission museum. The padres used printed music, some in large format that could be read at a distance. The San Antonio museum has a wall painting of the palm of an outspread hand with numbered fingers, a diagram used to teach music.[33] Some Franciscans in California composed music, but most scores were brought from Spain and Mexico.

Indian musicians connected their people to the church. When their job as mission neophytes (new converts) was music, that became their primary occupation. High mass with full musical accompaniment was celebrated eighty-six days of the year, requiring daily practice and intense study. Indian musicians received more attention, wore special uniforms, had access to extra training in the Spanish language, and were on especially friendly terms with the priests.[34]

Padre Narciso Durán of Mission San José, one of the most accomplished musical directors, reported that he had an Indian ensemble of thirty singers, accompanied by an orchestra. For the ceremony in 1809 to dedicate the new church building, he assembled and instructed the choirs of two additional missions, Santa Clara and San Francisco, in what must have been a once-in-a-lifetime moment of glorious harmony.

I was once brought up short when I read a text written by Padre Durán in which he stated that "[i]n the mission, the singers and musicians are trained from boyhood." He did not need to explain that putting Indian girls in proximity with boys to learn music might lead to sinful sexual relations. He did not lament, as I did, the diminution of joy and opportunity for girls in such a situation of deprivation.[35]

Juana's friendliness to one and all and her social comfort with many cultures suggest that one of the great equalizers, music, would have been a part of life she enjoyed sharing with others. Perhaps she sang as she worked with her herbal medicines or as she tended her patients. Music long continued as an important part of the world around her.

Three

BORN AND BRED IN BRANCIFORTE

Retirement Benefits for Special Soldiers

Ysadora Tapia de Briones gave birth to her last four children at Branciforte: Juana first; then two brothers who died there in infancy, Sipio Antonio and Silvenio; and another child who stayed close to Juana all her life, Epiciaca (also given as "Coipciaca, Epicacia, Egypciaca, Egipsiaca"). Another close sibling, Gregorio, had been born in Monterey two years earlier than Juana. That the formative years of these three Briones offspring occurred in such an unusual place as Branciforte probably contributed to their close bonding even later, when they came to live farther away from each other—Gregorio across San Francisco Bay to the north at Bolinas and Epiciaca closer at San José. In their younger days, when they were marrying and having children, they often lived near each other.

Family alliances must have factored into assignments at missions and presidios. Gregorio, Juana, and Epiciaca's marriages took place at Mission Dolores. Many of their children were baptized there and at Mission Santa Clara during the same time periods. Epiciaca married a Soto, as did one of Juana's sons. One census listed Epiciaca, along with several of her children, at Juana's ranch. In his will, Gregorio left 3,000 acres to be divided among his children, the ranch house and oxen to his wife, and an acre of land to each of these two sisters. A letter written by Juana to Gregorio's son, Pablo Briones, suggests that Juana, in her role as healer, cared for Gregorio at Bolinas in his final illness.

Juana's grandson Tomás Dimas Mesa, in his eighties at the time, mistakenly told a newspaper reporter that Juana had been born in Monterey, a reasonable error because by then Branciforte had been forgotten by mapmakers and nearly everyone else but historians, and even they tended to belittle that town of minor importance. Monterey had the cachet of being Alta California's first capital and thus easier to brag about.[1] Perhaps Juana had slightly altered the truth to simplify the past for a child and to improve his self-esteem by letting him imagine her being born in a place he had heard of. Branciforte could easily be mistaken for Monterey, if not examined too closely. In the early days, both were the only towns on that part of the coast, had missions for neighbors, and had originated during California's Spanish period.

On March 12, 1802, Ysadora Tapia gave birth to a sickly infant. Two days later at Branciforte's church, nearby Santa Cruz Mission, the priest entered the child's given name in the baptismal registry, Juana de la Trinidad. In case her godmother Trinidad Vicenta de Leon's provisional baptism had been imperfect, he baptized the infant officially to ensure her entry into heaven. If a baby's health appeared at all chancy, people attending a birth often performed a lay baptism in case the baby died before a priest could be reached.

Some historians consider the Villa de Branciforte to have been a utopia. More call it a failure. The two pueblos Spain had previously originated in California, San José in 1777 and Los Angeles in 1781, were at sites chosen by Governor Felipe de Neve for their agricultural potential. Residents received land if they were going to put it to good use and provision was made for a local government. The townspeople had to handle most of the infrastructure work themselves, such as marking boundaries by planting trees, digging irrigation troughs, and constructing homes within five years.

By 1795, however, planners for the founding of Branciforte decided that the government owed good housing gratis to the intended residents, all of whom were men, most with families, as payment for past services. This stipulation occurred because it had been observed that at San José and Los Angeles many settlers still lived in huts made of tule reeds, similar to Indian housing. Unfortunately for the *invalidos*, retired soldiers— including Marcos, Juana's father, and the rest of that small, select group at Branciforte—the government never did construct the vaunted adobe houses with tile roofs and more space than most members of the society enjoyed. Juana may have been happy with what her family had in her early childhood, although it would have failed to meet her father's expectations. She knew little of anything else. Having spent the first ten years of her life in a wattle-and-daub house, she would one day create such a house using a similar but far more sophisticated method. The *encajonada*-style house she had built on the ranch she purchased in her mature years used mud enclosed within wooden walls.[2]

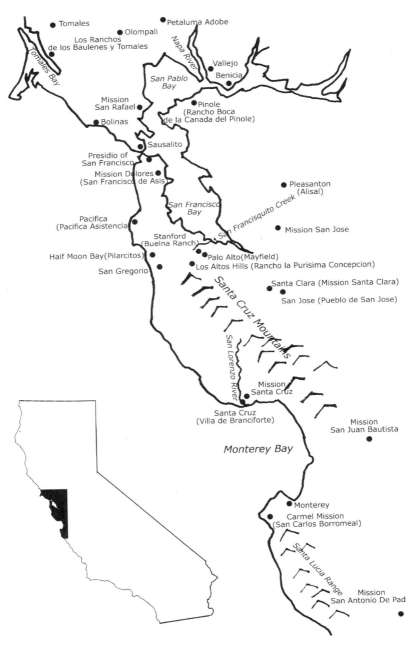

Juana's world. Only about 200 miles north to south and 60 miles east to west, eventually it was the home of people from nearly everywhere.

Newly arrived settlers recruited in New Spain mostly populated the Pueblo of Los Angeles, but the government offered pay and accommodations to artisans and their families to aid in making the Villa de Branciforte livable for long-time Californios. One family who came with that recruitment program included the child Candelario Miramontes, who later married Juana's sister Guadalupe and added another link in the chain of close family ties. Decades later, the Miramontes family founded a community now named Half Moon Bay north of Branciforte/Santa Cruz.[3]

In today's terms, the villa could be thought of as a retirement community for special soldiers such as Marcos Briones, who had by this time been a California soldier for at least twenty-five years. Designers called it a villa instead of a pueblo to emphasize the differences.

The government devised a protective, closely supervised atmosphere. Laws prohibited disruptive parties, late hours, excessive gambling and drinking, and concubinage. Priests had the task of reporting annually on the obligatory performance of citizens' duties: confession, communion, and church attendance. Because the Catalan Volunteers, the military group to which Marcos belonged, held themselves to the highest standards of military performance, hygiene, dress, behavior, and ethics, the government presumed that they would welcome such protective measures as surveillance and intervention in their private lives, and yet the philosophical underpinnings of their excellence was based on honor derived from self-reliance as opposed to authority imposed from upper ranks of society.[4]

It is no exaggeration to claim that the Catalan Volunteers deserve credit for the success of the first forays into California. That corps still had soldiers on active duty at the time of the founding of Branciforte, when twenty-five formed a detachment at the San Francisco Presidio. Their distinction shows in the Mission Dolores records, where the designation "Catalan" always appears beside their names. However, most corps members by then no longer came from Catalonia. As the original volunteers retired or died, locals such as Marcos Briones and other soldiers born in New Spain replaced them.[5]

Author Stephen Schwartz, who calls Branciforte a utopia, describes the Catalan Volunteers as following an intellectually based reaction against absolutism and a belief in individual achievement as opposed to imperialism of church and state. He defines their credo as one of "entrepreneurial energies."[6] The Catalan Volunteers' mantra of excellence entitled them to a better-than-average treatment partly in repayment for superb service and partly because they could be expected to be model citizens. According to officials, it would not be too much to ask them to compensate the government for its outlay in founding this community by policing the coast as reserve forces.

A heritage of such honor would leave its mark on these soldiers' children. By 1806, of the original six Catalan Volunteers for whom the government created Branciforte, only three remained with their families: Marcos, his brother-in-law José Antonio Rodríguez, and Joaquin Castro, who as a widower in his old age would one day marry a young Briones cousin, Rosalia. Castro and Rodríguez persisted at Branciforte longer than Marcos did and were rewarded with large land grants.[7]

Marcos would have known and learned from two men important to California, engineer Alberto de Córdoba and Lieutenant Colonel Pedro de Alberni. Born in Catalonia, Alberni was the highest-ranking military officer in California. He instigated the founding of Branciforte and had previously become legendary for his achievements at Nootka Sound on Vancouver Island.[8] When Alberni arrived at Nootka Sound, the soldiers there suffered from rampant scurvy, and the native peoples had little incentive to perpetuate the foreign presence by supplying food. When Alberni left the settlement two years later, friendliness between the Indians and the invaders prevailed. His kindly approach promoted friendship all around. He also achieved a cure for scurvy by devising a planting schedule for that unfamiliar climate and soil and handled the watering dilemma by putting his troops to work on wells and ditches. And, once again, music came to the rescue. Alberni composed a popular song that delighted both Spaniards and Indians.[9]

The kind of military discipline that saved soldiers' lives at Nootka Sound translated less happily for families at Branciforte, who took government intrusion with less aplomb. Alberni wrote to the governor, Diego de Borica, to say that workers would need to be brought from New Spain because Marcelino Bravo, Marcos Briones, Joaquin Castro, Juan Peralta, José Antonio Rodríguez, and Marcos Villela, the six men singled out to occupy Branciforte with their families, had accustomed themselves to erect military posture over many years of service and could not be expected suddenly to take up back-bending agricultural work. This letter gives us the only clue to Marcos's appearance other than his being called "mulatto" in the 1790 census.[10]

If Alberni spoke the truth about soldiers' way of life not preparing them for farming, Marcos may have been less of a farmer than his wife. Ysadora came from Sinaloa, along the western coast of mainland New Spain, where several rivers irrigated farmland. Marcos left his birthplace, the mountainous mining region of San Luis Potosí, at age seven, when he probably became familiar with military protocol by living where his father was stationed. Marcos must have become a soldier at a young age, like Alberni, who joined the service when he was twelve.[11]

Marcos was thirty-seven when he was targeted to be a settler at the new community of Branciforte. He may have been reluctant to move from Monterey, with the scenes of interest assured by the capital of Alta California, with the military headquarters of a large area that included the Santa Clara Valley, and with the comings-and-goings of a busy harbor, plus the companionship of his father, stepmother, other relatives, and longtime associates. Ysadora bore their eleventh child, Gregorio, at Monterey in 1800. Either she had not yet moved to Branciforte, or she remained in Monterey to be close to a midwife while Marcos went ahead to prepare a house and start their farming.

Governor Borica's efforts to make Branciforte an ideal community were more difficult that he had predicted. He was stunned at the poverty and discomfort of the workforce he had requested from New Spain. He wrote to the Marquis de Branciforte that settlers who had come in order to help build housing and install infrastructure at the villa arrived nearly naked and "some sick with syphilis." He said that those who were physically able were working at their occupations so they could purchase clothing and that he would be sending engineer Alberto de Córdoba to Branciforte as soon as Córdoba had completed his work at the Port of San Francisco.[12]

Córdoba, a military engineer temporarily assigned to California, had toured with Governor Borica to locate the Branciforte site. After rejecting two others, they remained for several weeks at Mission Santa Cruz, deliberately not telling the priest why they were there because missionaries often found civilian settlements near their churches to be a nuisance. The place Córdoba and Borica chose had trees, stone, and lime nearby that could be used for building. They neglected, however, to take into account the high banks of the San Lorenzo River and thus overestimated the potential for irrigation.[13]

Marcos's having known Alberni and Córdoba, both of whom were very familiar with the San Francisco Presidio and its area, and his marriage to a member of the Anza party would have given him a lingering sense of connection to that presidio, the place where he would one day reposition himself and his family.

Juana entered a society that totaled in all of Alta California about two thousand *gente de razón*, "thinking people," the term used in mission records to differentiate Hispanic people from Indians. Juana's advent would have been widely known. The addition of one at Branciforte made a noticeable difference in the local community's population of one hundred. Considerable danger surrounded a birth, so knowledge of the achievement, with mother and child doing well, would have been rapidly disseminated.[14]

In thinking about 1802, Juana's birth year, we may be excused for waxing metaphysical about that infant and about a political tsunami that would overwhelm her and her compatriots, which can be traced in some measure to President Thomas Jefferson. In 1802, in an offhand way that veiled the depth of his interest, Jefferson asked the Spanish minister in Washington, D.C., whether he thought his country might take offense if the United States sent some scientific, politically benign, exploring parties to the Missouri River. This vaguely worded antecedent of the Lewis and Clark expedition minimalized what actually happened two years later. The party traveled more than twice the length of the Missouri River. Yes, the minister had responded emphatically the year Juana was born, Spain would object, but, as we know, that did not stop Jefferson.[15]

Relations between the United States and California had improved when Spain, suffering from its war with England from 1796 to 1802, offered the United States access to Spanish markets worldwide. Spain had twin goals, to stimulate its economy and to buy neutrality from the United States. That young nation had established parity between its coinage and the peso, which, for Californians new to a business mentality, facilitated trade agreements.[16]

For the newborn Juana, such diplomatic comings and goings meant only that her community would one day gain from the expertise and viewpoint of American and European immigrants, many of whom, over the years before the Mexican-American War, had left their employment as sailors on whaling or merchant ships and had adopted somewhat the attitudes and even the language of the country.[17] Until 1812, when her life was rent by the lightning bolt of her mother's death, Juana lived among Hispanic people and Indians. The first recorded American settler, Cameron, alias John Gilroy, deserted his ship when Juana was twelve.

Marcos's absence from official correspondence except for three incidents in his years at Branciforte can be interpreted negatively—that he rarely held office, but then he could be described as a military, not a political, man. On the positive side, he stayed off lists of transgressors of the strict rules, which, besides monitoring personal behavior, did not permit such economic activity as killing or selling cattle without permission.[18]

One record can be interpreted to mean either that Marcos and others received stolen goods or that they believed what the Santa Cruz Mission manager, Francisco Morales, told them. He alleged to Marcos that the yoke of oxen he was giving Marcos had been received from the padres in payment for services. Morales explained to the authorities that he had stolen from the mission because he had no clothes. That accounted for the reason why he appropriated the oxen, but not why he gave them to Marcos. The oxen could have paid for any number of services, such as cooking or sewing done by Ysadora or someone in her household.[19]

Another item of official correspondence reveals intricacies of women's property rights. One list noted that in 1808 Marcos owned seventy cows, twenty-five mares, and three oxen, which put him roughly in the middle range of wealth in the community. In the previous year, his wife had complained to officials that he had sold land without her permission. By such a small clue, we can ascertain that she considered herself a partner in the ownership of family assets. It is significant that she felt confident enough to enter a legal plea and that she received a tentative reply agreeing that he should not have sold important family possessions without first telling her. Perhaps Juana inherited a bit of her mother's staunch sense of personal economic rights and received a life lesson she would later use to good effect: that she could ask government officials to intervene in disputes between husband and wife and that she should be minutely attentive to family finances.[20]

The family's assets in livestock increased reasonably well, considering the advantages that had been dangled before the Branciforte settlers: besides a house and a year's active-duty pay, they would acquire land, two mares, two cows, two sheep, two goats, a plough, a barrow, a hoe, and an axe. For their protection and militia duties, the men also were allotted a knife and a musket. The move to Branciforte thus put the family into a somewhat self-sufficient mode, even if they actually received less than had been promised.[21]

During 1812, a year of turmoil and devastation for the family, Marcos was a *comisionado,* a position that combined sheriff and civil administrator. His job description included encouraging rapport among citizens, assuring that all members of the town fulfilled their religious obligations and led virtuous lives, seeing to the accomplishment of public works by citizens and Indian employees, supervising the care and use of government-owned farm equipment, allocating water resources, overseeing the welfare of livestock, organizing the annual roundup, and reporting on everything to officials in Monterey.[22]

As overseer of livestock and protector of community assets, Marcos, along with his deputies, once moved mission sheep out of fields that residents claimed as their common lands. He explained to the Indian shepherd Maximo that if he took the sheep there again, he would pay with his life.

To make his point, Marcos and his crew burned Maximo's hut. When the padres complained about this action to José María Estudillo, *comandante* of the Presidio of Monterey, he responded like a soldier defending soldierly behavior. He wrote that he had found no record concerning whether that land had been allocated to the villa for grazing, but presumed that such a document must exist in the government archives in Mexico City. Of course, he did not need to mention that the process of notifying, locating, and replying from New Spain would in the best case take a year. Estudillo said that Marcos had asked him if he had records concerning whether the mission had permission to pasture sheep at yet another location, "to which I replied that I had not." As to the death threat, well, Estudillo said, let us not quibble over the "little whim" of Comisionado Briones.[23]

In 1812, Marcos moved with his children to the San Francisco Presidio, perhaps because of his excessive workload that year, but more probably because of the death of his wife at age forty-one, leaving Marcos with children at home, the eldest of whom was Luz, age sixteen.

Another crushing blow that year was the death of Padre Andres Quintana at Mission Santa Cruz, said to be of natural causes, although later his exhumed body supported the rumor that he had been murdered. A descendant of one of the alleged Indian murderers attributed the crime to Quintana's excessive cruelty. To discipline Indians, he had devised a whip with wire prongs that cut the flesh. A group decided they would no longer tolerate his abuse and killed him in a way that made his death seem natural.

He may also have been involved in a sexual relationship with an Indian woman. If Quintana in fact engaged in practices that the populace thought dishonored the priesthood and by extension their people, a negatively charged atmosphere could have contributed to a discomfort in the community that would have made departure a solution for Marcos.[24] Virtually everyone at the time, Indian, Hispanic, and Anglo alike, believed in omens, and the Briones family perhaps thought that, besides the deaths that deeply touched them, God was delivering a message through the earthquake of 1812. In the vicinity of Branciforte, where they were still living at the time, only buildings at Carmel Mission sustained damage, and the San Francisco Presidio was little touched, but most devastated of all was Mission San Juan Capistrano farther south. Forty people died there when one of the finest of the mission churches collapsed on them. Given the common belief that God sometimes took strong measures to punish or warn those who displeased him, many Californios must have gone to confession and said their prayers more fervently for a time.[25]

Whatever the reasons, Marcos gathered his family and left for the

San Francisco Presidio in 1812 or early 1813. Many retired soldiers, such as Juana's father and later her husband, preferred to make their homes at presidios, close to a lifestyle to which they had been accustomed since childhood. Had Marcos stayed in Branciforte, however, he might later, like Rodriguez and Castro, have acquired a large grant of land nearby.[26]

Mission Santa Cruz, founded as number twelve in the chain of twenty-one missions, never succeeded as grandly as some of the others. The Hispanic people there had only moderate experience in harvesting the mission's two main assets, marine and woodland products. Though Californios were surrounded by water, nearly all of them preferred horses to any other means of transportation. They played with a lasso on cats and dogs when they first learned to stand and began to ride horses almost as soon as they could walk. Boats remained beyond their purview. On one occasion in 1816, six soldiers refused to comply with an order to cross San Francisco Bay because they claimed that their military service in the infantry committed them only to foot or horse duty. William Thomes, a valuable source regarding Juana's dairy in San Francisco, says that at Santa Barbara no one owned a boat. The bay was full of fish, but Hispanic people ate it only when someone caught it for them.[27] One sailor who for three years starting at age fifteen cruised about California waterways to acquire hides and sell Boston merchandise, remarked that even the fine weather, "beautiful sheet of water in front of their homes," and a rich abundance of fish, crabs, oysters, and sea-otter furs did not tempt them into boats, of which they had none and wanted none. William Richardson, an early deserter from his ship in San Francisco Bay and thus one of the few experienced seamen in the area, hired Indian crews on his launches to distribute goods and collect hides and tallow around the bay.[28]

The community also neglected the other special Branciforte asset in the mountains, thousands of acres of *Sequoia sempervirens,* redwood, that they called *palo colorado.* The padres used the timber for support beams and preliminary structures. Historian Alan Brown observes that at Santa Cruz Mission (even as late as six years after the Briones family had departed), six men spent six days cutting out 25 twelve-foot planks. The lumber industry developed long after Juana's family had left Branciforte, but when she lived the second half of her life on the eastern side of the Santa Cruz mountains, she would hear and see logs being transported down trails to the bay, and she would use such lumber to build her home.[29]

The ten years that Juana lived in Branciforte set the tone for her life in terms of the people, mostly Indian, who composed her world. The hefty baptismal records of Mission Santa Cruz testify to the success of the ministry there. Indians of all ages were pouring into the mission from *rancherias* near and far. By 1801, the sequentially numbered neophyte baptisms reached one thousand. Ten years later, most Indian children baptized there had mission parents, although records do not keep track of whether all who were baptized stayed in that area. It has been suggested that Indians were less dependent on Santa Cruz Mission because of the abundant game in the mountains and fish in the bay, paired with a climate and soil less amenable to ranching than that in many other mission locales, where cattle and agriculture more drastically altered the ecology and deprived Indians of their usual wild food sources.[30]

For fifty years, until most Indians were virtually pushed out of the region, Indians lived in Juana's house or on her property—as patients, workers, family, and close associates. Some of the connections solidified by marriage included Mariana, Marcos's Indian stepmother for thirty-one years and in all probability the only mother he ever knew. This stepgrandmother died when Juana was four years old. One of Juana's Tapia uncles had a Nootka Indian wife. Marcelino Bravo, one of the six original soldier-settlers at Branciforte, married an Indian. From Juana's earliest childhood, Indians were an expected and normal part of her surroundings.

The egalitarian nature of Indian society, particularly in regard to women, could have been a model for Juana's later refusal to bow under patriarchal directives. Some Indian women held top leadership positions, a situation that many persons of European cultural derivation refused to recognize. The latter would select Indian men to deal with and would ignore women who acted like chiefs.[31]

The accomplished and influential Buelnas of Branciforte stayed part of Juana's life for many years. Joaquin Buelna, son of Juana's aunt Antonia Tapia de Buelna, was a poet, scholar, and teacher who established a primary school at Branciforte, one of the few schools in California. He at one time or another held most community offices. Historian Phil Reader says that Joaquin was "always a source of cohesion." In an era when few boys and fewer girls learned to read or write, Antonio Buelna taught "a select school for girls" in Monterey.[32]

Hispanic families taught their children socialization, religion, dancing, music, horsemanship, child care, cooking, agriculture, ranching, clothing manufacture, and all the work of daily life. Indians taught memory skills, ecology, hunting, harvesting natural land and water products, food storage and preparation, artifact manufacture, community, endurance, medicine, and spiritual values.[33]

In both cultures, children played games. Hispanic children rolled hoops, played blind man's bluff, rode hobby horses, played with dolls and cards, and pitched or skipped stones. Young Indian children played all day and, like the adults, did not have regular meals, but ate at any time. They swam, played a kind of tetherball and hide-and-seek, had small bows and arrows, threw javelins, played ring-around-the-rosie, and made their own bean shooters and slingshots. Indian girls sometimes had speed contests in basket making.[34]

Memory training featured prominently in Indian education. During the time of first contact, Indians would often surprise Hispanic people by giving information about recent events at a distance from their homes, a feat accomplished by specialists in memory and distance running. These specialists maintained their endurance with particular diets and exercise, practiced meticulous retention of exact messages, and were expected to be available when needed. Close contact with Indians during the first ten years of her life gave Juana an understanding of the advantages of an oral culture. In such a culture, one's word intertwined with one's honor.[35]

Spanish women cooked; managed the poultry yard, the orchard, and the vegetable garden; milked the cows and made cheese; sewed almost every item of clothing worn by their family members and others; and did innumerable other tasks that kept the family nourished and healthy. A girl child began her education in child rearing as soon as she was able to hold an infant and perhaps even before then, when she could entertain or distract a baby.

During Juana's youth, a few women—such as Apolinaria Lorenzana, Concepción Arguello, and Eulalia Pérez—taught reading and writing. Mission priests were directed to cease giving Spanish-language training to Indian girls after age ten, although boys could continue longer. When Juana's family left Branciforte for the Presidio of San Francisco in 1812, they went to an environment minimally conducive to formal schooling. In 1794, none of the soldiers in the ranks at San Francisco could write, and that situation was slow to improve.[36]

Juana's childhood at Branciforte prepared her for challenges to come. Her much older brother Felipe was already at the Presidio of San Francisco, father of a growing family that would some years later establish itself on the eastern shore of San Pablo Bay. Twelve-year-old Gregorio joined the San Francisco presidial military force and probably lived with his father. Marcos moved to a small, sheltered valley, less exposed to the elements than most sites on an otherwise cold, windy, foggy tip of a peninsula. His new home was right next to a fine water source, a place called Polin Spring.

Four

HEADING NORTH

A New Briones Home at the San Francisco Presidio

Many Spanish government regulations quickly became outdated or slept in files without affecting lives. Governor Diego de Borica had decreed in 1797 that retired soldiers must live at San José, Los Angeles, or Branciforte, but that anyone who chose to live at a presidio would be required to perform guard duty and, in any case, could be called to serve in emergencies. That decree most likely had been forgotten by the time Marcos moved to presidial San Francisco. Marcos might have taken on military duties, or he may have considered that distance and difficulty of travel made the governor's decrees less enforceable. Whether or not he performed any military functions there, certainly they were not a major focus of his life at that time.[1]

Had it not been for discomforting issues, such as arguments between the Santa Cruz Mission and the government that involved Marcos Briones as a representative of the government in 1812, Monterey would have been a more likely choice of residence if Marcos wanted to leave Branciforte. He might well have preferred to distance himself from arguments of that kind. The Monterey Presidio had been his headquarters throughout his career. Even when he lived at missions, his real home for most of his life was Monterey. His feelings in 1812, however, may have made the remote and relatively inaccessible San Francisco Presidio more attractive precisely because of its disconnect from the capital.

There was the undoubtedly irritating fact that the government had not lived up to its promises at Branciforte, particularly in regard to housing. San Francisco had the potential of giving him more control of his life, and he may have had information that ingenuity and hard work could provide better, sturdier housing for his family. As skimpy as pay and supplies had always been up to that time, after 1810 California soldiers received not another peso from Spain. In 1814, Governor José Joaquin Arrillaga— who was appointed in 1804, arrived in 1806, and served until his death in 1814—asked missions for donations to help alleviate soldiers' suffering. Such a situation could have offended Marcos. As one of only six retired Catalan Volunteers, he had been singled out for special privileges, and now scarcity extended even to the basic essentials, food and clothing.[2]

The San Francisco Presidio had the same shortage of supplies and salaries, but its distance from the governor and his cohorts could have been a positive feature. Doing business with foreign vessels and the settlement Russians founded in 1812 on the Sonoma coast, though discouraged by Spain, nevertheless offered a frontier survival mechanism. Government-imposed economic constraints grossly ignored everyday needs. Historian Robert Archibald traces some of the problems to an outmoded autocratic system that dictated every detail of personal life. Any error, oversight, shipwreck, or delay could affect not only well-being, but survival. In the first years of colonization, the late arrival of supply ships nearly caused the founding of Alta California to be aborted. At San Francisco, soldiers and citizens must have felt justified in stretching the rules against smuggling.[3]

An earlier encounter between Indians and representatives of the Spanish government, most of them born in New Spain, conveys a sense of the San Francisco Presidio's isolation as the Spanish Crown's north-ernmost outpost. Cattle and horses first entered Alta California in 1769. Long before this introduction into California, Spanish horses had gone feral and moved onto the plains east of the Sierra Nevada Mountains, but San Francisco Bay and the great rivers that empty into it had kept horses and cattle from spreading farther north. A full generation after the initial settlement of California, when no Hispanic people had yet gone to live north of San Francisco Bay, Indians on the north coast courteously asked a group of Spanish explorers to delay their departure by one day because their neighbors, hearing of the stunning spectacle, were in transit in hopes of getting their first look at horses.[4] The ocean and its rugged coastline, the nearly impassable Sierra Nevada Mountains, the desert to the south, and the rugged northern mountains made California in effect an island, cut off in great measure from ecological and environmental change beyond.[5]

Whatever the downside of homesteading at the San Francisco Presidio may have been, Marcos had already had every opportunity at Monterey and Branciforte to be friends with Lieutenant Colonel Pedro de Alberni and engineer Alberto de Córdoba and to learn from them about potential housing. Córdoba was said to have worked "tirelessly" for three years at the San Francisco and Monterey presidios and at the Pueblo of San José, but most devotedly at Branciforte, where he drew up plans for irrigation, fields, water supply, and lime kilns, and oversaw the acquisition of building materials and the construction of temporary housing, all a learning opportunity for Marcos.

Córdoba felt uncomfortable about government officials' insistence that he design the San Francisco Presidio in a static mode. He preferred to plan for mobility but had to follow instructions. Marcos, very much a man on a horse, would have agreed with him. As one of a tiny population at Branciforte, he and the others ignored the designated plan to arrange houses in a rectangle around a plaza, like a fort, with doors facing in, and narrow entry roads to the plaza at the corners. Instead, they created a Branciforte more like an Indian village, with room to stretch. The homes were close to each other, but did not share walls on both sides.[6]

Alberni, legendary innovator at Nootka, leader in founding Branciforte, and head of the San Francisco Presidio military for five years, had the distinction of taking over as commander-in-chief of the Catalan Volunteers when Agustín Callis, the troupe's founder, died in 1782, two years before Juana's parents married.

Alberni had brought twenty-five Catalan Volunteers to assist at San Francisco. He moved to Monterey in 1801, where Marcos would have had many opportunities to know him and Córdoba, both of whom harbored a deep sense of camaraderie with any Catalan Volunteer and had worked passionately to rebuild and reenergize the San Francisco Presidio. They could well have intuitively suspected that San Francisco, especially with its fine harbor, could become the intellectual and economic flashpoint of the region.[7]

Knowing about the place was one thing, but moving a family there another. Marcos had negotiated California's difficult terrain for most of his life. For people on foot or horseback, some canyons are so steep on both sides that a trail might better be called a slide. William Brewer, a geographer and U.S. government surveyor in the 1860s, wrote that a certain river wound about a canyon to the extent that his team had to cross it twelve times. He described another canyon composed of a series of side ravines they ascended and descended as they followed the trail that was nearly invisible because it was strewn with rocks, logs, and boulders. The California landscape could be very tough going for travelers.[8]

Marcos's showing up at places as distant as San Diego in his retirement years, when he accompanied a priest into Indian territory almost as if he were still on active duty, suggests that long-distance travel by horseback had become a mode of life for him. Soldiers like Marcos accompanied missionaries and government officials when they traveled, as he had accompanied Anza from Monterey to choose sites for the San Francisco presidio and mission. He might also have worked as a mail carrier on routes laid out over centuries by Indians.[9]

Terrain that single adults on horseback complained of was even more challenging when traveled with children. Lieutenant Ignacio Martínez, appointed in 1818 as San Francisco commander, said he had worried about relocating his four daughters from Santa Barbara, but that, although they all "took their falls," they galloped "their horses in their haste to reach 'their country,' as they called it." William Heath Davis wrote that one of Martínez's granddaughters rode like an angel, could shoot with the best of them, and could strike a bull dead with one slice of a blade. Her brother, Esteban Richardson, said he did not remember a time when he could not ride a horse. At age five or six, he would gallop to visit friends at the mission or at ranches more distant.[10]

Some histories imply that women traveled in clumsy, primitive *carretas*, carts used to transport hides and other goods, but that seems improbable. Horse-drawn coaches were an amenity in Juana's elder years, but not in her youth, when the only way to travel was on horseback. Various accounts, including a log of the Anza expedition, mention women riders in an explanation of something else. Any woman who has ever given birth to a child would be startled to read that the entire party would rest for a day after a woman gave birth because she could not ride a horse. Then she would walk for four or five days before remounting.

Two other bits from history in Juana's region substantiate the fact that girls and women excelled at equestrian skills. A granddaughter of María Antonia Mesa said that after Antonia's husband, Rafael Soto, died in 1837, she rode her horse to Monterey from her husband's Rancho Rinconada del Arroyo de San Francisquito to certify her title, a trip that even today by car over modern roads requires attentive driving.[11]

A contemporary of Juana's, María Antonia Pico Castro, was sixteen the year that Hypolito (Hippolyte de) Bouchard's crew invaded, looted, and burned Monterey. At the request of her mother, Antonia galloped back into the city from their place of refuge to recover an important book that contained her father's handwriting.[12]

The thrill of travel itself and the adventure of trying out a new country would not be lost on Juana at age ten or on her brother Gregorio, twelve, or on sister Epiciaca, eight. Ship captains would one day describe *rancheros'* unstinting hospitality, but the rancho period had not yet arrived in 1812, when only missions put up the few civilian travelers. In traveling from Branciforte to the San Francisco Presidio, Marcos and the children would have ridden horses and slept on the ground. He would have hired Indians to move the family's household belongings in a cart pulled by oxen and to drive the family's cattle, sheep, and additional horses. Imagining the scene requires also conjuring up a picture of thirty or forty dogs in the party. As one Anglo wrote, "it was no infrequent occurrence to see a ranchero ride into town with a string of dogs at his horse's heels."[13]

Marcos had several reasons to undertake a move that cut himself and his children off from their long association with people and place in the Branciforte area, a disadvantage surely, but he knew people anywhere he chose to live in California. His long military career and his theoretical pension gave him access to presidial resources, and the military gained by his presence because the Briones household could board their relatives and others.

Marcos's most compelling reason for moving probably derived from his close connection to Alberni, Córdoba, and the Catalan Volunteers, which gave him access to inside information about possible housing and other favorable conditions. At the San Francisco Presidio, the commander and engineer would have made good on the expectation that the Volunteers should have the best housing in keeping with their high standards of performance. Historical and archaeological evidence makes the supposition reasonable that Marcos knew where excellent though damaged building materials, the best water source, and good soil, otherwise in short supply at San Francisco, sat unused.

In 2003 and 2004, archaeologist Barbara Voss headed a dig at the site near Polin Spring where Marcos Briones and his daughter Guadalupe Briones de Miramontes lived next door to each other. A detailed map that purports to explain the presidio in 1820 led Voss and her team to look in the right place for the Briones house. They uncovered an impressive foundation and tiles from roofing and floor, unexpected because materials of that quality had not previously been observed by archaeologists or described by historians of the presidio. Other materials found there showed that the structure had been used for domestic purposes and that household items surpassed the quality of those at other nearby sites of that era.[14]

That the Briones family should have managed to live in such an impressive structure, and even that such a structure should have been built there, is difficult to explain, because ordinary people lacked access to mission resources. Churches and some living quarters have endured two hundred

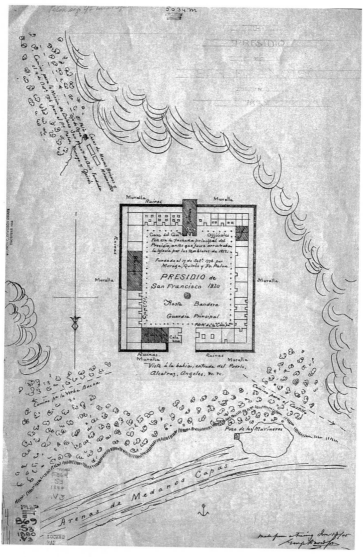

*The Presidio of San Francisco in 1820, with Polin Spring
in the upper left. This drawing by Edward Vischer was
commissioned by Mariano Vallejo in 1878. Juana's father had
earlier described some of the features to Vallejo. Note the label
for the "Casas de Marcos Briones y Miramontes" at the spring
and the damage to the fort from the 1812 earthquake, indicated
by the areas marked with diagonal lines and labeled "Ruinas."*

These sherds of table ceramics of British manufacture were found during the archaeological study of the site of the house of Marcos Briones. They are evidence of the family's prosperity at an early date.

years and more because of thick and sturdy walls of adobe bricks, beautifully crafted tile roofs, and stone floors, but during the era of mission construction nearly all the components were manufactured on site. This achievement required equipment, a large workforce, and, in the best circumstances, raw materials close at hand. San Francisco lacked timber, appropriate soil for bricks, and lime for plaster. The recent archaeological dig revealed two successive structures at the site. The first burned either partially or totally. The second utilized the remaining sturdy foundation. Dr. Voss concluded from a careful examination of the materials that the second building probably employed roof tiles and other useful debris not destroyed by the fire.[15]

When the Catalan contingent left the presidio, some of their housing may have remained vacant. The superior character of the Briones house foundation makes it conceivable that either Alberni or Córdoba had lived in the house that burned, one of far higher quality than other presidio living quarters.

Locating well meant living near freshwater, a lesson that Juana carried with her to each of her homes. Padre Juan Crespi observed water in all its manifestations—rivers, creeks, springs, marshes, lakes, and, to a lesser extent, the sea—in his diary of the Portolá expedition. His mention of water for the use of the animals, his fellow travelers, and appropriate mission sites figures so prominently that his diary might reasonably be called the Water Journals.[16]

Marcos settled his family near the best water source in the vicinity, plentiful and reputedly healthful. Indians traveled distances to partake of its waters. One story was told and retold, possibly jokingly, that Polin Spring enhanced fertility, which probably would not have been a motivating factor for Indians. They balanced their population with their resources. Hispanic people's goals were to populate the country with their own offspring, bring up children who would farm and manage livestock and honor religious directives that strictly forbade family planning.[17]

One story says that Polin Spring was named for a *polín,* a sturdy pole that was used to move heavy objects and that reminded some people of the penis. Another says that people who drank of its waters tended to give birth to twins. Both families who lived at Polin Spring helped substantiate the myth, although the Briones twins were born before the family lived there. Ysadora Tapia, Juana's mother, lived there as a child for a year, which perhaps contributed to the popular idea of her fertility, although ten or eleven children born to one mother was not exceptional. Juana's sister Guadalupe and her husband, Candelario Miramontes, had a very large family, probably twenty children. Juana's record was routine: of her twelve children, three were adopted, and four died in infancy.[18]

Polin Spring is still remarkable in these days of dried-up, covered-up, polluted waterways in San Francisco. El Polín pours all year from the aquifer at the rate of a gallon a minute through fissures in serpentine rock. The water is no longer notable for purity, but the area has a magical feel to it. One day early in the twenty-first century, a docent for the National Park Service who has made a special study of Polin Spring pointed out a small waterfall on the hill behind the Briones and Miramontes home sites. Hummingbirds seemed to be lined up in the air, waiting for their turn, one taking a swig and moving out to make room for the next.[19]

Such a sight might have enchanted Marcos and his family, but hummingbirds, like many other birds, probably flourished in the early nineteenth century and composed part of the ordinary background that included the sound of the sea or the view of deer nibbling on the hillside. The dense bird population surprised some persons new to the Bay Area before the gold rush. Captain William Phelps often mentioned birds in his 1841 journal. He wrote that a flock of California quail would number three or four hundred; one shot could bring down seven or eight ducks at a time; after one brief morning's hunt he returned to Mission Dolores with thirty-five ducks; geese covered large tracts of ground with their smelly effluvia; and numerous crows scavenged on the offal around houses.[20]

The Briones household might have used Polin Spring for watering animals, laundering clothes, and personal sanitation, but more likely they reserved the spring for drinking and cooking. Neighboring women may have gathered there to pick up their day's supply of water and to gossip. Several nearby ponds would have been good for laundry. Juana and her husband and children later settled near a pond just over the hill to the east. Laundry day was probably a convivial excursion at a distance from the residence, an occasion for conversation, singing, and relaxing while waiting for clothes and bedding to dry.[21]

Polin Spring now has a second name, Tennessee Hollow, for the First Tennessee Volunteer Infantry Regiment, which had a relatively comfortable campsite there in 1898 as part of the Spanish-American War. The valley had some arable soil, but military reports repeatedly emphasized how poor the San Francisco land was for farming. Nevertheless, a certain skepticism needs to be entertained in regard to such complaints. True, the Spanish settlers had no fields for wheat or barley, but products from small-scale farming could be exchanged at the mission, which had the wherewithal to reach lands farther away for grain. Reports about the people's nutritional hardship seem at odds with the list of supplies that the San Francisco Presidio furnished in 1792 at no cost to the English sea captain George Vancouver: eleven cows, seven sheep, ten *arrobas* of lard (one arroba equals twenty-five pounds), two steers and two calves, 190 calabashes, ten carts of other vegetables, many fowls, and four hundred eggs.[22]

Moving to the San Francisco Presidio meant Marcos could be with and give support to two sons, both older than Juana: Gregorio, who became a soldier in 1816 and remained in that position for eleven years, and Felipe, who had married Manuela Valencia in 1810. Felipe was a member of the guard at Mission Dolores, where he and his wife were bringing children into the world and thus could use some help from family members. Marcos and his two daughters would also have been in a position to make life easier for single soldiers by raising food to supplement unimaginative army supplies. There was no mess hall. Unless they could find a woman to handle food and laundry for them, soldiers had a problem because they received uncooked rations and washed their own clothes. Besides those issues of daily life, there was no hospital. Medical care was dispensed mostly by priests and women, although in the 1960s a ninety-year-old descendant of Felipe referred to him as a doctor.[23]

Juana and Epiciaca's help with the Miramontes babies would have been an inducement for sister Guadalupe to move her family next door to her father in 1815, a year that saw some important changes in the Briones family. In June that year, the priest at Santa Cruz listed Guadalupe and Candelario as having completed their religious obligations, attending mass on Sundays and holy days, going to confession, and receiving the sacraments. By December, Candelario was a presidial soldier, and they were in the Mission Dolores books as godparents to an infant born to a soldier and his Indian wife. Also in 1815, in Monterey, Juana's older sister Luz married Felipe García Romero, a widower with children, most of them grown. In San Francisco, Felipe Briones's second child was born, a son named Desiderio, one of two nephews who became close to their aunt Juana in later years.

Juana was of an age to be an important cog in the wheel to feed, clothe, and shelter her father and others, to facilitate their social and religious obligations, and to tend to their mental and physical health. Being a healer took longer to learn. Juana in her teens was still an apprentice. Little information survives about Juana's adolescence, but one story is rather surprising, given that she was ten years old at the time of the December 8, 1812, earthquake. She is still remembered today as the person who told the story that the disturbance caused a tidal wave that covered Portsmouth Plaza. Other evidence about Juana's home as a salon where important business and government men went for friendly conversation seems to be substantiated by such a report's having lasted to this day because of Juana.[24]

One reason that people still care about the plaza today is that it became Portsmouth Square. It was said that in 1833, before that place became the plaza, it was Candelario's potato patch, which the Miramontes family could have been farming for years by then. Another source called it the potato patch and vegetable garden of Candelario's mother, Victoria de Luna. The Briones family may have retained the memory of where the tidal wave struck in 1812 because of various connections to the place over the years and because the site became important to the U.S. government's takeover of California. The crew of the *Portsmouth,* a sloop-of-war commanded by Jonathan B. Montgomery, chose that location in 1846 for the first official raising of the U.S. flag at Yerba Buena, before it was named San Francisco.[25]

Juana's society had the habit of remembering stories and oral communications because most of them had no access to books or any other

Many early visitors mentioned the large Miramontes family, shown here. This photograph was given to me by Ernie Miramontes, now deceased. Ernie was a descendant of Candelario Miramontes and Juana's sister Guadalupe.

written material. For a time, the San Francisco Presidio had a school for soldiers. Male members of the family had more opportunity to get book learning than Juana did, scant as it was even for them. Advancement in the military was contingent on some degree of literacy. Brother Gregorio's various positions required him to read and write reports. He was the *alcalde,* mayor, of San Mateo, Sonoma, and Contra Costa, as well as *juez,* judge, of San Rafael, and he signed his land documents. Although book learning was secondary for men and less common for women, some women taught reading and writing to classes or to their own children. Californio Juan Bautista Alvarado's mother taught him to read, and he became one of the few who had a reputation as a bookish person.[26]

If Juana had any formal education, the death of her mother in 1812 probably would have put an end to that. She apparently did not develop a sense of need for literacy either for herself or her daughters, as indicated by the fact that one of them, Refugio Miranda de Mesa, signed land documents with an X as late as 1906, but at least two and probably all three of Juana's sons had some book learning.[27]

Being unlettered in the nineteenth century did not stop people from grand achievements. Jim Murphy, whose family purchased half of Juana's ranch in the 1840s, signed with an X, unlike the majority of new Californians. Historian Lisbeth Haas notes that Anglos who came to California tended to share a higher literacy rate than was common elsewhere in the United States; she attributes their having been convinced of California's commercial potential to their reading of articles, brochures, and books that described California as a near paradise.[28]

One feature of religion tended to discourage literacy. Some Catholic clerics wanted to keep heretical writing away from church members. When priests learned that Mariano Vallejo, Juan Alvarado, and Joaquin Castro assembled libraries in their homes and lent each other books, the three were excommunicated, a sentence that Alvarado managed to circumvent for them all.[29]

Inocenta Pico said that her parents took her out of school when she was fourteen and brought her home to learn to work so that she could become a wife, which she did the following year. Juana had stayed in the same home for her first ten years, but when her Buelna cousin opened a school for girls in Monterey in 1818, Juana lived at the Presidio of San Francisco and two years later would marry at age eighteen.[30]

Juana married Apolinario Miranda on May 14, 1820, at Mission Dolores. His mother, María de los Santos Gutiérrez, a Yaqui born in Culiacán, New Spain, was seven years old when her family joined with other members of the Anza expedition to found the San Francisco presidio and mission. Apolinario's father, Alejo Feliciano Miranda, first listed as a servant and later as a soldier, is said also to have been Indian, born in Potam, New Spain. María was eleven years old when she married Alejo. Apolinario was born in 1794 and baptized at Mission San Francisco de Asís (Mission Dolores).

As a Mexican Indian couple who diligently practiced their religion, Apolinario's parents, Alejo Miranda and María de los Santos Gutiérrez, bridged two cultures and advanced into a class favored with greater privilege, income, and status. In 1792, Alejo piloted the ships of the English explorer George Vancouver into anchorage in San Francisco harbor, maritime knowledge that Hispanic settlers notoriously lacked. Alejo had first arrived aboard a supply ship, the *San Carlos,* and possibly had been trained in seafaring duties.

Persons named Miranda had been active both in the Basque region of Spain and in the exploring contingent that helped found missions and settlements on the northern frontier of Mexico, the area of Sonora and Arizona, early in that history. At one time, because Yaquis knew the sea, their assistance was sought to access Tiburón Island in the Gulf of Mexico, where there had been Indian attacks on pearl divers. Whether Alejo Miranda owed his boating skills to early tribal training is conjectural. There was extensive interracial mixing on the frontier, which could account for his being both a Yaqui and a Miranda.

Alejo's first having been called a *sirviente*, then a soldier, then a corporal in charge of the guard of five soldiers in 1797 at the newly founded Mission San José, then his advancing to the rank of sergeant made him a highly accomplished newcomer to California. Apolinario's mother's having arrived with the honored Anza party was a distinction, but further evidence of her standing comes from her often appearing in Mission Dolores records as a godmother. Some historians of midwifery have noted that midwives often became godmothers of children born with their assistance.[31]

Hispanic people of the time took godparenting seriously for religious reasons, but also as a kind of backup guardianship for children. Priests wanted to be certain that children would be raised in the faith. Santos Gutiérrez was so respected by the church that when her husband was assigned to Mission San José at its founding in 1797, she was the godmother of the first Indian child baptized there. The priest who performed the baptism was Father Magín de Catala, who would much later figure importantly in Juana's life.[32]

After their marriage, Juana and Apolinario may have remained with her family at Polin Spring, moved to the presidio quadrangle, which is reputed to have been somewhat uncomfortable for families, or begun to construct the home that they would be living in by 1833, when he applied for ownership of land just over the hill east of Polin Spring. All three of her homes in that vicinity—Polin Spring, the Ojo de Agua de Figueroa, and Yerba Buena—were on the trail between the presidio and the mission. She also eventually had a house at the mission.

When Marcos went off on some travels, he might have turned over his house at Polin Spring to the newlyweds for a time, possibly even to two sets of newlyweds because Juana's sister Epiciaca married Antonio Soto two months after the Miranda wedding. In 1820, Marcos went to San Diego, where another daughter lived, Agreda, who married a second husband while Marcos was there. Perhaps he went for the wedding or because he had not seen this daughter in years. In 1821, Agreda, born in

1794 at Mission San Antonio and widow of José Pliego, married Francisco
Lisalde. Marcos was a witness to a marriage in November of that year at
San Diego, after which it may be supposed that he returned home to the
Presidio of San Francisco.

Wherever the Briones-Miranda newlyweds lived in the early years of
their marriage, they were part of presidial society. Juana would eventually take the initiative to diminish her dependence on the military, which
became less and less viable as an occupation for men. Growing up under the
tutelage of a father who partook of the advanced thinking of the time gave
her a good start on a career as what today we would call a businesswoman.
She became active in a new mercantile society that in California owed its
fundamental character to the Anglo world, but she never gave up her attachment and her loyalty to her people's culture under Spain and Mexico.

Part Two

MEXICO, 1821

Five

A PLACE OF ONE'S OWN
Personal and Social Change

No one wrote a description of the marriage in 1820 of eighteen-year-old Juana Briones to twenty-six-year-old Apolinario Miranda, but by then their world had passed beyond the worst of its survival worries and was taking pride in its unique identity, which included celebrations for ordinary souls that bore some resemblance to those for kings and queens. Californios created their own entertainment. From all accounts, they did a good job of elaborating on their dazzling equestrian and musical achievements, both of which entered into weddings before and after the solemnity of the church ceremony itself.

The pageantry surrounding a wedding melded the secular with the sacred, but there was less melding in the music. Priests sometimes complained about the style of popular music and dancing, but to no effect. In their descriptions of the area and culture, some astonished Anglos of Puritan background mentioned the crowds and the entertainment at weddings, as well as dancing that they considered somewhat lewd. Everyone came to a wedding, no need for personal invitations. Dancing continued either all night or all week or for three weeks, depending on who told the story.

For the Briones-Miranda wedding, the party traveled from the presidio to Mission Dolores. The bride would have been the star in a richly caparisoned cavalcade of horses—with strikingly artistic silver elaborations on bridle, saddle, and spurs, and the horses carefully selected both for beauty and ability, "resplendent," as one author described them. Juana probably was wearing white satin slippers that her husband-to-be had made for her. On the way to church, she would ride on her own saddle with her nearest male relative behind her on a bearskin thrown over the horse's haunches. For Juana, that relative was probably her father. She would then ride away from the ceremony sharing a horse with her new husband, Apolinario Miranda, visibly exchanging one man who had full authority over her life for another equally empowered to set the rules for her and enforce them, and adding de Miranda to her name.[1]

At the capital, two years after Juana and Apolinario married, the government created an extravaganza that outdid even weddings. Three days of fanfare at Monterey proclaimed "good-bye Spain, hello Mexico." Officials publicly took oaths to certify their acceptance of the deal whereby the Mexican flag would henceforth replace that of Spain on the Monterey plaza and throughout California. Inocenta Pico described the festivities there as including cannon salvos, parades, simulated battles, banquets, dances, and bullfights.

The revolution in Mexico, the replacement of Spanish rule with Mexican rule in California, and the liberal philosophy that inspired revolutionaries extended far beyond the formality of flag raising. Large-order change gradually reached every corner of Hispanic California and would later have a huge impact on Juana's life. Most important, Mexico revised the terms of understanding between church and state, which inserted a dark side into the gaiety for some Californios. Several friars began to prepare for departure rather than disavow their sworn loyalty to their king.

One woman who was a child at the time in San Diego remembered how Spanish soldiers had proudly worn single, long braids that, for a lucky few, reached their waists. The day after San Diego's chief official shouted out "Long live the Mexican Empire" at the flag raising, Juana Machado Alipaz de Wrightington's soldier father brought home his braid, which he had cut off because of some symbolism that is difficult for us to fathom today. He silently handed his braid to Juana Machado's mother, who cried.[2]

Regardless of feelings of loss and reluctance for change, many Californios sensed that Spain had not served them particularly well and that at least Mexico's relative proximity meant that important documents would arrive sooner than they ever could from Spain. One large-scale difficulty needed to be overcome, however, when the new government, while transforming the missions, would gradually wipe out that complex system of social-economic-political-religious interaction that still operated to oversee conditions of daily life.

Under Spain, government, military, and missions partnered to run California. Disagreement abounded, but having Mexico slate the missions to be dismantled threw off balance an elaborate, underlying system that had lubricated the sociopolitical machinery for more than fifty years. Churches provided the calendar and structure for holidays, beliefs, and life-changing events such as birth, death, and marriage. Fiestas centered in plazas in front of churches on Sundays and holy days, and people took their problems to priests, not lawyers, of whom there were few. On the positive side, secularizing missions meant that private landowning became feasible for hundreds of thousands of acres that missions had managed—land that was supposed to be returned to Indians, but was not.[3]

Mission Dolores reached its peak number of resident Indians in 1820, its forty-fourth year of operation. Building on that success, Franciscans had founded another church north of San Francisco Bay before Juana's marriage and another there soon after. Those two new installations, more outposts in hinterlands accessible only by boat than genuine new churches, did not for another decade replace the San Francisco Presidio's position as the main establishment at the edge of the northern frontier.[4]

Few soldiers moved across the water to that upper region bounded by San Pablo Bay in the early days of Missions San Rafael Arcangel and San Francisco Solano de Sonoma. Corporal Rafael García—Juana's sister Luz's stepson, who became crucial to the family—headed a three-soldier guard there and, until he died in 1866, continued to live in what came to be called the Northern Frontier. His sister, Ramona Romero García, married Gregorio Briones, and Rafael helped that branch of the Briones family acquire a large land grant along the waterfront, Bolinas—named for whales, *ballenas*. Today, from the Bolinas hills, one can gaze across San Francisco Bay to the towers of the city of San Francisco.[5]

The missions got things started for Hispanic settlers in this upper region. Besides the doctrinal advantage of proximity to more Indians as potential converts, the two northernmost missions staked out access to Fort Ross, founded in 1812 as a Russian business enterprise for hunting and trading on the coast, about ten miles north of today's Russian River. Californios found the fort a convenient place to exchange the food they grew for items produced in Russia or acquired elsewhere by Russian merchants, a bonus in a market-starved economy. The missions' seeming monopoly on foreign trade throughout California diminished when a growing number of ships managed to access avenues of import and export, trade that Spain had discouraged, but that Mexico sanctioned, in part because of its government's need for income from customs duties.[6]

Juana understood this economic system and tapped into several emerging opportunities in the first decade of her marriage, enabled by her ease in relating to people of many backgrounds and languages. In 1828, Mexico passed a colonization law that permitted immigration by foreigners if they pledged allegiance to Mexico and joined the Catholic Church. Within two years, 150 foreigners took up residence in California, but long before that deserters from ships had figured out ways to stay. Many just slipped into California without having their names or circumstances recorded. A few can be tracked historically. As early as 1792, ten years before Juana's birth, five or six men deserted from the English exploring team headed by George Vancouver, captain of the sloop *Discovery*. In 1804, an African American deserted from the frigate *McCain*. Thomas Doak deserted from the *Albatros* in 1816. Russians and native Alaskans left Fort Ross to integrate into the local populace. Antonio María Suñol arrived in 1827 on the merchant ship *Bordelais*, which remained for weeks to treat crew members with scurvy and departed without four who managed to hide well enough to escape detection. Suñol became an influential resident of San José and its environs. A small town today bears his family name. William Tecumseh Sherman noted that Andreas Hoepner, living near Sonoma in 1846, had "a pretty Sitka wife," which perhaps meant Russian, Aleut, California Indian, or a mixture and corroborates the theory that considerable intermingling and immigration occurred without leaving names or arrival dates.

In 1833, Juana helped four sailors from the whaler *Helvetius* hide out until their ship left without them. They were of diverse origins: Charles Brown of New York became well known in the San Francisco Bay Area; Gregorio Escalante from the Philippines remained connected to Juana's family as long as he lived; Elijah, a Connecticut Indian, was a cook; and Ephraim Frawell of Philadelphia was a tailor.[7]

Juana and Apolinario's situation during these far-reaching changes can be tracked with church and military records. During Apolinario's mission assignments, the family moved with him to the housing that missions provided for soldiers and their families. When not on such assignments, they could have settled for a decade or more on land across a steep hill from Polin Spring, adjacent to the presidio, before Apolinario applied for official title to that tract. The custom was that before requesting certified ownership of land, the applicant should establish a residence and even begin farming the land as a demonstration that the grant would be for direct support and housing for the family, not for speculation.

Wherever Juana and Apolinario lived, so did some of their relatives. In 1827, three infants of family members were born at or near Santa Clara Mission, fifty miles south of San Francisco: Epiciaca's daughter Raymunda Soto; Hilario Miranda (Apolinario's brother) and Juana Cibrian's son Francisco Solano; Juana's daughter María Rosa Isidora—all baptized by Padre Magín de Catala, about whom Juana would more than half a century later testify that he deserved to be canonically proclaimed a saint. This period of residence at Mission Santa Clara would have been an opportunity for Juana to become acquainted with the Indian Gorgonio and his relatives as they worked at the mission, and she later purchased a ranch from them.

Baby Isidora died when the family moved back to the Mission Dolores area. Most of Juana and Apolinario's other children were baptized at Mission Dolores, except for Tomás and Narcisa, who are known as their children from census and land dealings instead of from baptisms.

The rock-solid centrality of the church in people's lives made talk of secularizing missions a daunting chasm between present and past. The mission format had been central to Juana's life from her birth until her marriage and later. The Catholic Church remained, but the intensity of the relationship between priests and citizens lessened. Soldiers no longer protected priests. Priests no longer housed and fed soldiers and their families.

Brief mission records reveal the positive side of life in marriages and baptisms, but they also tell of tragedy. Three of Juana and Apolinario's daughters died in February 1828—Josefa, age five; María de Jesús, age three; and Rosa Isidora, age one. That year there was a smallpox epidemic in southern California among the Indians, who were more vulnerable, but not solely so. Some rudimentary knowledge of vaccination existed. The following year, the trapper James Ohio Pattie got himself released from prison in San Diego by offering to vaccinate people in the territory, but even if this plan worked, it would have been too late for the Briones-Miranda family.[8]

The Mirandas had other dangers to face as well, from animals and from people. William Phelps in his journal mentions an Indian boy thought to have been taken by a panther in Yerba Buena. At the San Francisco Presidio in August 1828, a five-year-old girl was raped, and she and her one-year-old brother were murdered while the parents were out at a fandango.[9]

No matter how much Juana and Apolinario may have found consolation in religion, they must have suffered deeply to have three of their young children die in one month and a fourth in the next year. They had company in their sorrow. Mission Dolores recorded a disproportionately high number of deaths in February 1828—fourteen, including the Miranda children. No other month came anywhere near that record. Other than five deaths in April and four in June, there was one death each in January, July, August, and November, and no deaths in the other five months of that year. Nineteen of the total deaths for the year were Indian neophytes, eight were gente de razón. A major disaster other than contagion would have been in reports for February, which leaves disease a virtual certainty as the cause of these deaths. There were fewer than half this number of deaths the following year. One of those was another of Juana and Apolinario's children.

Presentación, their first born, survived. Starting in 1831, ten years after her birth, so did the rest of their children. Tomás Miranda, said by genealogists to have been born that year and mentioned in legal documents and censuses as Juana and Apolinario's son, would one day work on his mother's Purísima Ranch, marry into the Bojorques family, which had longtime roots in California, and receive from his mother a parcel of the ranch.[10]

The year Juana married, Padre Catala at Santa Clara Mission baptized the first of her elder sister Luz's two illegitimate children, "Juan Bautista Briones, *pnc*," an abbreviation for *padre no conocido*, "father unknown." Also at that mission, Apolinario's sister Odorico Miranda de Galindo bore a child in 1823 soon after her husband, Rafael, died. Her father, Alejo, stood in for him in the role of parent at the baptism. Three years later Odorico brought for baptism a "pnc" child. Bearing an illegitimate child was a serious breach of social expectations at that time and place. Mission baptism records show, however, that "padre no conocido" was not entirely uncommon. In an article about marriage patterns at that time, Gloria Miranda writes that the society treated sexual indiscretion with secrecy when possible and that priests gave precedence to happy unions over pressing too strongly for marriage to repair illegitimacy.[11]

Many authors of gender studies have written about the disparity wherein societies often admire men for indulging in sexual freedom, while finding women contemptible if they share that propensity. As Michael Gonzalez notes, prominence and respect were not denied open philanderers such as Pio Pico and Carlos Carrillo, widely known for their economic and political successes. Ann Twinam detects a social norm in which women who gave in to passion outside of marriage often paid for their indiscretion with years of religious devotion and seclusion. In a family history with elements of fiction, Marin Pepper writes that Juana's sister Luz was physically disabled and thus devoted herself to good works. Luz has been the family mystery woman, in contrast especially to Juana and to others of the Briones clan. Even her name had irregularities. From her marriage to an elderly man who died within two years of the union, Luz bore one child, María Isidora García de Rosales. Luz's husband usually preferred to use his mother's name, Romero, instead of his father's, García. Two of his children chose different last names, Rafael García, of the Tomales grant north of Bolinas, and Ramona Romero, who married Juana's brother Gregorio.[12]

If rape caused pregnancy and thus a "pnc" child, women admitted it reluctantly. It made them damaged goods and was considered to be at least in part their fault. In one drastic case, three young girls at Branciforte were lashed for having been raped by their stepfather. Women's shame about rape made it an underreported crime, and although priests complained that soldiers raped Indian women, prosecution seldom followed. In *Women and the Conquest of California,* Virginia Bouvier notes ways that the people of the time and historians have underplayed rape as a social and legal issue. She mentions as an example an archival index in which the viciousness of the rape of two young girls, one of whom died, is described with the benign title "Misconduct at Mission San Carlos."

Prostitution seems an unlikely explanation for "pnc" in a society with virtually no cash and in which women relatives and friends took in needy people. When sailors began invading the land, it was said that some Indian women agreed to payment for sex. Indian society did not condone adultery, but it had a more flexible understanding of sexuality than Catholic society. The abbreviation *pnc* was given as shorthand for all the possibilities, but some were more possible than others. Luz might have been the mistress of a prominent married man, and, if so, the relationship would have been hushed up for his sake.[13]

Luz or any woman of dubious sexual conduct was out of the running for property ownership, but when the Mexican government detached land from mission operations, many other Californios saw therein relief from a stagnating economy. Some women obtained grants, often as widows. Several of Juana's male associates seized the opportunity to acquire large estates. Juana's siblings acclimated more slowly. She of all her family inclined most toward accessing economic opportunity, a temperamental difference that drove a wedge between herself and Apolinario.

Apolinario's status as a soldier of the San Francisco Presidio made him eligible to think more grandly than he actually did. He had less distinction in leadership positions than José Peña, a lieutenant and a teacher whose property acquisitions had a certain majesty about them. When Mexico allowed the acquisition of former mission land, Peña jumped in early, applying in 1822 for seven grants and receiving permission to occupy one square league of cattle-grazing land, more than 4,400 acres, without having a definite title at first. His land eventually shared a boundary with the ranch Juana purchased twenty-two years later. Soon after her purchase, he and his wife were guests at her house.[14]

Luis Peralta, of a family Juana had known since her childhood at Branciforte, obtained land in 1820 on the east side of San Francisco Bay, roughly in present-day Oakland and Alameda. Both Peña and Peralta, like many landowners of the time, left ranch labor to others while they lived in town, an option that would have been available to Marcos Briones or to Apolinario had they wished, but neither of them jumped at the economic opportunity of the period, however tentatively Mexico changed the rules at first.[15]

Juana's husband applied only for the comparatively small piece of land called the Ojo de Agua de Figueroa and waited until 1833 to do so. He probably chose that year because most San Francisco soldiers were moving to the settlement being developed by Mariano Vallejo on the new Northern Frontier, but, given the customs of the time, Juana and Apolinario may actually have occupied the Ojo de Agua long before he requested certified possession.

Their choosing the Ojo de Agua testifies once again to the importance of water in locating a residence. Proximity to the vast Pacific and one of the best bays in the world offered business opportunities, but vastness, however useful for trade, meant nothing without clean daily water to sustain life. The spring, the creek, and the pond at the Ojo de Agua dictated the plot's selection as the first place the couple acquired—or, more accurately, that Apolinario acquired.

He applied to the commander of the San Francisco Presidio, José Sánchez, for one hundred *varas* square (a vara is a little less than a yard). His request followed the standard pattern. He would soon retire, had already begun using the land for agriculture and cattle, and had constructed a provisional dwelling. Sánchez signed his approval the next day, September 16, 1833.[16]

Apolinario's attitude regarding this important issue of real estate had some admirable qualities. He and Juana's father may have developed or may have inherited a sensibility that many of the Indian cultures around them demonstrated, that individuals should acquire only what they need, but Apolinario and Juana disagreed on what they needed.

Both of them had had ample opportunity to learn personally from Indians, and they both also had Indian ancestry. Apolinario's parents were Yaqui. Juana's father, though listed as "mulatto" in the 1790 census, had a sister, Guadalupe, who was listed in the same census as "mestiza." When Marcos was about eighteen years old, his father, Vicente, married at Mission San Luis Obispo a northern Chumash Indian woman who died in 1806 at Carmel Mission, giving Marcos an Indian stepmother well into his adult years.[17]

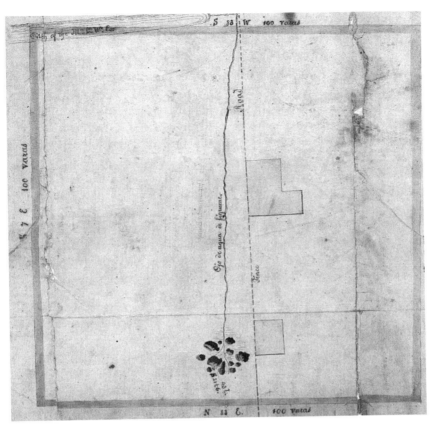

The Ojo de Agua de Figueroa. This map was based on Charles Brown's testimony in 1854 that affirmed the legal ownership "by Mrs. Bryones and others"—that is, Apolinario Miranda's widow and their children.

Spain at first introduced 150 soldiers, missionaries, and colonizers into a California Indian population of an estimated 65,000 in the coastal area. By 1820, there were 22,000 Indians in the missions and 3,400 gente de razón in California. As a youth, Juana lived as a member of a minority among an Indian majority. In California from 1769 until the U.S. conquest in 1846, it is reasonable to assert that, exclusive of racial considerations, two cultures collided, European and Indian. A priest, Geronimo Boscana, had lived in close association with Indians for twenty years in southern California at the time when he wrote that he found them "incomprehensible." One can extend this cultural divide to Apolinario and Juana in regard to property ownership: he who favored the Indian outlook, she who preferred a more acquisitive style.[18]

Although both Juana and Apolinario thus had close ties to Indians, lived close to Indians in California, and absorbed some Indian viewpoints, their advantage lay in being part of the landed ruling class, for whom Indians were mostly servants and laborers. Success in business and leadership positions are remembered in histories. Juana could not be a leader because of the exclusion of women from all offices of authority, but economic achievement was possible for her, though difficult. Success in business led to the preservation of much information about her life story for posterity.

Common law of the Mexican period considered husband and wife effectively as one person. He acquired land in his own name, but his wife could acquire the land entire as his heir, which she did if he died intestate. Under the laws in effect in Mexican California, Juana and her children would inherit the Ojo de Agua when Apolinario died, but under the U.S. government she then had to meet the challenges of an unfamiliar legal system and a foreign language, as well as laws that were highly disadvantageous for women.

When the U.S. government gained control of California, its requirement that landowners must prove up their titles meant operating within a legal system that favored aggressive individualism over familial well-being. U.S. civil law considered married couples as "disunited . . . with disseveered interests in property"—that is, a partnership in which the husband made the decisions. These changes were especially significant for Juana after Apolinario died and she had to prove her claim to the Ojo de Agua and other plots of land she owned. She kept her case for the Ojo de Agua afloat from her first application in 1852 until twenty-two tenacious years later. Why she never remarried could have related to her difficult first marriage or to her knowledge of law or to both.[19]

Married women living with their husbands had more favorable legal rights under Spanish and Mexican systems. In most states of the United States and eventually in California, a *femme couverte* feature dictated that married women's rights resembled those of minor children. U.S. jurisprudence limited a widow's inheritance to a portion of the estate, usually half, even if the property had been hers before marriage. Spanish law allowed women to inherit property entire, a measure of economic equity that held only briefly after California became part of the United States. In the state constitution drawn up in 1849, representatives considered themselves generous by stipulating that laws would be passed to register a woman's separate property, which would be assumed to belong to the husband if the wife neglected to handle the necessary legalities. The alleged benefit, which quickly ended in any case, was that women should be allowed to possess any separate property at all.

If single, a Hispanic woman could acquire a grant in her own name. If married, she could inherit property or receive it as a gift in her own name. Juana's brother Gregorio willed property specifically to his daughters and not to their husbands.[20]

Marriage difficulties between Juana and Apolinario did not come out into the open until eight years after he applied for ownership of the Ojo de Agua de Figueroa, in which he repeated the universal claim that he needed it to support his family. The year 1833 was one of unusual turmoil at the San Francisco Presidio, reflected in the name chosen for Apolinario's grant, honoring Brevet Brigadier General José Figueroa, then governor of California (1833–35). Ojo de Agua, "Eye of the Water," referred to the spring and the watercourse clearly delineated on the *diseño,* the customary drawing of a property being requested of the government, using physical features as boundaries and lacking the sophisticated survey with instruments that Americans introduced. Water ran in the open at Ojo de Agua until 1912.[21]

One after the other, Juana's places of residence connect beauty with utility and possess uncommon depth of character. The Ojo de Agua stands out in a city replete with unusual corners. Its western boundary shows on ordinary San Francisco street maps as a rectangular notch in the otherwise straight Lyon Street border of the presidio, straight because no claimant other than Juana won suits for title to lands that impinged on the presidio. Six tall, elegant residences now grace the indentation that juts into the wall of the former army base and present national park. In proving up her claim as Apolinario's widow, Juana hired the best attorney in California, Henry Wager Halleck, which assuredly helped.

Still today, the unforgettable character of the Ojo de Agua comes from the combination of the natural and the built environments. Climbing the hill on the property's southern border would have been a workout, except that in Juana's time people and animals would have taken an angled instead of a straight path. Serious exercisers today trot up and down the hill's 125 steps, a stairway built in 1915 to beautify the place for the Pan-Pacific Exposition down Lyon Street toward the bay. The stairs extend Lyon Street for pedestrians. Motor vehicles go around.

For Juana, living next to a steep hill had the advantage of deterring horses and farmers, thus promoting a habitat where native plants could survive to be used for food and for her stock of herbal medicines. The Ojo de Agua boundaries, running in an east–west direction below the steepest part of the slope, roughly paralleled the entrance channel from the ocean to the bay and paralleled a stream that ran right through the middle of the property (and now goes into underground pipes).

A neighbor who lives in one of the houses on the presidio side thinks the original pond dampens the first story of her house and nourishes the thicket at the foot of the Lyon Street stairs. Two huge redwoods prosper there on a vegetated oval 20 feet across and 150 feet long. Bumpy cobblestones around the thicket bring to mind an era before the plucked, pruned, and paved modern city. The dense undergrowth has been citified, but by imagining its more wild state, a visitor might well believe that there, Juana listened to the land, and the land reassured her.

No buildings intervened between Juana and Apolinario's view of the bay, the Marin headlands, and what is currently known as Alcatraz Island, a view that now can be enjoyed from upper stories of houses on the property. Perhaps seeing so many sailing vessels coming into the harbor gave Juana the idea of setting up a post where she could sell merchandise to them.[22]

Although on adjacent wild places some grass grew for a few additional cattle and nature gave gratis some foods to be harvested—strawberries, blackberries, and other wild foods—Apolinario claimed barely enough land for subsistence farming, 1.8 acres. The impending retirement he mentioned on his application implied that the land would be his pension. Like other soldiers who continued to serve after receiving land, Apolinario was still on the presidio roster three years later.[23]

By 1833, when Apolinario applied for his land, two of the three Briones siblings who had married within two years of each other—Juana, Epiciaca, and Gregorio—had chosen to move away from the area, and Juana and Apolinario had that option. The settlement being founded in 1833 to create a new northern frontier may have prompted Apolinario's decision to apply for land near the presidio instead of taking an assignment to move again. He and Juana would stay where they both had spent most of their lives. Apolinario may have had enough of uncomfortable assignments. Just three years earlier, he had served at Mission San José, where he had lived formerly as a young child when his own father's military duty took him there. Apolinario had possibly requested that assignment in order to care for his ailing father, who died at nearby Mission Santa Clara in 1830.

The change in mission life instituted by the new Mexican government increased everyone's awareness of the power of government to affect lives.

Many Mexican governors were unpopular, but José Figueroa had pleasing ways about him. He was Mexican and mestizo and thus fit comfortably into a society where having racial categories dictate class had become if not entirely outmoded, at least less fashionable. He also brought a strong intellectual bent to his work, quoting philosophers such as Miguel Cervantes and Jeremy Bentham in support of his mission secularization plan, expressing a refreshing attitude toward a possible better future. People called him "Father of the Country." That his intellectual predilections appear in tune with Juana's could be taken as a clue to the couple's naming their property in his honor.[24]

Figueroa handled one matter of an extremely delicate nature, expelling Spanish priests and replacing them with ten born in Mexico, who took over the seven missions from Monterey's Carmel northward. He also brought print type with him from Mexico, and the *Manifesto á la Republica Mejicana* became the first item printed in California, though the printing process took so long that Figueroa died before its completion. His proposed equitable distribution of mission land to Indians and settlers hit a Hispanic population hurting for economic improvement who thought of Indians as laborers, so not every detail of his proposals gained popular approval.

In a society based on oral communication, the *Manifesto* received wide distribution and discussion. A literate member of the community would read it aloud to a social or public gathering. News also traveled via *corridos*, popular musical narratives focusing on vital current information. The major adjustments indicated in the *Manifesto* had been proposed previously but were insufficiently backed up. The change deeply affected an economy dependent on large tracts of grazing land. As practical as the policy appears in retrospect, however, civilian administrators seldom activated it as intended.[25]

Figueroa also took steps to discourage Russian incursion into what Mexico considered its territory. He sent Mariano Vallejo to the Russian enclave of about three hundred persons to purchase supplies, but actually to spy. The Russians' Fort Ross showed Vallejo a nonreligious economic and organizational structure that incorporated Indians, which he subsequently adopted with modifications to develop the Northern Frontier.[26] At the San Francisco Presidio, Figueroa saw firsthand the demoralization of unpaid troops with few supplies. Establishing a northern colony addressed both Russian and local troop problems. The presence of a presidial force in Sonoma would discourage Russian expansion, and the soldiers could support themselves on the land. The idea sounded somewhat like another Branciforte, but without quite so much government intrusion on individual lives and without stipulations making it sound like a utopia.[27]

General Vallejo moved most of the San Francisco Presidio soldiers to Sonoma, which deprived Juana and Apolinario of many of their social comforts, but they had connections in the north. Five years before Vallejo's move, Apolinario's brother Juan Miranda was *mayordomo*, overseer of maintenance and operation buildings and land, of the Sonoma Mission. Juan was married to María de la Luz Mesa, whose family descended from Anza expedition settlers. Years later, two of Juana's daughters and a niece married Mesa men.

Vallejo made the Sonoma Mission his headquarters and welcomed potential settlers, including some of the newly arrived Mexican Hijar-Padres colony in 1834, which many locals resented, suspecting that members of the colony intended to appropriate land that Californios thought more rightly belonged to them. Juana, six years older than Vallejo, shared his generational viewpoints. He was a highly prominent and influential Californio, so his liberal ideas made him a target for at least one Catholic historian, Zephyrin Engelhardt, who describes secularization as dishonest and calls Vallejo and his cohorts "young, conceited and unscrupulous upstarts . . . overgrown schoolboys . . . crude youths [who] lacked thorough religious training . . . [and held] Voltarian ideas." Engelhardt uses the expression "silly nativism" about Mexico's order to expel Spaniards younger than sixty.[28]

People who did not know they were being influenced by philosophers nevertheless shared Enlightenment ideas. James Sandos assesses Franciscan thinking—disseminated through the mission system—as "medieval." Contrasting enlightened with medieval would have been beyond most Californios' ken, but the concepts can be discerned in events nonetheless. Juana and Apolinario admired Figueroa, and though surely they had no name for Enlightenment thinking, they leaned that way and, like others of their comrades, wondered where their government might go—toward being a province of England, France, or America or toward being its own country. They preferred not to be called Mexican. A contemporary wrote that some Californios responded to "Who goes there?" with "California libre" (free California).[29]

If Juana and Apolinario factored in mercantile opportunity when they decided to stay where they were near the San Francisco Presidio, then they showed more perception than most of their compatriots, who had not found ways to make a living from the trading vessels in San Francisco Bay. In the same year that Apolinario received official possession of the Ojo de Agua, four sailors "took French leave" from their Boston whaler and sought refuge at a house at the presidio where an "old lady" (she was thirty-one) named Juana Briones hid them. She got her brother Felipe to come for Charles Brown and Ephraim Frawell and take them in a boat to his ranch in the East Bay for safety. Elijah and Gregorio Escalante apparently could be better hidden in the local population.[30]

The situation of these four sailors can be contrasted with that of Juana's father-in-law, Alejo Miranda, who stayed behind in the area when his supply ship left. Sailors from Spanish or Mexican government vessels had the option of settling permanently, unlike deserters from American and English merchant vessels, who, if caught, would be flogged and forced to return to duty, with all shore leave canceled.

Brown subsequently lived on the Ojo de Agua for a year or so. He said that Apolinario had a fence around the property, a corral, fruit trees, and the rest of the ground in cultivation, and that when the family moved to town, Apolinario stayed behind to operate the farm. The diseño shows two structures beside the creek, one of which could have been a barn. Brown later said that after Apolinario died, Juana continued to grow crops but had to move the cattle out because people in the area were killing them.

Two years after Commander José Sánchez conferred the Ojo de Agua on Apolinario, the Briones clan brought three infants to be baptized at Mission Dolores. Gregorio Briones and Ramona García Romero brought Juana Ynocencia de los Dolores. About two weeks later, Apolinario Miranda and Juana Briones brought María Antonia del Refugio, who would in later life always be called Refugio. At the end of the month, Francisco Silvestre was baptized, born to Luz, father unknown.

When Luz at age thirty-nine gave birth to a child, she had been a widow for eighteen years. The family did not consign her to begging in the plaza, but neither did they stretch to give her ownership of possible means of support. When Juana later distributed portions of the Rancho la Purísima Concepción to relatives, Luz was not among them, although she has been described variously as living with her father and with Juana. One of the parcels from Juana's ranch went to Antonio Romero, who may have been Luz's stepson or stepgrandson.

The family record in childbearing went to Guadalupe Briones de Miramontes, but Juana had a big family as well. When Apolinario applied for the Ojo de Agua grant, he and Juana had three living children of the seven they had parented to that time. The energy that was pouring into the locale must have diverted Juana somewhat from the deaths of her children. Immigration brought new ideas. Mexico's rescinding of Spain's rigid economic policy had let in fresh air. Ships that came to buy rawhide from a country swarming with cattle needed supplies for their crews, especially food, and a sailor would actually pay to borrow a horse from people who formerly thought nothing of lending a horse for no charge. Juana did not need a dictionary, a philosopher, or a textbook to explain to her that there was such a thing on earth as payment for hard work.[31]

Apolinario did not accompany Juana when she set up a second home at Yerba Buena. People called the Ojo de Agua the "Miranda grant," but they called the homestead down the road "the property of Juana Briones." She applied for it in her own name. Apolinario died in 1847, having lived his entire life at missions, at the Presidio of San Francisco, and, for at least fifteen years, at the Ojo de Agua de Figueroa. Like most of his contemporaries buried at Mission Dolores, no tombstone exists for him in the present graveyard.

Six

YERBA BUENA

Neither the Mission nor the Presidio

Juana Briones created the city of San Francisco. If that claim seems overblown, try this: Juana Briones was the first resident of the area that developed into the earliest version of the city of San Francisco. If that statement ignores Indians, then it can be said that she was its first non-Indian resident. If that leaves out the presidio and the mission, the presidio is now a national park, and the mission area was included as part of the city only as San Francisco grew. If San Francisco would have become a major metropolis anyway and being its first resident does not really matter, there is a certain irony in the fact that several very prominent men of the 1850s disparaged San Francisco and invested in Benicia because of its better climate and in Sausalito because of its better port. Juana's residence had the name Yerba Buena, the original pueblo, which was later renamed San Francisco.

Juana Briones's young womanhood pivoted around a place sequentially named Yerba Buena, the City of San Francisco, and North Beach (now a neighborhood in the city). Yerba Buena first simply put a name to a vicinity before two men received government approval to make part of that area a pueblo, giving them more control over a defined space where they hoped to build wharves, develop a business neighborhood, and install government facilities, such as a customs house.

The name "Yerba Buena" allegedly originated from the healthful herb Juana harvested near her home and served as a tea to her guests. A member of the U.S. occupation force, Lieutenant Washington Bartlett, changed the name to "San Francisco." Like William Richardson and Jacob Leese, who first applied for pueblo status, Bartlett was business oriented and thought

Yerba Buena Cove. This drawing by Daniel Wadsworth Coit, ca. 1848 or 1849, may be the only existing view of William Richardson's house. The people looking down at the cove are on the eastern slope of Loma Alta. Its western slope, not shown, overlooks Juana's house.

the name "Yerba Buena" would mean nothing to the American shippers who brought money and business into the harbor. He thought people would recognize the name "San Francisco." Maybe he copied the practice used for the naming of New York Harbor, San Diego Bay, and Monterey Bay, where the main settlement had the same name as the harbor.

North Beach now seems oddly named. The beach was moved when entrepreneurs sank ships and pushed hills into the bay to create land they could sell. Instead of centering around La Playa de Juana Briones (Juana Briones Beach), the North Beach neighborhood of today centers around Juana's former corral and dairy farm, now called Washington Square. A state historic plaque there reminds passersby of Juana, although one of the volunteers who helped the plaque project, Muriel Sutcher Knapp, had a more imaginative idea to remind visitors of Juana. She recommended that an artist be commissioned to create a statue of a cow, or perhaps a cow and calf. Perhaps one day this idea will come to pass.[1]

William Squire Clark, who arrived in the area in 1846, said he assisted in making the first survey of "the old part of town," meaning Juana's part of town. In an oral history interview, he said that prominent people stopped by Juana's place and implied that Yerba Buena was named for her tea:

MEXICO, 1821

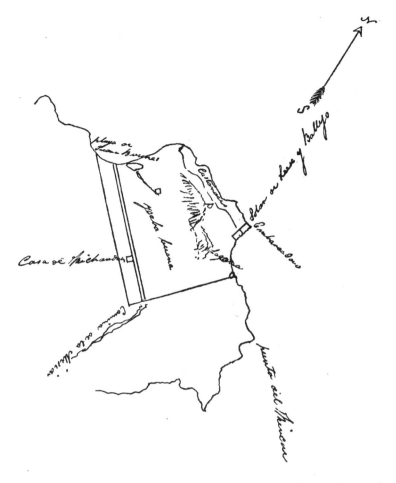

La Playa de Juana Briones. This third map of Yerba Buena is a tracing of the 1839 map that Jacob Leese and Salvador Vallejo submitted with their application to Governor Alvarado for approval to build wharves at Yerba Buena cove. The two houses are William Richardson's and Juana's. Also shown but not named are Briones Lagoon, adjacent to Juana Briones Beach, and Loma Alta, the high hill east of her house.

Yerba Buena by which it was known for an interval was a nickname given, it is said under the following circumstances. There lived near North Beach a widow named Brueauo [sic] who gathered herbs from the side of Telegraph Hill from which she decocted a very palatable tea. The local territorial officers at Monterey, the capitol, in taking their excursions to the different missions around the Bay, including the Mission Dolores, and at this point always partook freely of this delightful tea, hence the name Yerba Buena (Good Herb).[2]

Juana's sensitivity to change and to developing opportunities fits well with the notion that in her home at Yerba Buena knowledgeable people relaxed while they discussed issues, ideas, and current events. Her social side facilitated her achievements. She "had the faculty of dramatizing events so that her listeners could picture them vividly," according to Marin Pepper, who was born at Bolinas during Juana's elder years and knew descendants of Juana's brother Gregorio.[3]

The story that Yerba Buena got its name from Juana's tea could have derived from a feature of banter. When one left the capital for the windy tip of the peninsula, it may have been common to say, "I'm going there for a sip of *yerba buena*," in lieu of reviewing a tale of work in progress or admitting to alcoholic refreshment. Perhaps officials winked when they said they thought they would be going to have tea. Saloons came later. Juana once applied for a license to purchase a barrel of *aguardiente*, brandy, the Californios' only liquor.[4]

The certain date by which Juana had set up her outpost is 1838, but some evidence suggests a possible date twelve years earlier. If Yerba Buena did get its name from Juana's tea, as Clark said, then she could have been living there as early as 1826, when the English captain Frederick William Beechey entered the bay. His exploring sloop, one of forty-four ships that entered the harbor that year, desperately sought fresh food and water before continuing their search for the Northwest Passage. They paid attention to their surroundings, drawing up a geologic map of the San Francisco Bay Area, thought to be the second ever created for North America. Their careful notes about their surroundings included the information that the ample vegetation of the land east of the presidio (where Juana's place lay) gave the area the name "Yerba Buena."[5]

Other sources give later dates for when Juana set up her own household at Yerba Buena. Alfred Robinson, a reliable observer who arrived in 1829, represented a Boston firm with permission to trade at various ports. He said Juana built her house at Yerba Buena in 1831. If we accept this claim as fact and remember that Apolinario applied for the Ojo de Agua grant two years later, we can ponder differences in their personalities and the dissension that later plagued their marriage. Apolinario might have resented being upstaged by his wife. The fact that she had property that everyone accepted as hers might have convinced him to certify that another property would be identified as his. Visitors never mentioned Apolinario in connection with Yerba Buena. Most Anglos referred to the business and household adjacent to Loma Alta, later called Telegraph Hill, as that of the "Widow Briones," following the common nineteenth-century practice of referring to any woman with children but no husband on the premises as a "widow."

John Hittell wrote in his history of San Francisco published in 1878—while Juana still lived at her ranch in the Santa Clara Valley—that Juana had settled at Yerba Buena by 1836. William Richardson and María Antonia Martínez's son Esteban mentioned that he clearly recalled his parents' saying that Juana moved toward the cove to be near his family and that the Richardsons helped her build a temporary house in 1835. A newspaper reporter said she moved to Yerba Buena in 1838, but Charles Brown, the sailor she helped, testified that she moved there in 1842. Historian J. N. Bowman wrote in a 1957 article that she built her home at "Washerwoman's Bay" in 1837 or even 1836, temporarily in the first year, but permanently in the second.[6]

All these interpretations play into the subject of who settled there first. Hubert Howe Bancroft wrote in his multivolume history of California, published in 1886, that William Richardson of London and Jacob Primer Leese of Ohio were first, and in a footnote he added that Juana Briones was third. During the period when Bancroft was collecting documents and interviews and assembling major West Coast histories, women were worth interviewing only if they had a famous male family member, but even then Bancroft seldom wrote about the women themselves. Juana's presence in his work is somewhat unique. He even put her in his *California Pioneer Register*, which is said to be a listing of men. That he entered her name in a footnote with regard to the founding of Yerba Buena suggests that it was impossible for him to leave her out entirely. Bancroft could have, but never did, arrange for his oral history researchers to contact Juana, as Charles Brown recommended he should to the man who interviewed him.[7]

The government's role in deciding matters inserted another complication in this history. In 1834, the Mexican Departmental Legislature authorized the election of an *ayuntamiento*, municipal assembly, for the San Francisco presidio, mission, and an undefined area in between them. The need for governance arose because the two institutions that managed civil affairs had essentially departed: the military moved to Sonoma with Vallejo, and the mission had been secularized, no longer overseeing its former domain and leaving many buildings empty, into which Hispanic people moved.

Juana's father, husband, and brother Felipe were appointed as electors of the new assembly. The electors chose her brother Gregorio as a councilman and Francisco de Haro as the first alcalde for the area, whose job would relate mostly to the residents around the mission, where he lived. The central government at Monterey instructed de Haro to help lay out Yerba Buena Pueblo at the cove, and he thus became its first mayor.[8]

To set up an official pueblo, Richardson and Leese had to get permission from Monterey. Under the former Spanish law, pueblos were to measure four square leagues, about 18,000 acres, with a maximum size for house lots and one lot per family, requirements that the Mexican government followed but adjusted. Some regulations could be sidestepped—for example, the regulation that for a place to receive status as a pueblo, a specified number of "male heads of families" had to be present.[9]

Had the gold frenzy never occurred, San Francisco geography could have dictated a series of hamlets separated by daunting hills, chaparral, sandy stretches of flatland, and mud. When the tide went out, even the cove where ships anchored became a mudflat. William Tecumseh Sherman wrote that in 1849 a horse's legs entangled in bushes hidden in the mud could cause a rider to be thrown and drowned.[10]

Ships entered the channel between the Marin headlands and the presidio, passed La Playa de Juana Briones on the south, rounded imposing Telegraph Hill on the right, and swooped into Yerba Buena cove. The hill cut the two coves off from sight of each other. Several sailors wrote of climbing Telegraph Hill and being surprised to see Juana's large establishment spread out below. Seaman William Thomes visited her home often for milk for his ship, and he came to know and respect Juana:

> Lewey proposed that we should climb Telegraph Hill, and take a view from its summit. We pushed on, and after a short walk, stood on the top, and from our elevation could look all over the beautiful bay, and note the islands, and the rocks, covered with sea fowl and seals, and the low, sandy spit that ran out, like a crescent, with the end pointed toward Goat Island. In the rear of the town were vast sand mounds, ever changing, while at the foot of the hill, on the Golden-Gate side, was a large adobe house, and outbuildings, the residence and ranche [sic] of Senora Abarono [sic], a rich widow, where I afterward used to go for milk every morning, unless off on boating duty.[11]

No telegraphic equipment had yet been installed the year that they stood on this hill, so instead they actually looked down on Juana's buildings to the west from Loma Alta, "High Hill." In 1835 and 1836, Richardson and Leese selected sites south of that hill and developed the area at a more protected anchorage than Briones Beach. That they officially called the new area "Yerba Buena" can be interpreted to mean that they considered the pueblo an extension of the place where Juana lived.

The triumvirate had mutually supportive roles. Juana sold milk, almost certainly other farm produce, and sewing services. Leese set up a store. Richardson was captain of the port and hired Indian mariners to pick up hides and tallow around the bay. As captain of the port, he also directed boats entering the harbor to the Yerba Buena landing place in which he had invested.[12]

Richardson had arrived in 1822. He either had a falling out with his captain or deserted from the British whaler *Orion*. He married María Antonia Martínez, the girl who had ridden horseback with her father from Santa Barbara. In 1829, the Richardsons moved to Mission San Gabriel in southern California, where Antonia's Arellano relatives lived, her mother's family.

When José Figueroa passed Mission San Gabriel in 1833 on his way to take up his duties at the capital as the new governor, he convinced the Richardsons to travel with him back to the presidio area. Figueroa needed William to facilitate launch transport for trade around the bay, to carry troops and settlers to the Northern Frontier, and to collect customs. A side benefit for Richardson as port captain was being able to board ships first and acquire products before they were subject to customs duties, although no one claimed that Richardson himself used such illegal tactics. William Heath Davis described some ingenious schemes for evading taxes, such as hiding valuables in water casks with a foot or so of the popular Boston pilot bread on top in case a customs agent inspected the keg.

Richardson directed ships to Yerba Buena cove once they entered the harbor, giving them access to Leese's trading post. Leese's partners for a brief time, Nathan Spear and William Hinckley, lived in Monterey, where they influenced government decisions. Figueroa's successor as governor, Mariano Chico (1836), lasted three months before locals ousted him for being overly attached to Mexico and the old ways. During his short term of office, he instructed the alcalde to grant Leese a lot near the Richardsons.[13]

Richardson and Leese had experience and support in their lines of work. Juana was self-taught. Growing up within a mission context, she had observed the value of an outpost. Mission populations reached the thousands in some cases. Cattle wandered afar, and large fields were needed to feed a concentrated populace in the urban-style setting of a mission. The padres created *asistencias* where Indians could live at a distance to grow crops and tend cattle and sheep. Juana followed that example by managing her small assets as missionaries did their large ones. Mission Dolores had set up an asistencia at Pacifica, closer to the ocean, with housing, a chapel, and a ranch run by Indians. In 1817, three years before Juana's marriage, the church founded another such outpost north across the bay, San Rafael, where sister Luz's stepson headed the guard and managed the farm. In Juana's version of an economically beneficial outpost, she could sell produce grown on the Ojo de Agua family farm and operate a dairy, where fewer cattle could be profitable, unlike cattle used for meat or hides, which ranged over thousands of acres. Her outpost was also located where boats could come in to buy produce for sailors on board ship, and close to the emerging center of population at Yerba Buena cove.

Juana's management of the dairy impressed Thomes. In his usual ironic tone, he provided considerable information about Juana. He admired her energy in overseeing her employees, her ability to do the job when they couldn't, her friendliness and generosity. He wrote in 1884 that if Mexican men had "some of the energy of that buxom, dark-faced lady, California would have been a prosperous State . . . and we would have had to fight harder than we did to get possession."[14]

Juana's home site between Telegraph Hill and Russian Hill enjoyed several ecological advantages. The hills trimmed the wind's sails. Wild plants could be harvested from steep hills that horse traffic went around. One Christian minister in San Francisco in the 1850s advised patients hospitalized for scurvy to go out on the hills and pick a plant that he called "wild lettuce," probably the miner's lettuce that still pops up uninvited in local gardens. Another antidote for scurvy would have been wild berries.

Access to freshwater once again played a role in choice of a home site. Two springs rose near Juana's Yerba Buena house and coursed down the slope toward the bay, forming a pond that was first called Briones Lagoon and later Washerwomen's Lagoon. The latter name implies that her household handled laundry at a short distance from the residence to avoid contaminating the cooking and drinking water and that laundry might have been one of the establishment's businesses. In a few years, during the gold rush, men would send their laundry to Honolulu or Canton rather than pay what they considered the exorbitant charge of eight dollars a dozen.[15]

This painting by Frederick Tobin, ca. 1850, shows Juana's house at North Beach, the largest house in the middle left, with outbuildings. Juana developed it in the 1830s as a second residence and a base for her business enterprises and medical practice. The buildings in the cove were probably constructed by immigrants responding to the discovery of gold.

Although Juana's Yerba Buena place appears isolated in one sense, it had a cordial component in that the trail between the mission and the presidio went right by her property. Living on a well-traveled trail provided contacts and information for a community-oriented person. The same trail went by her father and sister's households at Polin Spring, a convenience for someone who throughout her life maintained close ties to her family.

Juana could have listed beauty as one of her property's assets. Sand and precipitous hills predominated elsewhere, but Juana's soil was more amenable to agriculture and sloped gently to the bay. The moods of the highly visible bay changed from season to season and sometimes from moment to moment, its waters whipped to a fury by winds from the Pacific Ocean or baked to an eerie calm by a hot sun. The view to the north across that stretch of water stimulates spiritual thoughts. Hawks and eagles swirl above heights that disappear during hours when fog makes those ridges seem imaginary. At other times, thick, low fog drifts in from the ocean, making the ridge tops appear to be floating on clouds.

Juana's reasoning about her move can be deciphered from her personality. She adventured toward success in difficult endeavors and carefully assessed what she learned from others' experiences. No contemporaneous author left a comprehensive account of her life, but many mentioned her, and several commented on her commercial endeavors. Definite information confirms that at Yerba Buena she sold milk and sewing services and provided medical care. It may be reliably presumed that she also dealt in produce such as fruits, vegetables, beef, chicken, and eggs, and that she rented horses and saddles to sailors. Others managed pocket farms or practiced medicine, but Juana was unusual in that she made a profit and at the same time was impressive enough in character and personality that many people remembered her and wrote about her.

Juana's place at Yerba Buena contributes to an interpretation of one aspect of Juana and Apolinario's relationship. Their marriage may have been amiable when she originated the second farm. They may have thought of it as a vending place for produce from the Ojo de Agua. Their family of children grew from one to seven, plus an adopted child, in the decade between 1831 and 1841, suggesting that economic potential, not marital problems, triggered her development of that second home. From Apolinario's point of view, however, the enterprise had the unintended consequence of Juana's learning that she could manage without him.

Their marital problems undoubtedly had festered earlier, but they reached a point of no return when Juana was one-month pregnant with their last child, José Aniceto, later called Dolores. They had been married for twenty years when she brought suit against Apolinario in 1840 for physical abuse. For the first of such accusations, justices often held a hearing to promote reconciliation, with two *hombres buenos* (men in good standing) as witnesses, one recommended by each side.

Juana said that Apolinario beat her and did not support the family. He said she resented all his requests for companionship and normal wifely obligations. Beneath their testimony one can read that she was too independent for him and that he was too overbearing for her. His abuse appears to have worsened after Dolores's birth. The baby was four months old when a scandalous drama played itself out. Juana's Indian manager dashed to the sheriff, Francisco Guerrero, to ask him to intercede, apparently fearful that Apolinario would injure Juana. Another man had tried to protect her. Guerrero put Apolinario in the guardhouse.[16]

Guerrero had brought the community badly needed legal training. As one of a group of educated, liberal thinkers experienced as teachers, artisans, businessmen, and government officials, he had arrived in 1834 with the Hijar-Padres colonizing party from Mexico. Governor Figueroa and many Californios mistrusted members of this party, fearing they would take over the best land at the secularized Mission San Francisco Solano eighty miles north of San Francisco, where he had put Mariano Vallejo in charge. Figueroa expelled them, but about two hundred settled in various places, including Guerrero at Mission Dolores. His carefully kept records preserved information about the delicate matter of Juana and Apolinario's disintegrating marriage.[17]

The entirely male composition of the legal system created a daunting prospect for women who had to use that system. Juana was the only woman present at that first hearing, but, in any case, not too much could remain hidden in so small a community. Apolinario, Guerrero, and Alcalde Francisco de Haro signed their names to the transcript; Juana and Tiburcio Vásquez signed with a cross.

Women held a decidedly inferior position within marriage law. Miloslava Chávez-Garcia writes in her analysis of marriage and women's status in Los Angeles to the 1880s that men held complete authority over households, including the right to punish wives and children physically. Men interpreted the limits permitted by law. Juana's complaints assisted her, but genuine solutions came slowly, if at all. The society considered marriage indissoluble, making any final and definite resolution of problems unlikely.[18]

Apolinario's literacy should theoretically have made him better able than Juana to deal with legal complexities. In 1844, in his own fine handwriting, he composed and submitted a summary of his position regarding Juana's complaints against him. The summary indicates that he had begun to realize that Juana might be causing him serious problems, that he might actually be imprisoned or exiled. If Juana had any literacy at all, her confidence in it was apparently so low that in several documents she explained that she had hired an amanuensis because she could not read or write.

After the second time Juana went to Guerrero for protection, Apolinario may have been angered even more. If she had previously attempted to live with him at all, at this time she uncompromisingly moved out of the Ojo de Agua residence with the children and tried to keep her husband at a distance. His anger smoldered and would flare up more seriously within a few years.[19]

Had Juana's Yerba Buena locale been less ideal, she probably would have looked for a place farther away from Apolinario. Perhaps she considered her later purchase of the large ranch thirty-five miles south as a way of distancing herself from him. Although symbolism would have been of little interest to her, it does factor into an assessment of her decision to locate at Yerba Buena. By creating a refuge and a business between the military base and the church, she mediated in a physical sense between those institutions. She put economic potential for the support of her children ahead of physical or spiritual protection of herself.

The geography of Juana's various homes makes a pleasing metaphor for her life. She distanced herself gradually from the culture of the military, away from her soldier husband and the expectation that he or his employer, the army, would look after the expense of raising a family, and moved toward a culture that embraced both the secular and the religious.

Freedom to make a living had never been a given in Juana's world during her youth. Before she was ten, Californians experienced the apparent dichotomy that the Spanish government both tracked down persons who traded illegally and admitted the need to compensate for scarcity. By the 1840s, the Mexican government encouraged outside trade and minimal law enforcement, which both hampered and helped the economy. Some of the items Captain William Phelps brought from the eastern United States to sell in California in 1841 give an idea of what California lacked: mirrors, rugs, cloth, thread, tape, cotton hose, ribbons, needles, suspenders, pencil cases, artificial flowers, boots, shoes, paper, pans, pickaxes, tablespoons, forks, knives, ladles, chest locks, wrench hammers, and various foods and spices such as confectionary, chocolate, nutmeg, cloves. When Juana's daughter Narcisa died in 1879, part of her estate consisted of two hundred dollars worth of gold coin in a bank. Gold coinage was relatively common in California in the 1870s, and yet that cache could have dated to Juana's early business operations. Some Spanish, Mexican, and U.S. gold coin circulated in California before the gold rush. Juana might have been one of the merchants who managed to work for cash, although many Californians bartered cow hides and tallow for manufactured goods, deals often made onboard vessels set up like stores. Deathbed wills often included statements such as "So-and-so owes me two cows" and "I owe So-and-so four sheep."[20]

Like a few businesspeople, Juana could tap into the modified cash economy that began opening up as early as 1822, when Mexico took over the government of California and such notable Anglos as William Hartnell, John Rogers Cooper, Nathan Spear, William Heath Davis, and William Richardson started arriving, staying, and over the years contributing the novelty of commercial stores on land in place of mission warehouses, military commissaries, and shipboard trading posts.

Juana's dairy adapted both to the emerging mercantile economy and to the local ecology. Sand made large-scale ranching impossible at Yerba Buena. Everyone had horses, but usually also sheep, goats, and pigs, possibly fruit trees or grape vines, and always at least a small vegetable plot. At some homes, chickens ran freely indoors and out. During a night's lodging at one ranch, an Anglo visitor rolled over onto a nest of eggs in his bed. Juana's Yerba Buena property, besides providing a home for a large family, had the capability of small-scale production as well as important access to a market.[21]

Housing varied in the area. Eloise McLoughlin Rae, wife of the manager of the local branch of the Hudson's Bay Company, described her home as a long building with a hall in the middle opening onto a store on one side and a house about the same size on the other. Archaeologist Barbara Voss writes that the "Latin American" style of the area "failed to appeal to the architectural sensibilities of Europeans and New Englanders." Her insight points to conflicting interpretations of housing. Alfred Robinson referred to Juana's "rude little cottage" as the only residence between the landing place and the presidio. By contrast, a descendant of Juana's sister Guadalupe said Juana had "the most imposing home in San Francisco."[22]

Where the Briones-Miranda family stayed at various times and who owned what at a given moment were far from static conditions. In 1838, Juana applied either for the first or second time to the alcalde for ownership of her Yerba Buena lots, an indication of her sole-proprietor status. Her joint home with Apolinario was considered to be in the presidio, an area of housing and use that had by then little to do with the buildings that once composed the fort itself, which had largely become rubble by the 1830s. Apolinario would sometimes have been absent on military assignments. The family had the option of going with him to missions. Possibly not all the family members were at Santa Clara Mission when Apolinario was assigned there. The eldest daughter, Presentación, might have stayed behind with one of her aunts at the San Francisco Presidio.[23]

Besides trying to confirm her ownership of the Yerba Buena land, Juana took another major, life-altering step in 1838 when she applied to adopt the Indian child Cecilia Chohuihuala. Her application indicates the attachment that people in her neighborhood felt to the Northern Frontier or to a belief that Vallejo's jurisdiction included them: she applied not to the governor or the local authority, but to General Vallejo of Sonoma.

There must have been a question about why Juana did not just take in the child. Families frequently adopted children informally, although even foster children were seldom Indian. Rich Hispanic people sometimes assigned an Indian girl to care for each newborn child. Juana speaks in the adoption papers of the Indian girl not as a servant, but as a child of the family in accord with other instances of Juana's unusual recognition of equality across racial, cultural, social, religious, and age divides. The application mentions that Juana wanted to certify Cecilia's adoption officially so that she would become a legal heir, which ultimately never occurred because Cecilia predeceased Juana by thirty-six years.

Mission Dolores first recorded Cecilia's surname as "Miranda," subsequently as "Briones." Her becoming a bona fide member of those two families of substance and position undoubtedly added to her potential to marry John Burwood Cooper, who was also known as Juan Bautista in the custom of using the Spanish version. Cooper had two prominent Anglo relatives, Thomas Larkin and John Rogers Cooper. Larkin, a prosperous merchant who became U.S. consul, had an American wife. John Rogers Cooper, ship captain turned merchant and landowner, married Encarnacín, a sister of wealthy Mariano Vallejo.[24]

Juana and Apolinario had their first child, Presentación, in 1821; their next four children, born in the next eight years, died before reaching age five; then, during ten years starting in 1831, three boys and three girls who lived were born to them every two years in this sequence: Tomás, Narcisa, Refugio, José Julián, Manuela, and José Aniceto (Dolores). Neither Tomás's nor Narcisa's baptismal record appears at the missions Juana and Apolinario apparently attended or in the comprehensive database compiled by the Huntington Library, but all census and legal records list them as their children.

It is hard to figure how people housed so many, gave temporary shelter to others, and at the same time operated businesses out of their homes. One explanation is that they lived and worked mostly outside. In at least two known cases, Juana took in needy children. In 1840, Carmen Pinto complained to Sheriff Guerrero that the aunt with whom she lived treated her harshly. He granted her request that she should live with her godmother, Carmen Cibrian. Juana then added her situation to the case, saying that she already cared for two other Pintos, her godchildren. The Pinto and Briones families were related and were neighbors before and after Juana was born, at San Antonio Mission and at Branciforte. Juan Pinto's wife was Manuela Tapia, Juana's maternal aunt.[25]

A woman told a representative of *California History* magazine in 1946 that her ancestors, Mr. and Mrs. Robert Duncan, came from New Zealand to Yerba Buena with their five children. After Mrs. Duncan died in 1847, "Senoras Briones-Miranda and Vicente Peralta" brought up the "motherless" children.[26] Juana was not unique in caring for children in need. There were no orphan asylums. Historians of Bolinas tell that Gregorio Briones and his wife brought up a young girl whose family died in a shipwreck off the nearby coast. Another story alleged that four illegitimate daughters of Gregorio's son Pablo and an Indian woman lived with Pablo's parents. All thought themselves to be Gregorio and Ramona's children until Gregorio died and named in his will only his wife, children born to him, one of his sisters, Epiciaca, and Juana's daughter, Presentación.[27] Juana would probably have known her sister Luz's stepdaughter Carmen García de Barreto. When Carmen died in 1865, her obituaries claimed that she had taken in scores of homeless children and had raised seven orphans, making her Juana's companion in spirit if not in fact.

Juana's habit of foster care might be a reason why she acquired yet another home, aside from the Yerba Buena residence, or maybe she just wanted a place closer to the church. In the birth year of her last child, 1841, she had a second home at Mission Dolores—a second home, not a third, because the Ojo de Agua by then had become Apolinario's only. Unlike the Yerba Buena place that Juana pioneered, she was not first or foremost at the mission. Many local Hispanic people had already congregated there and made use of the former mission housing, so much so that the mission became known as the Hispanic part of town and Yerba Buena as the Anglo part.

Seven

UNDER MEXICO
Family and Friends Disperse

In 1841, an especially eventful year for Juana and her extended family, Juana's adopted Indian daughter Cecilia Briones married John Burwood Cooper. No one has managed to count accurately how many Anglo men married Indian women in the San Francisco Bay Area, but definitely they were few. Marrying a Hispanic woman facilitated land ownership. Marrying an Indian woman seldom had economic benefit.

John and Cecilia settled in San Francisco and had four children. When asked about this Cooper family, a descendant called Burwood "a common sailor." His uncommon tombstone at Mission Dolores suggests, however, that being a sailor meant much to him. Many sailors went to sea quite young and never entirely quit being sailors. The still mostly legible words on his monument read:

> Though [illegible] winds and Neptune's waves
> Have tossed me to and fro
> Yet joy [illegible] decree
> You plainly see
> I am harbored here below
> With many of our fleet
> In hopes our admiral Christ to greet.

He died nine years after Cecilia, who has no visible tombstone.[1]

One of Juana's nieces also married in 1841, Ysidora, daughter of Juana's brother Felipe, to José Francisco Peralta, of a prominent family. His father, Luis, lived in San José, where he had been head commissioner of the Spanish pueblo and where his adobe home has been preserved as a historic site. He sent his sons to operate the family's 19,000-acre East Bay ranch, property that historian Richard White says they lost to a swindler. It is now Oakland, Berkeley, and Alameda.[2]

In 1841, Juan Prado Mesa, three of whose sons would one day marry into Juana's family, was the titular presidio commander of a barely functioning military. Only a few Hispanic people still lived at the Presidio of San Francisco, among them Apolinario and possibly also Juana's father and her sister Guadalupe. Instead, foreigners clustered around Yerba Buena cove, with Juana's home on the periphery. Hispanic people clustered around Mission Dolores. Difficult trails kept those three habitats relatively separate. Eloise Rae said that because of the difficult sandy trail, she went only a few times from Yerba Buena to the mission and never saw a wagon go there. Entrepreneurs later constructed a plank road, which sounds inventive but never worked well. The mission community would in today's terminology be called an unincorporated village. During the mission period, the vibrant compound had included the church, a granary, guard barracks and family quarters, priests' housing and offices, Indian family and single housing, storage rooms, workrooms, kitchen, and infirmary, with a cemetery, orchards, vineyards, vegetable gardens, corrals, and a plaza nearby—all resources that local people accessed when a parish church replaced the mission, as mandated by Mexican rule.[3]

The community that centered around the former mission rarely receives attention from historians, but many Hispanic people made it their home. Juana accessed that place for additional housing and for her legal, social, and spiritual needs. One of her friends throughout her life, Charles Brown, former deserting sailor who testified in her claim for the Ojo de Agua land, married a daughter of the prominent political leader there, Francisco de Haro. They occupied former mission housing for more than thirty years, or rather she did, because Charles frequently went off to follow his occupation of harvesting redwoods and establishing the peninsula's first sawmill near Juana's Purísima ranch. Another mission resident, Francisco Guerrero, also married to a de Haro daughter, was the magistrate who heard Juana's petitions several times when she applied to the court to intervene in her marital dispute. By 1841, he was the leading civil officer—mayor, justice of the peace, and port collector.[4]

A horrifying event occurred in 1841 on the Northern Frontier when Mariano Vallejo's brother Salvador led a massacre of Indians at Clear Lake, north of Sonoma. Battles had occurred previously, and troops had put down Indian uprisings or brought back Indians who had fled the missions before secularization, but the slaying of more than 150 defenseless Indians shocked the citizens. The event was hardly unique, but times had changed, and many Indians had become incorporated into communities.[5]

Among the positive happenings of 1841, land transactions gave Juana an example she later followed. Her son-in-law to be, Robert Ridley, acquired the 8,900-acre Rancho Cañada de Guadalupe de la Visitación y Rodeo Viejo with a house in what is now Brisbane, south of San Francisco. Juana's sister Guadalupe's husband, Candelario Miramontes, acquired the Pilarcitos Ranch, more than 4,000 acres on the ocean coast. Other people Juana knew made similarly grand acquisitions that year. Three Castro sisters, María de Los Ángeles, Candida, and Jacinta became owners of the 12,000-acre Rancho Refugio near Branciforte. José Peña, the first alcalde of San José Pueblo, got confirmation of his ownership of the 8,000-acre Rancho Rincón de San Francisquito, near where Juana would move within a decade.[6]

The significance of the arrival in 1841 of the first overland expedition of pioneers from Missouri hardly made a dent in daily life for Hispanic people. Before this time, Anglos had deserted from ships or come as employees of businesses, and the Spanish had socially accepted them, but members of this party were not looking for social acceptance. One of the members of that group, John Bidwell, age twenty-two, was hired to replace Robert Ridley to dismantle Fort Ross and to transport its moveable goods to John Sutter on the Sacramento River. Russian business interests decamped and shut down Fort Ross mainly because they had harvested sea otters to the point of extinction for their gorgeous and lucrative fur.[7]

One traumatic incident in Juana's life, though hardly important to the larger populace, happened in October 1841. At Mission Dolores, Justice of the Peace Guerrero conducted a hearing soon after a fracas at the "casa de Juana Briones," the only evidence that Juana had a house there. Witnesses said that either more than twenty or more than forty sailors, Kanakas (Hawaiians), and Californios stirred up the trouble. Several men threw stones at the home and people, forced entry, and stole aguardiente, a serape, and some cloth. They attacked Juana's nephew Desiderio Briones with wooden clubs. The intrusion happened on a fiesta day, usually held in the church plaza and usually including horse races, bull and bear fights, music, dancing, and drinking. At Juana's place, noisy men diverted attention from the thieves, some of whom were apprehended. Hispanic men on their way to the fiesta heard women shouting and hurried to investigate. Those who testified in court included Desiderio, then twenty-six, who had tried to fight off the robbers.

That October day at Juana's house is one of the few examples we have of Juana's voice other than in letters, land documents, legal cases, and other testimony. The judge's legal report stated that she asked the men's indulgence, that they be considerate of her sick father. Her sister Guadalupe was also present, probably sharing nursing duties. Local citizens often substituted for the nonexistent police force, as Desiderio did that day, along with other men such as Blas Sibrian and Francisco Moraga.[8]

By 1841, Juana's marriage had irredeemably fallen apart. She registered her third complaint to the authorities a little more than a year after son Dolores's birth. She testified that Apolinario publicly and loudly abused her, was a poor example to their children, and left family support to her.[9] The society hardly stood firm against abuse. For instance, one woman in San Rafael almost died in 1846 after her husband beat and stabbed her for having sold his partly full bottle of liquor to an Indian. He told her he would kill her unless she kept his attack secret. She had long suffered beatings, but when she nearly died, her relatives went to the judge of the prefecture of San Rafael, who assigned Juana's brother Gregorio to validate testimony about her wounds.[10]

Some California women who attempted to flee mistreatment were put in safe houses, where their freedom would be limited for their protection. Such a restriction would have been inappropriate in Juana's case. She was called upon as a healer, managed a large and prosperous business, and gave a home to many employees, foster children, sick people, and her own family. Leaving was not an option for her, but it was for her husband, who did not seem to care for family members, anyway.[11]

When the difficulties between her parents were occurring, Presentación was of an age to be eligible for marriage. William Heath Davis, a year younger, could have been with the family simply as a social visitor, as a potential suitor, or as a business contact with Juana on behalf of his uncle and employer Nathan Spear. Davis described his visit to Juana's house during the Easter season, when young people enjoyed a tradition that many Anglos found quaint. He wrote that Presentación, a "sprightly and pretty girl," broke on his head several eggshells filled, in the custom of the country, with colorful fragments of paper, cologne water, or some other substance to amuse without harm. One stealthily attacked while avoiding repayment in kind. Davis had brought along several festival eggs without managing to break even one on her. When he left, Presentación said in Spanish, "You came to shear, but you have been shorn." Davis noted that the incident happened in North Beach, the name for the neighborhood by the time he wrote of the incident, where the family was at home, near

Easter in 1841. Three years later Presentación married Robert Ridley. Six years later Davis married María de Jesús Estudillo.[12]

Juana became the godmother of the first Ridley baby, Clara, born in 1845. Two years later they had a son, Roberto de la Cruz, whose godparents were Presentación's sister Narcisa and one of the deserters Juana had helped, Gregorio Escalante. Everyone knew Robert Ridley, who was funny and entertaining and likable. His enterprises suggest a person always on the lookout for the next deal. He worked briefly for Sutter, then as a clerk for William Rae, then he rented a bar and billiard parlor from Jean Jacques Vioget, a surveyor who made the first map of Yerba Buena. Ridley kept the map up on the wall in his saloon, where, as if it were a town hall, people came to apply to purchase lots.

Ridley hired John Brown to manage that business and then sold it to him and moved to the mission area to originate the Mansion House bar. In Yerba Buena, he built a house that he sold to William Leidesdorff and bought two of Juana's North Beach lots from her. He applied for a large grant in Sonoma, which he traded to Jacob Leese for one on the peninsula, and he ran unsuccessfully for the office of alcalde in Yerba Buena.

In 1846, the Bear Flaggers arrested Ridley because they thought he would favor the Mexicans. They imprisoned him at Sutter's Fort, along with Leese and Mariano Vallejo. The Bear Flaggers were a small group of men who created a foray near the home of Mariano Vallejo in which their actions made it appear that they were taking over California—whether as their own country or for the United States was unclear, possibly even in their own minds. The flag they created was the basis for the flag that the state of California would adopt, the image of a bear representing the large number of bears that thrived in the area at the time. According to a man who worked for Ridley, when the Bear Flaggers arrested him, he did not send word to his family about being taken to Sutter's Fort, but he did think to take along two bottles of liquor.

Ridley's contentious and somewhat unorthodox way of doing business sounds unstable. Besides never settling for long on any endeavor, he took pride in the gargantuan quantity of liquor he regularly consumed. He died at age thirty-two. One can rather sadly observe that Presentación's husband combined features of her parents, a father who drank and a mother who engaged in business. Ridley's unfortunate exaggeration of both characteristics created a fractured lifestyle.[13]

Presentación absorbed some management expertise from her mother and an understanding of the Anglo business world from her husband. Several receipts for payment of rent to her show that she handled financial matters carefully. In 1854, to prove her claim to the Rancho Cañada de Guadalupe y la Visitación y Rodeo Viejo in what is now San Mateo County, Presentación hired the brilliant lawyer Henry Wager Halleck, who was considered so influential in the state that one historian said that in 1849 Halleck, the secretary of the first California constitutional convention, was, "in large measure, its brains."[14]

During the 1840s, the families of Juana's siblings Felipe, Gregorio, and Guadalupe moved, at least part-time, to outlying ranches. Felipe's son Desiderio moved to San José, where he was appointed *juez de campo,* overseeing agricultural fields assigned to residents. He married Teodora Soto at Mission San José in 1843, a year after she applied for a grant of more than 13,000 acres adjacent to Felipe's Pinole grant. This area, where many Mirandas and Briones eventually lived, largely defined the easternmost limit of Hispanic settlement in the Bay Area of the time. Parts of the eastern branch of the coast range reached more than five thousand feet and discouraged setting up households beyond that natural divide r.[15]

Felipe, owner of Pinole Ranch, was the brother who had taken in two deserting sailors at Juana's request. He and his wife, Manuela Valencia, baptized at Mission Santa Clara in 1796, parented fourteen children. Felipe had one of the longer entries in the death records of Mission San José. In 1840, he died at the hands of the Bolbones (Volvon) Indians when he attempted to retrieve horses they had stolen. His widow applied for and received Pinole after his death. Briones Regional Park and Briones Reservoir in Contra Costa County still remind the local populace of Felipe's family.[16]

Twelve years Juana's senior, Felipe figured in her life less prominently than Gregorio, who was closer to her in age. Juana and Gregorio were important to each other even to the last years of Juana's life. During her Yerba Buena period, Gregorio, still a soldier, for a time had East Bay assignments, after which he joined Vallejo in Sonoma. That move north led to his applying for the Bolinas grant in 1842. William Richardson, who had also moved north, helped him mark the boundaries and draw the required map. Gregorio's brother-in-law, Rafael García, had moved to the northern segment of that land at Tomales Bay and relinquished the southern portion to Gregorio.[17]

Juana established long and deep connections with the families at Bolinas-Tomales, which led to the almost wondrous public finding in 2007 of the only known photograph of her. With charcoal or crayon, an artist enhanced the image that had been weakly printed on salted paper. There is no name on the portrait, but the process and the probable age of Juana at the time the photograph would have been taken, in the 1850s, substantiates

Juana's brother Gregorio Briones, who essentially founded the town of Bolinas and was possibly her dearest sibling.

the García family's belief that the subject is indeed Juana Briones y Tapia de Miranda.[18]

At Mission Dolores, Juana, other family members, and close associates were devoted churchgoers, as noted in marriage and baptism records. Some frequently recurring names during this period were Apolinario's brother Hilario, who married Juana Cibrian (Sibrian, Sebrean). A Cibrian married one of Juana's nieces in Bolinas. Gregorio Escalante, referred to as a "Manila man" by Charles Brown, his fellow deserter from the whaling

*Juana Briones in a photograph enhanced to create
what is described as a "crayon or charcoal portrait."
Seven generations of relatives of Juana's preserved the
original and in 2007 donated it to the Point Reyes
National Seashore Archives. The curator, Kirsten
Kvam, believes the picture dates to the 1850s or 1860s.*

vessel, served often as godparent with or for Juana's family members. For decades, the three Briones sisters—Juana de Miranda, Guadalupe de Miramontes, and Epiciaca de Soto—alternately gave birth and served as godmothers. That the church, not the government, kept the records of births and deaths says a great deal. The government relied on the family and the church to mediate a viable social system.

After the birth of her last child in 1841, Juana entered a new phase. She and the community had matured. The military declined, the population rose. The few Indians who remained at the secularized Mission Dolores worked for local people. More Anglos arrived and contributed to revising social dynamics. In 1830, the population of the San Francisco presidio and mission, including the land between them, had been 131. By 1842, many soldiers and their families had moved elsewhere, but the population had increased to 196, a demographic difference of considerable consequence in so small a place.[19]

In December 1842, Marcos Briones died without receiving the last sacraments due to forgetfulness of old age, according to a priest's notes in the mission's death register. If Marcos had been alone when he died, this might have been excusable, but it is also conceivable that he had separated philosophically from the Catholic religion and did not want a priest. He did not hire anyone to write a will for him because he owned no land, the major asset to bequeath in those days.

No images remain of Marcos. Few official records and fewer stories tell of him. Mission Dolores seems the most fitting place for his burial. One of his memorable moments, from the viewpoint of our day and age, was his accompanying as guard, at age nineteen in 1776, Juan Bautista de Anza to locate sites for the San Francisco settlement. Mariano Vallejo, one of the few Californios who could be called an intellectual, knew Marcos and said he was "intelligent." Another clue attests to Marcos's honor, integrity, determination to excel, and demeanor as a Catalan Volunteer. Marcos Briones—soldier, son, husband, father, grandfather, citizen—may have been with the Portolá expedition. If not, he arrived in California soon after. He lived under and fought for Spain, then, after he retired, under Mexico. He came to California young and lived long. What describes him best is to say he was a Californian. No tombstone honors him now, or his son Gregorio, who asked to be buried near his father in the Mission Dolores cemetery.

Having been born in California, Juana was even more of a Californian than her father and more of a San Franciscan, having lived there all her adult years to the time of her father's death. Had it not been for the American occupation and especially the gold rush, La Playa de Juana Briones might have remained Juana's main, lifelong residence, with her house at the mission a second, less business-oriented home. But then she may have thought of a big ranch as a way to supply homes and incomes for her children in their maturity, the way Peralta thought about his big ranch in the East Bay. Things did not work out that way for her, though, once foreigners swarmed in, swamped the area, and took over its management.

SAN FRANCISCO

A Case of Mistaken Identity

Before 1842, what Juana did and how she lived seemed less specific to her and more an extension of other people's lives. She had set up a business and two homes on her own, but when she reached age forty, she took more complete charge within complex circumstances. Divesting herself of her husband and acquiring land constituted related endeavors. Her marital dilemma affected her ability to achieve self-sufficiency. Juana mainly wanted to get rid of an abusive husband, but even she hardly understood some of her problems in their entirety, culturally and legally entangled as they were and resistant to solutions. There is no glossing over Juana and Apolinario's worsening marriage. They lived in separate houses in a small community, not exactly within shouting distance of each other, but at least a quick ride apart. Any possibility of unity or friendship had evaporated.

Apolinario's making fun of Juana turned malicious. He wanted other people to know how little she deserved his affection. She testified that he shouted demeaning words at her. Her temperament and her high standing among people of every status in her community and in her church would have made his private and public disdain all the more intolerable. His demeaning her in front of the children must have been doubly hurtful.

Although safety was a serious issue for Juana in regard to her husband, giving up her home and moving elsewhere were not reasonable options for her. When she gave birth to her last child during this stressful time, the godparents were her sister Epiciaca and Gregorio Escalante. It is possible that during this period of danger, Escalante was helping to protect Juana and the children.[1]

Juana said that Apolinario insulted, beat, and wounded her. The couple's deeply contentious relationship continued over the next six years. Juana appealed to the courts twelve times from 1840 to 1846. Her most frequent contacts with officials occurred in 1843 and 1844, none in 1845, probably because Apolinario was incarcerated in San José that year to separate him from his wife. In February 1844, Apolinario wrote a letter saying he was an elector and expected to have some of the more important political people, including the governor, intervene on his behalf. He had begun to realize the possibility that he could lose his liberty, which ultimately happened. Later that year Juan Prado Mesa made arrangements to transport the prisoner Apolinario Miranda.

By the time Juana took uncommon steps to effect a definitive, legally recognized separation, she had already experienced her disadvantage as a married woman attempting to acquire title to the land she occupied in Yerba Buena. She felt deeply the injustice of living with a man who did not respect or support her and, beyond that, within a system that hampered her ability to provide for herself and her children. She had somehow to convey this urgency to authorities. In her attempts to acquire the title, by always mentioning that she supported the family without Apolinario's help, she frankly admitted the economic dimension of her complaint. Men had the right to punish wives and children, but that depended in part on fulfilling their obligation to provide for their families.[2]

In terms of the economy of her day, Juana knew that only land promised genuine security for their children someday. But the alcalde failed to certify Juana's ownership of the Yerba Buena lots, probably because he considered their marriage intact even if they did not live together. Women could possess land, but for married couples, husbands applied for grants in their own names. When the local authorities did not address her dilemma adequately, Juana realized that church sanction of the separation would encourage government officials to take her seriously. She went not to her local priest, but to one in Santa Clara, who wrote for her to the bishop in 1844. Perhaps the local priest would not do as she asked, or perhaps she preferred to distance herself from gossip. She may also have preferred talking to Padre Rafael Moreno at Santa Clara because he personally knew the bishop, Francisco García Diego y Moreno, with whom he had traveled to California in 1833. Juana herself may also have known the bishop. He had headquartered at Mission Santa Clara when he first came to California and before he became bishop.[3]

However much Father Moreno may have sympathized with Juana, he had a duty to explain that other wives endured as much or worse. She knew from her lifetime of churchgoing that the greater the obstacles, the more certain the heavenly reward, and that God repaid with eternal joy those who endured hardship, especially those who persevered without complaint. Her knowledge of doctrine gave her reason to admit something she would have preferred not to mention. Yes, her husband beat her, which she would tolerate as a test sent by God, but serving God required her and her husband to set a good example for the children. Apolinario's failure in that regard must not be tolerated. She held forth the incontestably worse possibility that he had either threatened or accomplished, which is unclear, incest with their eldest daughter. Juana said that fortunately this daughter was married now, but the example of their father's liquor-influenced behavior continued to damage all the children: "y ha querer poner en practica sus acciones nefandas no solo exigiendo de me imperiosamente y con puclicidad el debit conugal, sino aun queriendo abusar, como lo intento varias veces hacer con mi hija Ma. Presentacion, que ya afortunadamente esta casada." A full translation of the letter in Barbara Voss's dissertation "Archaeology of el Presidio de San Francisco" reveals the sexual accusations that other historians have hinted at by referring to "unpaternal actions." Juana wrote that she did "not fear to shoulder the conjugal cross," but

> I fear the destruction of my unfortunate family due to the scandal and bad example. . . . [His] only concern is drunkenness and all the vices that come with it, and [he] no longer cares about feeding his family, a burden that I alone carry. . . . [M]y own labor and the labor of my poor family sustain my husband, providing him not only with clothes and food, but also paying for his drunkenness. . . . [A]s soon as he is a little tipsy he begins to utter his blasphemies, swear, and to put into practice his abominable behavior, not only publicly and imperiously demanding the conjugal debt from me, but also wanting to abuse it, as he has tried to do several times with my daughter María Presentación, who fortunately is already married. . . . How will I excuse myself before God, if I do not seek . . . all possible means of ridding my family of such a bad example?[4]

Drinking by itself would hardly have justified divorce. Some historians have said that Californios drank moderately, but records occasionally mention overindulgence. Francisco Sánchez, who owned the grant that is now the town of Pacifica, stayed at various times at the Portsmouth House in San Francisco and paid with cattle for his board and beverages. Juan Alvarado escaped from his government duties at Monterey for occasional alcoholic binges at his ranch near the present town of Salinas. Even some priests drank excessively.[5]

Annulment or divorce were almost unheard of, although occasionally some instances occurred, as in Monterey, where María Lucia del Carmen Bolcoff obtained a divorce in 1847 from Pierre Richard, or he from her—both were equally interested in terminating the marriage. Ambivalence about marriage extended to every social sector, private and public.[6]

The letter that the priest in Santa Clara wrote on Juana's behalf went to Bishop García Diego. When he had arrived as part of Governor Figueroa's party, he was in charge of nine Zacatecans who were Franciscans from a primarily Mexican seminary. They had been assigned to the northern missions from Soledad to Solano to replace Spanish priests. Part of their mandate was to make former mission buildings and land more available for use and occupation by Indians and Californios. Not yet a bishop at the time, Padre García Diego examined conditions in California and returned to Mexico, where he made his application to the pope for permission to replace missions with parishes. As he observed, missionary activity no longer made sense in the territory. The Indian population had either converted or been absorbed into the general society or fled to Indian country. While in Mexico, García Diego was appointed the first bishop of California, eliminating the position of father-president of the missions. He set up headquarters successively in San Diego, Santa Clara, and, by 1844, when Padre Moreno wrote to him for Juana, in Santa Barbara.

Almost immediately on receipt of this communication, Bishop Diego wrote to William Hinckley, the mayor of Yerba Buena, who was married to a Martínez, a family with long and close connections to Juana's family. Diego explained that Juana had provided documentation to the ecclesiastical court that her husband had disobeyed civil orders against harassing her. He formally requested that Hinckley take measures to protect her and the children. Hinckley apparently put the matter to Apolinario, but with limited success. Juana complained of Apolinario again two years later. An Anglo businessman said that Hinckley was "a man with good powers of speech and persuasion," something he needed to deal with Apolinario, a respected landowner, descendant of founders, retired soldier, and father of a large and prominent family. Except for Juana's adopted Indian daughter, who used the name Briones, their children were Mirandas.[7]

Juana's 1846 document of complaint raises the question whether she was truly illiterate. Every other extant communication from her is written by someone on her behalf, and perhaps this one was, but it does not include her usual statement that someone is writing for her because she cannot read or write. There is a remote, yet unlikely, possibility that she could write but had so little formal education that she preferred not to disclose her inferiority.

Juana's purchase of a ranch in 1844 can be interpreted as a potential escape from Apolinario, but one she would have been reluctant to use immediately because of her many responsibilities and commercial interests at Yerba Buena. For a person who was accustomed to a congenial social atmosphere and who had resided for thirty-two years in the vicinity of the San Francisco Presidio, the relative isolation of a ranch would have seemed disadvantageous.

Apolinario died a year after the last complaint, which sounded as desperate as ever. His health may have precluded any further government action in his last year of life. He died in 1847 at age fifty-four and was buried at Mission Dolores, as were two of Juana's elder brothers that same year—José, single, age sixty, and Antonio, married, age sixty-three.[8] If Apolinario's grave at Mission Dolores ever had a tombstone, it is no longer visible.

Juana's first request for certification of her ownership of Yerba Buena land that she was already using had gone to Alcalde Francisco de Haro in 1836 or 1838. Her application for land almost a decade before Apolinario died was unusual. Only widows or single women or women who had inherited directly owned land—but not married women. In 1844, she mentioned that this request was the second or third time she had petitioned, but it was not until January 1847 that Alcalde George Hyde confirmed her title, nine months before her husband died. Governmental reticence in handling her request for land that everyone considered to be hers taught her a lesson, so that when she looked to purchase a ranch, she knew to cover every angle. One of the angles was church sanction of her status, and though she did not specifically gain a divorce from the bishop, he validated her separation in the opinion of the local authorities.

In Yerba Buena, on the land finally allocated to her, Juana's house angled across her six lots at the corner of present Filbert and Powell Streets. What is now Washington Square can reliably be assumed to have been the corral that Thomes mentioned in his memoir. Juana had a dairy already in good working order in 1843, when Thomes's captain assigned him shore duty to purchase milk "every morning" from Señora Briones. Thomes was more than an ordinary sailor—he was writing a book and was hired to represent business interests—but he did not expect the first-class treatment that captains routinely counted on. Juana, however, did not feel the disdain that other people showed toward ordinary sailors. Thomes and Juana "struck up quite a friendship. She always welcomed me with a polite good-morning, and a drink of fresh milk."[9]

This friendship corroborated numerous instances of Juana's ability to relate positively to people across myriad differences. In another part of his reminiscences, Thomes mentions the exclusion of ordinary sailors at Larkin's in Monterey. When everyone else was offered a glass of wine, "we were not invited." In Yerba Buena, Richardson's daughters "flew at higher game than common sailor boys" and "knew their stations in life and were well aware of ours," very different from his welcome at Juana's place. Thomes wrote that captains went ashore confident of a hearty welcome, but even chief mates, second in command, expected no such reception and more often passed on ship leave or returned early if they did go ashore because of their cool reception.[10]

Thomes found Juana's milking interestingly different from the tame East Coast style of operation. California cattle had to be handled like wild animals. He said that "Pedro" went to milk the cow, which was in a corral with a dozen others plus calves. After one was milked, Pedro went on to milk the others. Juana may have had a reputation for especially good milk. On one occasion, Thomes and Lewey were sent to her to get milk because John Sutter was aboard, and the captain required a meal that expressed the quality of ship cuisine—for the captain and his honored guest, that is, not for ordinary sailors. Besides the drink of fresh milk Juana gave the errand boys, they hid containers in their pockets to take aboard for their own coffee. Another fine point Thomes mentioned was Juana's milking the cow herself when Pedro could not. She used a technique known by dairy operators, that a cow will put down milk for its own calf. She then continued milking the rest of the cows. Thomes wrote, "She knows her business."

John Ackerman, a youth who arrived in the area in 1844, said he would be hired by Anglos in town to do errands, one of which was to get milk from a family named Briones at North Beach. Juana's bartender son-in-law Robert Ridley was noted for milk punches at his saloon in a rickety Mission Dolores building, which he called Mansion House in the humorous way for which he was known. He may have been cashing in on Juana's reputation for fine-quality milk and on his own for liquor.[11]

Juana's herd was growing along with the hide and tallow trade, and her space in Yerba Buena was limited. From her difficulties in getting her Yerba Buena lots approved, Juana realized that she would be up against discrimination if she attempted to acquire a ranch for pasture. Women who took such action, as she did in purchasing the Rancho la Purísima Concepción in 1844, were considered to be preempting the natural perquisites of fathers and husbands. Men and a few women obtained land as grants at no cost. She probably realized that this option was unlikely for her, and for that reason she took the opportunity to purchase, which was somewhat

Mission Dolores, ca. 1860, after the buildings attached to the church had come into private ownership. This stereographic view has Mansion House (Robert Ridley's saloon) in the center.

uncommon at the time. She had found a niche in a favorably evolving economy. Whaling vessels put into port for supplies. Local farmers learned to grow foods that the sailors preferred—potatoes, cabbage, pumpkins, onions. The government encouraged foreign trade. Thomes's remark that Juana knew "her business" was right. She had a knack for economics, and a large trade in the sale of hides and tallow had dramatically opened up.

Hispanic California ranchers had skill working with cattle that many visitors described as the finest they had ever seen, using exquisitely trained horses. Added to that, cattle flourished almost beyond belief on California grasses, except during rare periods of drought or flood. Ships that took away raw hides returned with manufactured goods, some of which previously could be obtained at missions when they were in full operation. Indians continued to make many fine products such as saddles, bridles, and shoes, but their workshops declined along with the missions. Men making riatas from horsehair were observed working alongside Juana's Yerba Buena household, labor that would have been part of her cattle business, and because she was attuned to marketing, some ranchers may also have purchased such equipment produced at her establishment.[12]

Ships departed for eastern ports—to "Boston," as Hispanic people said—with as many as forty thousand hides in one cargo. They brought back shoes of California leather made not by artisans, but in factories. The associated tallow trade was by no means a minor component of the economic benefit. Davis estimated that Californians exported 62.5 million pounds of tallow between 1826 and 1848, mostly to Peru for candle making. Californians used some of the tallow to make their own soap and candles, both difficult processes. If Juana were to attempt such large-scale operations, she needed more space than Yerba Buena afforded, but the disadvantage was that ranching involved less sociability. She and most of her compatriots were accustomed to the companionable life of pueblos, presidios, and missions, which were combination living and work environments. A large ranch could have on its staff various artisans such as shoemakers and dressmakers, a model that Juana already imitated in her pocket-size ranch at Yerba Buena, but neighbors were farther away.[13]

Houses in town usually had a chicken coop and a vegetable garden in back. As a mercantile society evolved in Yerba Buena, the government restricted residents from acquiring big properties there and passed laws to discourage land speculation by stipulating that lots be sold one to a person, which some residents such as Captain Joseph Folsom circumvented. He paid various people a small fee to buy lots under their names and then transfer them to him, but he died before he could enjoy his property, which lawyer Henry Wager Halleck then administered. The village that Americans chose to name "San Francisco" became the centerpiece of towns around the bay, but not everyone recognized that potential. William Tecumseh Sherman wrote in his *Memoirs* that he would not have stooped so low as foolishly to purchase land "in such a horrid place."[14]

Juana must have occasionally congratulated herself on her prescience in buying the Purísima Ranch when she did. She could have had no inkling of the major shift that would occur in the six years after her purchase. She was making a good living at Yerba Buena and had staff there. She would be able to reside part of the time in town and part at the ranch, where she could leave daily operations to Indians, a work arrangement that may have been included in the understanding between Juana and the Indian who sold the ranch to her.

Presentación married Ridley in January 1844, but some of Juana's other children, from three to thirteen, were just reaching an age when they could begin learning ranch management. Apolinario's Ojo de Agua de Figueroa was measured in the Spanish equivalent of yards, and Juana's new rancho in leagues, a measure on land equal to 2.6 miles. As it happened, she purchased the ranch just in time, two years before a U.S. Navy ship, the *Portsmouth*, pulled into San Francisco Bay as part of the Mexican-American War of 1846.

After a short interval to look around and assess the situation without flashing their guns about, the Americans hoisted their nation's flag over the Yerba Buena plaza and onetime potato patch. John Brown named the other people besides himself who were on hand to watch the American flag go up: Captain William Leidesdorff, John Finch, Joseph Thompson, Mrs. Robert Ridley (Presentación), Mrs. Andrew Hoepner, Mrs. Captain Voight, and Richard the Third, a local character.

Presentación Miranda y Briones de Ridley watched that flag rising over country where her mother's parents and her father's mother had pioneered on behalf of Spain. William Heath Davis made a list of the residents of Yerba Buena, the mission, and the presidio at the time, claiming to exclude none. His list of 148 included Juana and five young children. Tomás, the eldest not married, was listed separately, and the baby, Dolores, was not included, perhaps because he was only five and not seen much. Others on the list with connections to Juana were Apolinario and three servants; Presentación Ridley and one servant; Robert Ridley; Mrs. Montgomery, who later married Talbot Green and then Joseph Wallis, who became Juana's lawyer after Henry Halleck departed California to become army general; and Gregorio Escalante, a baker. At the presidio were Guadalupe Briones de Miramontes and her husband, Candelario, six of their children, and Luz Briones. Even if Davis missed some, which he claimed he did not, Yerba Buena was tiny.[15]

Many of Juana's compatriots did not share her meticulous attention to securing her legal status as a property owner. Ignacio Martínez, a leading member of the Bay Area community and father of Richardson's and Hinckley's wives, received a huge land grant in the East Bay along the southern shore of Carquinez Strait. In 1834 and again in 1837, he asked for validation of that grant because he had "mislaid the papers." Martínez perhaps neglected to consider that his former position as presidio commander might someday cease to assure his economic viability. He assented to Felipe Briones's claim that Felipe occupied the Pinole Ranch with Martínez's knowledge and consent. Felipe's wife, María Manuela Valencia de Briones, authenticated her full ownership after her husband's death.

A similar case of loose interpretation about boundaries and certification occurred in a ranch adjacent to Juana's owned by her Buelna cousins. A place on their grant occupied by Juana's sister Guadalupe was so commonly accepted as hers that her name appeared roughly in the middle of the diseño, with no boundary lines and no indication that she ever applied for it. The Stanford University golf course now encompasses Guadalupe's unofficial parcel.[16]

Governmental silence and delay greeted Juana when she first applied for approval to purchase the Rancho la Purísima Concepción, but she succeeded on her second attempt. The date of the letter from the bishop to the alcalde about her marriage, July 1844, and her application to the governor for permission to purchase the ranch, October of the same year, suggest her understanding of the connection between her marital status and her potential for owning land.

Although Juana then could have moved lock, stock, and barrel to the ranch, Yerba Buena remained her first place of residence, a situation that owed something to her good relations with and understanding of new arrivals, regardless of their provenance. Most other Hispanic people preferred to live among their own at the Mission Dolores village. By 1846, of eighty-four lot owners in Yerba Buena, fewer than half had Hispanic names.[17]

Immigration accelerated in the decade of the 1840s. Before the influx became a human stampede with the gold discovery in 1848, both Indian and Hispanic people could access the economic opportunities. Fairly soon, though, Indians were pushed out entirely, and Hispanic men found themselves at a disadvantage, both for money-making work and for marriage prospects. Societal change, Tiburcio Vásquez said, turned him into an outlaw. At parties and dances of his own people, the Anglos would shove him and his friends out, monopolizing the women and the event.[18]

Most immigrants were single men, both before the gold fever and after it raged, but families too came. The Stephens-Murphy party of 1843 brought a large family, the Murphys, some of whom would soon enter Juana's life by taking a lease on about half of the Purísima Ranch. Another member of that party, Sarah Armstrong Montgomery, lived in Yerba Buena in 1846, when, with so few residents, everyone knew everyone. In so small a town, she and Juana shared the dilemma of being afflicted with husband problems. Allen Montgomery had abandoned Sarah. Her second husband,

Talbot Green, was found to be a bigamist who had embezzled from a Philadelphia bank. Perhaps with such bad luck, Sarah preferred to avoid another disaster when she married a third time. Her lawyer brother set up a trust under his oversight by which she owned a fine piece of land adjacent to Juana's ranch on the peninsula. Under that trusteeship arrangement, she also owned the elegant house she and her husband, lawyer Joseph Wallis, built on the land. Sarah advocated women's property rights and suffrage. She hosted Susan B. Anthony and lobbied in Sacramento. Like Juana, she built a house in Mayfield and moved there in her elder years. The two women's paths and interests thus intersected at many points, and given Juana's unusually good relations with Anglos, the women would almost certainly have been friends.[19]

During these tumultuous years, Juana developed her personal circle of friends and acquaintances, expanded her business interests, and dispensed medical treatment—all accomplishments that built on her willingness both to help and to learn from diverse people, including Indians, who were not exotic, unusual, or wealthy, but were part of daily life. It was common to hire them as household or ranch workers, but Juana may be the only one among her people who was said to have had Indian women construct her Yerba Buena house. Perhaps this fact was only partly true, but it resonates with other truths and was remembered because someone thought it indicated that Juana hated men. She could never have succeeded as she did, though, if she hated men. They had full charge of all the major institutions of the society. There were many instances in which she helped nephews, male patients, deserting sailors, and her own male children, who inherited from her along with her daughters. She also had lifelong friendship with two of the sailors she helped desert, Gregorio Escalante and Charles Brown; long and close association with several of her brothers and their families; and positive relationships with priests.

Instead, the story about her house being constructed by Indian women reveals that Juana knew that within many Indian tribes, women were the construction experts, a job that the European patriarchal mission system had reassigned to men according to their interpretation of appropriate gender roles. They called in Indian women only when the women were badly needed to help make adobe bricks or carry materials in support of men's work. Indian women were the carriers and load bearers in their own society, and they constructed their family homes.

As the story went, Juana's Indian women builders used a construction technique called rammed earth, which she also adapted later for her home at the Purísima Ranch. Harry Peterson, who was the curator of the

Stanford family museum for nearly twenty years, wrote about the Indian women's methods. He wrote that they cleared blackberry vines from Juana's Yerba Buena home site, gathered driftwood at the beach, put it upright in the ground to form inner and outer walls about two feet apart, and filled the crib so formed with brush and stones, which they cemented together with mud. A two-foot-thick wall would have given excellent insulation against the cold and fog that sped through the entry to the bay. If Indian women did build Juana's Yerba Buena house, she demonstrated once again her insight into the knowledge and abilities of people from many walks of life.[20]

Indian women who had learned sewing at the missions would also have been on Juana's staff, and her children worked as well. Juana mentioned in one of her marriage depositions that she and her children supported Apolinario with their labors. Juana's sewing business is known from one letter dated April 23, 1846, from William A. Leidesdorff in Yerba Buena to Mr. J. P. Leese in Sonoma:

Dear Sir,

My launch goes to Sonoma for the purpose of taking over some few articles for Captain Fitch, and to bring me back some hides & flour. Therefore the launch will not be able to bring down the wheat for Mr. Thompson. However next time will do. I inclose [sic] you the order. Dona Juana Briones wishes me to say to you, that in case there should be any room in the launch, to be good enough to send her some of the grain you have for her.

She also wishes you to give your wife her respects, or rather muchos saludas, and say to her that the articles which she has here belonging to your wife, are under way sewing and will soon be done. No news here of any consequence.

I remain your Obt. Sevt.

Wm. A. Leidesdorff[21]

The woman who had articles being sewn at Juana's place was a member of the California elite. Leese's wife was Rosalia Vallejo, sister of Mariano Vallejo, head of the Northern Frontier. She would have sought out the finest workmanship available.

Two years later, in 1848, a visitor to the Purísima Ranch mentioned that the two older daughters did the cooking. They were brought up differently from the Vallejo girls, each of whom had an Indian to care for her, and from Brigida Briones, possibly Juana's niece Benedicta, whose Indian servant carried her kneeling mat to church for her. In Juana's family, everyone old enough contributed to the common welfare. At the date of this Leidesdorff letter, only eight Indians lived at Mission Dolores, a center that had once housed twenty looms to process the wool of eleven thousand sheep. Indian women who had handled the manufacture of cloth and clothing thus needed jobs, and they made good, well-trained employees for Juana.[22]

Juana's household economy accommodated her medical career, which sometimes required her to be away from home ministering to sick people or attending a birth. One healer of the eastern United States recorded in her diary that her family contributed to household income. Laurel Thatcher Ulrich's analysis of Martha Ballard's records shows that Martha's midwifery practice became more active when her daughters were old enough to take up weaving. Martha, who kept her diary until 1812, lived in Maine, but her circumstances as a woman doctor resembled Juana's. During Martha's working life, professional doctors began to move into the field, as they did into California shortly after Juana purchased her ranch. Nevertheless, Juana was still sought out because some patients preferred less drastic cures than those of trained doctors.[23]

At this time, Americans were arriving on every side—John Fremont from the north, the first overland party of settlers from the east, another following two years later, U.S. warriors with a navy sloop-of-war in San Francisco Bay, and occupation forces in Monterey. Times were in flux, but Juana in the mid-1840s probably had no idea that she lived at the cusp of a cataclysmic divide that began with this trickle of overland travelers.

Members of the Bidwell-Bartleson party in 1841 had no intention of becoming either Mexican or Catholic, the Mexican government's requirement for owning land, or of marrying Hispanic California women. Some members of that party five years after their arrival took part in the Bear Flag Revolution, a series of events that brought harsh politics into Juana's family with Ridley's imprisonment.[24]

Ridley had arrived in 1840 and married Presentación only two years before the U.S.S. *Portsmouth* arrived in 1846. Politicians and businesspeople talked together at his saloon, and Ridley certainly tried to smooth the waters between Anglos and Hispanics. Edwin Bryant, who wrote a rather detailed book about his experiences, *What I Saw in California*, attended a fandango "given by Mr. Ridley . . . whose wife is a Californian lady. Several of the senoras and senoritas from the ranchos of the vicinity were present." Bryant wrote that women smoked, and "they puff it with much gusto while threading the mazes of the cotillion or swinging in the waltz." On Ridley's return to San Francisco after his incarceration at Sutter's Fort, he ran for mayor against Washington Bartlett. Sailors were shuttled ashore to vote in order to assure Bartlett's victory.[25]

The arrival of military personnel created excitement but no drastic revision of local custom until word of gold came down like a cyclone from the mountains in 1848. The earliest miners came from elsewhere in California, as well as from Mexico, Peru, and Chile. Many of them had previous experience with mining that was helpful to inexperienced newcomers from other regions, but before long, certain miners, including Hispanics and Chinese, were treated as taxed immigrants and potential victims.[26]

The U.S. Army and Navy trailed speculators behind them like a horse pulling a plow, but with gold as an incentive, the population came to include people of innumerable languages and religions. Anglos adopted California systems until they could install their own. The existing infrastructure facilitated the exploitation of the gold fields. Boats with food, supplies, and information plied the rivers back and forth to the gold country from San Francisco Bay. Established travel routes and a working overland, north-south mail system made conquering the area, accessing resources, and installing a new government relatively simple.

Food production, housing, and craft and trade workers, as well as innumerable horses and mules for travel and transport, all within a compatible European-based society, enabled the entry of large numbers of immigrants who could hastily start mining, farming, and business enterprises, such as Leland Stanford and his brothers, who opened stores catering to miners in the foothills. Stanford later became one of the wealthiest people in California and Juana's neighbor.[27] And the Stevenson regiment that came by ship from New York intending to help fight the war with Mexico had families aboard, the women being called "laundresses."[28]

Religious change nearly as drastic as economic and social change accompanied the U.S. conquest. Between 1769 and an imprecise date, as late as 1833 in some places, Catholicism had shared power with government, concentrated the economy largely in its purview, and set the parameters of daily life. Even after the church lost its huge landholdings, the religion had remained central to belief and custom. When news of gold spread around the world two years after the U.S. invasion, Protestants, Mormons, Jews, and Chinese with long-standing, unifying, traditional clan and philosophical attachments began arriving. They overwhelmed the Catholic religion, but did not obliterate it.

Some Protestant ministers claimed that God had kept the gold hidden until Americans, the chosen people, were in control. One minister commented on the morally reprehensible "carnival nature of the Sabbath"

*San Francisco, ca. 1850. This lithograph by the French naval surgeon
Louis Le Breton shows extensive housing built by gold seekers near both
coves and on Loma Alta (Telegraph Hill) in the center. The travelers
are approaching from the Mission Dolores Hispanic neighborhood.*

when people poured out of mass onto the plaza for festivities. As early as
1850, Congregationalists, Presbyterians, Methodists, Baptists, and Epis-
copalians had begun ministering to San Franciscans. In 1854, an act was
passed "to prevent Noisy, and Barbarous Amusements on the Sabbath." In
San Juan Bautista south of San Jose (now spelled without the accent under
the U.S. regime), Hispanic people terminated their Sunday bullfights after
being fined for breaking a law against the fights.[29]

How each group interpreted and stereotyped the other showed up in
Yerba Buena, San Francisco, and Mission Dolores. The Anglo military
people who were there because the United States was at war with Mexico
referred to the Hispanic people as "Mexicans," yet by this time they no
longer thought of themselves as Mexican. They had divested themselves of
several unacceptable Mexican governors, called themselves "Californios,"
and for six years, from 1836 to 1842, had paid allegiance to Juan Bautista
Alvarado, a native-born governor.[30]

At the same time that Anglos misinterpreted Californios, another
situation indicated convoluted religious-cultural divides. Sam Brannon,

the leader of a Mormon contingent that came in by boat from New York, had seen to it that they came well supplied with guns to enforce acceptance of the Mormon republic they visualized themselves forming. Mormons had been expelled from three states and refused admittance to Arkansas, but to Hispanic people they acted, looked, and spoke just like the rest of the Anglos, with one difference. Because there were more families among them, they melded better into the population, needing help with children and family illnesses. Although Anglos' bigoted accounts of Mormons had frightened Hispanic people in Monterey, Mormons found themselves accepted in San Francisco as they had seldom been elsewhere. The curious contradiction here was that Mormons were outcast Anglos being accepted as good citizens by Hispanic people, but Hispanic Catholics would soon be treated with disdain by the mostly Protestant Anglos, whose anti-Catholic fervor blossomed after California gained statehood in 1850. Once Anglos were securely in charge, some Anglo journalists and elected officials began to describe people such as the alleged Hispanic murderers of John Marsh as having "low foreheads" and as sharing the "inherited ignorance and revengeful disposition of their breed."[31]

Disdain sometimes traveled in the other direction. After witnessing her husband and brother taken as prisoners to Sutter's Fort, Rosalia Vallejo de Leese refused to learn English, her husband Jacob's language. She said that John Fremont threatened to burn down their houses with the people in them if she did not write a letter for him and that "those hated men inspired me with such a large dose of hate against their race . . . I have abstained from learning their language." She later divorced Leese for having squandered her dowry and opened a business in Monterey to support her family.[32]

Juana had facility with language, experience relating to Anglos through her work at Yerba Buena, and was not easily discouraged, but danger where ruffians abounded made staying in San Francisco problematic, especially if one had children. In 1848, men attacked a group of Chileans who had a tent city on Telegraph Hill, looting, burning, killing a boy, murdering a mother, and raping her daughter.[33]

Such criminals abused anyone who looked Hispanic, but Juana had not as late as October 1849 moved definitively to her Purísima Ranch. A man who first arrived that month took a jaunt soon after leaving his boat and observed Juana's Yerba Buena holdings in operation at Telegraph Hill. It was he who mentioned having seen Indians weaving riatas outside a shed there.[34]

Safety mattered most, but aesthetic changes also might have been disheartening. Streets that looked regular on a map disregarded natural features. Anglos ran straight lines on paper for streets and boundaries. They even cheated by selling underwater lots where hills would be pushed into the bay and ships and wharves sunk to make land. Some abandoned ships became housing or even prisons, then were left to rot and sink to make new land worth money.[35]

Many people have wondered why the tip of the peninsula named San Francisco became an economic center. Sausalito to the north had more freshwater. Richardson had named it "Sausalito" because ship captains would recognize the name as "Little Willow" and expect to find water. He also appreciated the deep, sheltered harbor.[36] Benicia, northeast of San Francisco, had good access to the river route to the gold mines. Mariano Vallejo had named the town for his wife, Francisca Benicia Carrillo. The U.S. Land Commission later invalidated his claim, but some important businesses opened there. In 1849, the commander of the Pacific, General Persifer F. Smith, put his headquarters on land donated by two business leaders in Benicia. In 1850, the Pacific Mail and Steamship Company set up shop there. Benicia was the state capital for two years, and promoters used the name "Athens of California" to advertise the quality of the town's schools.[37]

But there were several reasons for San Francisco's rise in population and prosperity. It was adjacent to one of the best farming regions in the world, the Santa Clara Valley, where Juana settled for the second half of her life. Access to Monterey through the Santa Clara Valley also favored San Francisco. Monterey could be reached more readily by land than by sea due to the vagaries of ocean transport. Prevailing winds and currents created the implausible situation that the same trip by sailing ships between Monterey and Los Angeles took twenty-four hours going south, but two weeks going north.

Something about Juana made her memorable. After she left San Francisco, her Yerba Buena land was for many years called the "Spanish lot." What is now Washington Square, a large city park with a state historic marker honoring her, has been referred to as Juana's vegetable garden, her potato patch, or her corral. It could have been all three, separate from the lots she claimed. After Robert Ridley purchased three of her lots in 1849, she retained the rest until 1858, perhaps imagining that life would return to normal there, which it never did. In 1862, a year after the U.S. Supreme Court certified her and her children's ownership, she sold the Ojo de Agua property, the last of her San Francisco holdings.[38]

From being called Loma Alta for half Juana's life, the Telegraph Hill of her later years symbolized the way her world flipped. A fifty-mile telegraphic connection installed from San Francisco to San Jose in 1853 and to Los Angeles in 1860 contributed to a diminishing appreciation of her oral-based culture. The telegraph connected to Omaha in 1861. Another world-revising technological achievement was completed in 1869: the railroad across the Sierra Nevada. The railroad almost seemed miraculous, replacing covered wagons that had followed a route infected with deadly cholera. It did not seem outrageous to claim even before the railroad had crossed the mountains that this phenomenon managed to annihilate distance and outrun time.

Amid all the hoopla about so inventive a generation, seemingly no one cared that the good herb that flourished on the hill next to Juana's Yerba Buena house and from which she made tea probably breathed its last in 1881, when the U.S. Army quarried Telegraph Hill for road-building material.[39]

Part Three

PERSISTENT STRUGGLES ACROSS REGIMES

Nine

"THIS WOMAN WHO CURED ME"

Nineteenth-Century Medicine

Juana's lasting as a historical figure rests primarily on her financial acumen because business information tends to get explicitly written down, preserved, and admired when it is successful. Her occupation as a healer was also written down, albeit less explicitly. Who taught her medicine and when and where she was taught can be accurately surmised because the teachers available had to be people where she lived or people who visited where she lived because she had no books. It is known that healers generally learned primarily from family members and from other healers in their communities who had particular knowledge of herbal medicine—most of whom in Juana's case would have been Indians.

One of the letters written for Juana to the alcalde of Yerba Buena asking for protection from her husband is the only instance when she herself refers in print to her career as a doctor. She said that her husband took an opportunity to steal valuables from her house while she was out caring for a patient. She thus knew that the recipient of the letter would be familiar with the requisites of her occupation as a healer.[1]

Lore constitutes the primary source about Juana as a curandera. More than fifty years after her death, Robert O'Brien, a newspaper reporter who specialized in San Francisco history, wrote an article that contained a story told to him by Marion Cowan, a North Beach resident and novelist whose nom de plume was B. M. Bower. She told O'Brien that one damp and chilly night the fire in Juana's house went out. Fearing that the cold would harm the sick Indian girl in her care, Juana saddled her horse, galloped to the presidio, returned with a burning brand, and thereby saved the girl's life. O'Brien called it a "heroic ride."[2]

Whether this story rings true in every detail matters less than that it corroborates other information about Juana and that it gives us insight into the rigors of daily life. Juana's "heroic ride" also confirms other instances of her healing across barriers of race and culture. She had close relationships with at least some Indian people and some foreigners, made her home a hospital, and energetically pursued solutions.

Another San Francisco newspaper a mere thirty years after Juana died ran a stunning article entitled "The Remarkable Story of Juana Briones" by Harry Peterson. He called Juana "California's Clara Barton" when Barton was still famous as "the [Civil War] Angel of the Battlefield" and founder of the American Red Cross. Peterson had attended school in Mayfield while Juana lived there in her old age. Had he been writing about an American war hero, he might be thought of as given to laudatory ideas, but he was part of a society imbued with ethnic discrimination. Few of Juana's people under U.S. rule served in important government positions, held high-paying jobs, or were thought particularly worthy of note by historians.[3]

Peterson specialized in California history and held several impressive positions in the field, such as heading field operations of the California History Department of the State Library. While holding one of those positions, as curator of the Stanford University museum, he wrote a never-published book about the university's history. He thought Juana's importance to the community mattered sufficiently that he included a chapter about her. He wrote that Juana "became the best known and the best beloved woman in California, [was a] ministering angel . . . among rich or poor, the doors swung open in cordial welcome. Her very name was a talisman. In the Indian villages she was received with awe and reverence, and at the missions every padre was her devoted friend."[4]

The mid–nineteenth century offered few options for medical care. Some California residents thought foreigners had access to exotic cures from distant places, which ship captains especially had access to, and ships often carried medical supplies to minister to their crews. On one occasion, after protesting in vain that he was no doctor, Captain Phelps treated two patients, one with a dose of Peruvian bark, one with sulfur. If they did not cure, he said, at least they would not kill, a prudent observation at a time when doctors still used bleeding and calomel, a mercury compound, as curatives.[5]

When wagon trains heading west became like modern traffic jams, cholera, a disease first identified in 1817, killed travelers and resident Indians on the plains where water flowed too slowly to clear out bacteria. Some of the travelers rapidly hooked up their oxen to their wagons and fled in terror, leaving sick and dying comrades on the ground, or they buried the dead in shallow graves in their eagerness to escape a contaminated locale. Hispanic people knew nothing of cholera when they first settled California, but in 1833 people still remaining at missions contracted cholera even as missions were becoming parish churches. Central Valley Indians caught from trappers cholera and other diseases formerly unknown there.[6]

James Abbey wrote in his diary that in the California mining district in 1848 he "came across a poor fellow lying in front of a log cabin—severe diarrhoea. I left him a bottle of Brown's cholera mixture and directions how to take it." Abbey's two sentences support the proposition about a difference between male and female dispensers of medicine—women tended to nurse patients, men supplied a remedy and departed. Chester Lyman, a surveyor boarding at Juana's Purísima Ranch house in 1848, mentioned that there were two sick people in the house: "an Indian girl, of fever, and a man, a sailor, apparently a Portuguese, who has a very bad cough"—again testimony about Juana's difference from the dispense-and-run mode and her attention to patients of diverse backgrounds.[7]

Some historians have excoriated Franciscan missionaries for the decline in Indian population from disease, but the Central Valley suffered epidemics without help from missions. During that season when cholera entered the region and Anglos were still a novelty there, some trappers heading north to Oregon noted a dense Indian population. When they traveled back through the Central Valley the following year to Santa Fe, where they sold beaver skins and California horses, they saw far fewer Indians alive. They even came upon empty villages where homes had collapsed with the dead inside. That disaster could have been caused by cholera or by the first invasion of malaria. When snow melted in the Sierra Nevada east of the valley, much of the great lowland turned into a mosquito-breeding swamp. John Bidwell said that he lost so much blood from mosquitoes in the Sacramento Valley that he could barely walk.[8]

Across the American continent, Indians died from European diseases to an almost unimaginable extent. Smallpox, measles, cholera, malaria, syphilis, diphtheria, typhoid, and respiratory diseases harmed everyone, but especially Indians, who lacked the partial immunity Europeans had developed. California's topographical isolation meant that local Indians' contact with Europeans came late. Indians still were at a loss in dealing with unfamiliar illnesses when Juana was an active curandera.[9]

As inadequate as nineteenth-century medicine appears, it is gratifying to read occasional sensible advice, like that of James Tyson in his *Diary of a Physician in California,* where he advised travelers to avoid drinking much water and to add a bit of an alcoholic beverage to it when they did;

to avoid working in the heat of the day, which would also give time for food preparation, including vegetables, on which not only health, but life depended; and to adopt hygienic habits of person and living space. Tyson admitted, however, that although he did not believe in bleeding, miners, even some in good health, insisted that he provide it, and his complying at least earned him a healthy fee, an ounce of gold.[10]

Medicine as practiced by Hispanics and by Anglos illustrated one of the cultural divides, on one side primarily humanitarian and on the other mainly economic. One incident involving the Robles family gives an example of such a difference of opinion. Juana had known the family since her childhood at Branciforte and again as her neighbors in the Santa Clara Valley. In 1847, for $3,500, brothers Secundino and Teodoro Robles purchased José Peña's Rancho Rincón de San Francisquito, adjacent to but double the acreage of Juana's ranch. Because the U.S. invasion had begun the previous year, the brothers had little time to contemplate their good fortune before various difficulties arose.

In the 1850s, Secundino was involved in a number of quarrels and at one time received a knife wound on his upper arm, severe enough that death seemed lurking. An Anglo doctor cured him and gave him a bill, which Secundino considered excessive. Hispanic people expected their fellow human beings to take care of them with little, if any, compensation. Secundino thought that Dr. George W. Bull's services reciprocated the extensive hospitality he had received from the Robles family. Dr. Bull, however, thought that Secundino owed him six hundred dollars for treatment, medicine, and supplies such as bandages and plasters. The case went to court, where testimony was given about whether Bull was actually a doctor. Secundino won.[11]

Juana apparently believed that she would be repaid somehow, but, if not, she nevertheless dispensed care as her purpose in life. In "The Remarkable Story of Juana Briones," Peterson wrote that Juana, with "poultices and herb tea," nursed and cured a dying sailor. When his shipmates asked how much they owed her, she said she did not charge, her patient's good health was her payment. Before their ship departed, they left at her door "a red lacquered Chinese chest in which were a pair of blankets, several pieces of good linen and many personal articles."

Secundino Robles had a reputation as a highly accomplished horseman, a generous host and parent, and a rich landowner, but with a mindset that eventuated in financial collapse. For example, to get cash to take his family to a circus, he pledged land for security on a seventy-five-dollar loan from an Anglo and later paid off that debt with fifty acres.

This Chinese chest resembles one a group of sailors gave Juana to thank her for saving the life of one of their shipmates. The Bolinas Museum acquired the chest, containing family papers, after the death of Pablo's daughter Rose.

By contrast, the achievement of Juana, for whom remuneration for medical care was secondary and who bestowed a parcel of land on each of her children, had to do with personality differences. In 1920, an obituary of one of Juana's sons said he owned a large amount of land south of Mayfield. The eldest Robles daughter about the same time owned no land, and she finally and reluctantly sold her two cherished rebozos for two hundred dollars because she "had to eat." Robles probably thought he enjoyed life more than Juana did, if he thought of such a comparison at all, but Juana would not have agreed with him. She enjoyed a different kind of satisfaction. They started out as neighbors in childhood and became neighbors again as adults, but in most other ways their paths diverged.[12]

Juana learned to be a curandera when huge health problems prevailed worldwide, no schools of medicine existed where she lived, and there were few schools of any kind, so the questions arise, where did she receive her education in doctoring, and what gave her the confidence to treat a wide clientele? Peterson again comes to the rescue, but what he tells us is not news; it simply validates worldwide information about the way people gained medical knowledge. He said that Juana learned medicine from her mother and from Indians.[13]

It would have been strange indeed not to learn from Indians who were so much a part of her world during her formative years, and, to this day, remedies used by indigenous people of many countries inform the European-based pharmacopoeia. Historical records maintained by the conquering culture detail what Indians learned at missions, but learning in the other direction seldom got written down; mostly it was just part of everyday life. Some stories about herbal medicine have been preserved, though. In 1846, when U.S. troops invaded the Los Angeles area and approached Antonio Coronel's home with guns drawn, he got out fast, thinking he would soon return. When this plan became impractical, he found himself wondering what to do because he had left the house without shirt or shoes. He applied to an Indian chief he knew for help, who thought they should travel to the mountains where his tribe had camped in order to harvest acorns. Despite the sandals the chief had made for Coronel, his feet became a bloody, painful mess as they hiked. When he limped into camp, an "old woman" washed his lacerated feet with an infusion of herbs that, he said, relieved all pain instantly and made his feet "tougher ever since."[14]

José María Amador told of a time when he and other men, including Juan Prado Mesa and Desiderio Briones, went into the Central Valley to retrieve horses that Indians had stolen from Amador's Rancho San Ramón. He described in detail his company's various injuries and in particular his own arrow wounds, which he expected would be fatal. An Indian doctor treated him with three roots: the first cleared infection by making blood gush from the wounds, the second enlarged the openings for removal of the arrowheads, and the third treated the gaping wounds. Indians carried him home. Instead of dying, Amador returned to normal health within a month.[15]

Stories about wonder cures would have circulated widely. Only a few have been preserved. Learning from such valued teachers must have been a cherished privilege for Juana and a resonant connection for her to oral culture, in which tales of memorable moments teach facts. Juana's mother had the opportunity to learn from Indians early, while their medicines were still at their most potent. Historian Douglas Monroy observes that the failure of Indian medicine to treat unfamiliar illnesses that came with first contact caused them to distrust their own remedies. Syphilis, in many ways the worst of all, passed to women through sexual relations with infected men, but could also be transmitted through an open cut, from soiled bedding or clothing, from tubes medicine men used to remove pus, or even from suppurating sores on an infant born to a syphilitic mother. A sense of loss and devastation could be expected when even the shamans and herb doctors in whom people trusted wasted away in a maze of oozing sores, lassitude, anemia, blindness, and other deformities caused by syphilis.[16]

European respect for Indian medicine had a long history. A Jesuit missionary took quinine, the bark of the cinchona tree, to Italy in the 1600s. Junípero Serra had an infected foot on his first journey into Alta California in 1769. An Indian muleteer cured him with a herbal poultice he used for mules' saddle sores. In his report of 1812, Father Luis Martínez of Mission San Luis Obispo described how powder of ivy cured deep lacerations over a man's entire body from a bear mauling. At some missions, the priests grew, stored, and studied herbs based on information they gathered from books and from Indians. Some medicines were shipped to the missions, but priests had to rely extensively on local plants. Confusion arose because of California's relatively unique ecosystem. To make the best use of local remedies, Mission San Antonio de Padua, long the home of Juana's parents, hired a skilled herbalist, Juana Caravajal.[17]

Herbal medicine was more complex than simply knowing which plant was good for what. The correct part of each plant had to be harvested at a specific time. Certain roots had to be dug before the plants flowered in early spring; leaves might need to age away from sunlight in a dry place; flowers had to be gathered when they first opened, fruits at maturity, bark at times of the year when it could be stripped without harming the tree. The curandera had to know when and how to use the plant, the storage and preparation requirements for different plants, and where and when to locate particular plants. An owner of the Juana Briones house in the 1980s found on the property a *mano y matate,* a stone mortar and pestle, that might have been an Indian artifact or a tool Juana used to process some of her medicinal herbs, or both.[18]

Peterson's point that Juana learned from Indians is substantiated by her circumstances. His second point, that she learned from her mother, is probably true. Medicine was a career that tended to run in families. At Mission San Diego in 1822, Juana's sister Agreda baptized a child who died at birth, meaning that Agreda probably was the midwife. Little information has survived about Juana's mother, Ysadora Tapia, but some information about her medical skill came from interviews with the Murphys, some of whom settled in the Santa Clara Valley in 1843 and knew Juana well. They told an author writing what he called the Murphy family saga that Juana learned herbal remedies from her mother. That evidence is slim, but Juana had at least two other relatives with impressive credentials as curanderas from whom she could have learned, directly or indirectly.

Juana's paternal aunt, Guadalupe Briones de Olivera, actually earned a salary at the Purísima Mission as a nurse, a highly unusual validation of her skill. The priests hired Guadalupe as a nurse to replace Padre Luis Gil y Taboada, known for his medical talent, when he was transferred to another mission.[19] Guadalupe earned food and a monthly wage of five pesos. The mission kept careful records of the value of goods she took from the mission storeroom in lieu of money—shoes for her children, stockings, soap, Dutch linen, flour. At this time, starting in 1817, Juana was fifteen years old and would have known about her aunt's major achievement. Guadalupe had been at the San Antonio Mission when Juana's parents lived there, so the families had the opportunity to share medical knowledge, and Guadalupe had the opportunity to learn about herbs from the Indians there.[20]

Juana's elder sister Guadalupe probably received no salary officially for her work as a healer at Mission Santa Clara, although she would have received some special privileges. Father Magín de Catala influenced Juana's life in many ways, one of which was that, according to testimony by someone who knew Guadalupe, he had a great deal to do with making Guadalupe a "famous" midwife "called by natives and strangers." Catala himself instructed Guadalupe in midwifery because he was impressed with her. Her prudence, piety, and inclination to charitable works were so far beyond others that he selected her as his student. Guadalupe and Juana were next-door neighbors at the Presidio of San Francisco during Juana's teenage years, when she was precisely at the best age for absorbing the intricacies of medicine.

William Heath Davis wrote the most dramatic appraisal of Guadalupe's medical ability that has come down to us. He had the habit of clearly identifying people, no small matter when extended families were common and names changed over time. It was easy to mistake one for the other because both Juana's aunt and her sister were named Guadalupe Briones, both were recognized for their skill in medicine, and both had connections to missions. Davis was clear about whom he meant:

> Doña Guadalupe Briones de Miramontes lived formerly at the Presidio of San Francisco, near "Polin" the name of a spring of water celebrated for certain virtues. She is now (1889) a resident of Spanish town in San Mateo County, and a very old lady . . . over a century. . . . I have been informed that she is hale and strong, and is able to insert a thread through the small eye of a needle, preparatory to her habit of daily sewing with her hand. It was this woman who cured me of a malady and saved me from death years since. I was afflicted with the neuralgia in the head from my youth, and I had been on the point of death, but Doña Guadalupe's simple remedy relieved me of suffering probably to the end of my time.[21]

If only he had explained what the simple remedy was! Spanishtown was the name given to Half Moon Bay in San Mateo County, and if there were any doubt otherwise, the Polin Spring reference solidly identifies this curandera as Juana's sister, not her aunt.

Carmen Miramontes, Juana's niece and Guadalupe Briones de Miramontes's daughter, lived into the twentieth century. Her being known as a healer happened when there were more written records. In a manuscript dated 1902 in the archives of the San Mateo History Museum, an anonymous author says of Carmen that people of the "coastside . . . still remember her today" as a "combined doctor and midwife." She was married in 1852, a time when families gathered from far and wide for weddings. Juana and her children would have traveled to Half Moon Bay for the festivities. As often happens in tracking generations, this author mistook an aunt for a grandmother, claiming that Carmen learned medicine from her mother, Guadalupe, who learned it from her mother, Juana, the one "often called the Widow," who "possessed the most imposing home in San Francisco." Both points mentioned make Juana Briones de Miranda the Juana intended—in other words, Carmen's aunt, not her grandmother, was her mentor.[22]

Neither student nor teacher would undertake so demanding a relationship without mutual trust, one reason why family ties provided a close source of medical apprenticeship. An individual also had to show exceptional interest and aptitude in youth. A small error in judgment or in recognizing and handling herbs could cost a life. Grandparents' wisdom is often credited with passing on medical knowledge, but three of Juana's grandparents died before she was born, and her mother died when she was ten. In all probability, she gained much of her knowledge from her sister Guadalupe, ten years her senior. In this case, confusion about generations may have occurred because Juana the student surpassed Guadalupe the teacher.

The suggestion that Juana's brother Felipe had notable medical skills rests on one remark by a descendant, John Briones, who was for many years a prominent citizen of the town of Martinez. He said incorrectly that his ancestor Felipe had been born and educated in Spain. In fact, Felipe had been born at San Antonio Mission and probably had little if any book learning. John called him "Doctor" Briones, and perhaps he got that right. During Felipe's lifetime, from 1790 to 1840, there were seldom more than one or two formally trained doctors in California at any one time. Felipe might have been a folk doctor.[23]

Another male Briones of the generation following Juana and Felipe's became a doctor and is still remembered for that contribution to his community. That Juana trained her nephew Pablo Briones in medicine still remains a cherished tradition in Bolinas, the town originated by Pablo's father, Gregorio.

Gregorio, his brother-in-law Rafael García, and Juana's brother-in-law Juan Miranda helped Mariano Vallejo in the early years of establishing Sonoma. All stayed on. At first, Gregorio sent his fourteen-year-old son Pablo to tend his cattle on the southern part of Rafael's land and to live with Rafael's family. The northern part, the Olema Valley near Tomales Bay, was later confirmed to Rafael, but he lost it in the 1850s and died poor. Gregorio applied for the southern section in 1842, using a map that William Richardson, who had acquired his nearby ranch the previous year, and several other men helped him draw up, using a 50-vara measuring tape flung from horseback, somewhat guessing at the boundaries.

Bolinas is a town very much isolated from other communities by a lagoon, San Francisco Bay, and the ocean. Few visitors find the town unless they have reason to find it. The Bolinas community's physical and psychological isolation has meant that its residents have valued and carefully tended its history. They remember that Juana was summoned to take charge when smallpox hit in 1853. At that time especially, her nephew Pablo became interested in her work. Under her guidance, he became "the beloved doctor of Bolinas for fifty years." (One of Pablo's daughters, Rose Briones, born while Juana was still alive, kept family documents in a red-lacquered Chinese chest, possibly the one that had been given to Juana in payment for curing a dying sailor.) In 1853, the desperate community sought Juana's help, but she was incapable of staving off much of the tragedy, and husbands of two of Gregorio's daughters, Francisco Cebrian and José Valenzuela, died of smallpox. It was said that the first step Juana took was to separate the sick from the well—a wise move, although not original with her. Quarantine was a known treatment. Juana's not being susceptible to smallpox herself could have developed from her work in milking cows, with their potentially beneficial cowpox.[24]

By the time the Bolinas residents were afflicted, inoculation would have been ineffective even if Juana had had access to the vaccine. Possible protection had been known for half a century, but knowing was easier than delivering. In 1803, the Spanish king ordered that vaccine be taken to the New World, a noble intention accomplished horrendously. Twenty-two boys age four to ten were taken as living reservoirs, one vaccinated from the pustules of another until the ship arrived, at which time one of the children's bodies would be harboring live serum. Most of the boys who survived were put in an orphanage in Mexico City. In 1821, a Russian ship brought vaccine to Monterey; and in 1828, James Ohio Pattie, a trapper, claimed to have vac-

*Pablo Briones, Juana's nephew
whom she trained in medicine.*

cine and to have charged the government to use it for ten thousand people, although the effectiveness of the dried pus he had on a cloth is doubtful.[25]

The memory of Juana's assistance during the Bolinas emergency persists because the community loved and trusted Pablo. A small piece of paper was Pablo's business license from the Internal Revenue Service. He paid ten dollars for it. Portions of the form filled in indicated that he was authorized to practice medicine, exclusive of surgery. In the caption to a picture of the license, Marin Pepper, author of *Bolinas*, states that Pablo "was . . . a 'natural doctor,' using the herbs and salves his aunt Juana Miranda had taught him about. Pablo Briones was depended upon in times of epidemics, accidents, natural disasters and, yes, childbirth."[26]

Two separate stories connect Juana's and Pablo's excellence in setting bones, suggesting that he learned from his aunt. Charles Brown stated in his manuscript "Recollections" that one of his three fellow deserters, Elijah, the Indian from Connecticut, was a good cook but not very smart. Elijah stood on a tree limb as he sawed it off. When it fell, Elijah fell with it and broke his jaw, and "Juana Briones cured him."

A detailed story about Pablo—said to be a small, kind, courtly man with a "healing way about him"—tells that he would gently massage bones back together. At that time, broken bones often led to lifetime disability. Jack Mason wrote that though Pablo lacked book learning, he had learned "all he needed to know of herbs and healing from his grandmother at Yerba Buena." That Juana would be recalled as "grandmother" instead of as "aunt" again fits the tradition of grandparents as the storage house of inherited wisdom. Pablo, born in 1823, three years after his aunt married, had the opportunity to learn bone setting from her. He twice treated Albert Ingermann's grandson George, whose family liked to point at him with pride as he ran around like a normal child, saying, "He walks as good as new." Mason wrote of Pablo that "Bolinas believed in him."

Pablo also resembled Juana in his attention to economic aspects of his life. Like her, he fit his medical career into other ways of earning a living. He worked as a veterinarian, operated his own cattle ranch, drove stage to Olema, owned a sawmill that, when the lumber had been fully harvested, he redesigned to make into a house, and other ventures. In 1849, he moved up the trail from Bolinas to Dogtown.[27]

Stories about Juana's prowess as a healer came from people who knew her personally or could have spoken with people who knew her or knew of her. She died in 1889. Someone born in 1870 might have known her, and if this person lived to be eighty years old, he might have reported in 1950 based on his own experience and knowledge of Juana. Some remembrances became public as early as 1895, and more surfaced around 1920. If we allow for a lack of precision in memory or even for a lack of precision in firsthand reports, stories can be trusted to have a kernel of credibility if they fit a pattern.

All the stories that have survived about Juana in regard to her occupation as a curandera are consistent with a portrait of a respected, admired, working doctor. The second half of her life, the part during and after the U.S. invasion, recedes somewhat because the now dominant Anglo culture denigrated hers while proclaiming its own superiority. Nevertheless, intriguing stories of medical practice by the Californios and the Indians have emerged from that period, one of them about heat treatment that was used by both Juana's people and Indians. There were some mineral hot springs in southern California where Apolinaria Lorenzana at Mission San Diego would take syphilitic women for several months of treatment. Mission San Antonio had hot springs nearby. Indians of the San Francisco Bay Area used sweat houses, called *temeschals*. When a mission priest would occasionally decide that such steam baths were bad for health, Indians would construct them in a hidden place.

Guadalupe Vallejo, Mariano's nephew, wrote that sick people drank the water of hot sulfur springs and buried themselves in mud near the spring. They would be brought on litters, helped into the mud, protected from the sun with boughs overhead, and left all day with food and water near them. It was said that, lacking hot springs, Juana heated water, added dirt, and had a trench dug about a foot and a half deep and lined with cowhides. She and her Indian assistants then lowered the patient onto the cowhide and poured the hot mud into the bath.[28]

Mary Gates, an author who interviewed many people in Juana's locale, wrote a small book published six years after Juana died in which she referred to Juana as an herbalist. Gates imagined a scene with a group of local Hispanics at the home of Juan Prado Mesa, near Juana's ranch. Describing each person doing something illustrative of his or her character, she wrote, "The widow Briones is seated upon a broken millstone, with her lap full of herbs, and apparently examining another."[29]

A biographer of the Murphy who purchased half of Juana's Purísima Ranch wrote that the younger Martin Murphy admired Juana's energy in ranching and that she was using the ranch for the hides trade, but also that she still found time to nurse the sick and, in particular, that she treated people in Indian villages near the ranch. The author said Martin "was a good friend" of Juana's, confirming her difference from Hispanic women who had little tolerance for people who spoke English. Juana found likeable traits in Anglos and Indians, people on opposite sides of the Western social spectrum. Peterson's comment in his Stanford University history that "[i]n the Indian villages she was received with awe and reverence" seems less extravagant in light of a similar opinion by Juana's contemporary and next-door neighbor.[30]

A photograph taken in the 1880s or 1890s shows the back of Juana's house at the Purísima Ranch with the kind of rough lattice work that would have been used for drying herbs and food items. One Santa Cruz historian wrote that just about every home with Spanish residents had red peppers hanging on the side of the house. Josefa Buelna, a descendant of Antonia Tapia, Juana's aunt, spoke to her high school graduating class in 1886 about what she called "Spanish Santa Cruz," where the gardens were better kept and more impressive than the houses and always had a collection of various medicinal plants.

Even though they dried some of their medicines on a rude trellis, folk doctors were sometimes trusted more than educated doctors. Antonio Osio, Juana's contemporary, wrote in his memoir, in part as a joke and in part as truth, that a Colonel Telles became gravely ill in Monterey in 1843, and "[f]ortunately for him, the troops did not have a doctor, so he was treated with folk remedies."[31]

Nineteenth-century medicine lacked knowledge of beneficial ways to care for mental illness, which was rarely mentioned, although the church sometimes kept track. Maynard Geiger's book on Franciscan missionaries in California mentions Tomás de la Pena Saravia, who was at Santa Cruz in "a completely demented condition"; José María Fernández, who suffered hallucinations due to a blow to the head; Pedro de la Cueva, with undiluted alcoholism; and Eulalia Callis, who was considered a mental case for being wildly angry with her husband. (Although the Callis problem dated to the years when Juana's parents were first married, perhaps Juana was fortunate that she did not get so tagged after her adamant refusal to abide her husband.)[32]

In an undated, unsigned letter in the archives of the Portola Valley Historical Association, a member of the Martínez family that owned the ranch that shared a northwest border with Juana's wrote a pleading letter to the effect that the recipient had to come to get "mother," the girls could do nothing with her, she wanted to kill herself, didn't want to be shut up in the house, and was crying all the time. In some ways, physical illness could be more directly dealt with than mental.

Juana's youngest child, Dolores, was sometimes mentioned in public records as being a "mental defective." A resident of Mayfield who knew him said that he was "a hard drinker" and "not too badly off mentally." Charles Brown said he was "a little crazy." Such comments leave open to speculation exactly what they meant, but it must have been sad for Juana to be honored and respected for her ability to cure others but not be able to cure her own child.[33]

Ten

"THE TROUBLESOME SERVICE
OF THE MISSION"

Challenges to Indians

In 1844, Juana bought Rancho la Purísima Concepción from Indians, Gorgonio and his relatives, a most unusual way of acquiring land. It is therefore important to cull any possible information about Juana's connection with Gorgonio, his tribe, and their status in the Santa Clara Valley at the time of her purchase.

They had learned the skills they needed from the mission and stayed as the workforce after Juana purchased the ranch. When someone complimented a California cowboy on his exceptional ability, the cowboy would often say it was because he had been raised with Indians. That explained it: everyone knew Indians were the best. Juana needed cowboys and agriculturalists on her ranch.

Indians kept figuring in Juana's life from her birth to her elder years. Hispanic women within a household had congenial opportunities to exchange ideas equitably with everyone living or working there. Historians have somewhat neglected Indian life in the Santa Clara Valley because of the tendency to concentrate on places that became big and famous, such as San Francisco or Los Angeles, or places where Indians came in contact with Europeans later or fused tribal identities. Anthropologists preferred to study Indians with cultural features as undiluted as possible. Whatever scholars cared about, the fact was that Santa Clara Mission was highly unusual in distributing land to Indians, a situation that facilitated reciprocity between Juana and Gorgonio and his people.[1]

Gorgonio's having not only received but persisted in arguing for legal possession of a large parcel duplicated Juana's experience in Yerba Buena. She and Gorgonio and his people could have shared information about their experiences in dealing with the government and encouraged each other. Gorgonio's success eventually resulted in Juana's legally acquiring his ranch, which soon proved to be a refuge and a living for her and her family when the United States took over California.

A number of stories testify to Juana's direct contact with various Indian individuals. She helped the Indian Elijah desert from his ship with three other sailors and "cured him" of a broken jaw, and she was said to have been caring for a sick Indian girl in Yerba Buena, later to have a sick Indian girl under her care at the ranch, to have adopted an Indian girl, and to have employed Indians as her workforce.

Juana's proximity to Indian life gave her innumerable opportunities to establish friendly relations with Gorgonio and his tribal community, in which a woman, Calistro, either was the head of the tribe or shared that position with Gorgonio. Hispanic leaders could not accept the reality of Indian women's high positions and their sharing of leadership. European culture presumed that a single ruler, a king or, rarely, a queen, occupied the top rung. Women were not eligible for president, general, bishop, governor, sheriff, mayor, or priest, and Indian ways violated this basic premise of European culture.

Instead of sole leaders, most Indian tribes had experts in different categories. The women's equal participation in that hierarchy so irritated some people that few Indian women would be remembered by name. Information has survived about Toypurina, a southern California Indian woman, because she fomented a rebellion. At the sentencing for her war crimes, Governor Pedro Fages expressed his disgust that Indian warriors took orders from a woman.[2]

Lucy Thompson (Che-na-wah Weitch-ah-wah), who wrote her reminiscences in 1916, said her people had no chief. Their first contact with invaders had occurred eighty years after Portolá's pioneering expedition. This Yurok woman of the rugged Klamath River valley in northern California wrote that those who failed to settle differences could not participate in the area's most important religious and social gatherings where decisions affecting all would be made by the group.[3]

Fray Juan Martín of San Miguel Mission wrote in 1814, "Not even in their pagan state had they any caiques or chiefs. Only in their battles would they have a sort of captain to whom they submitted. Outside of that all considered themselves equal. Nor did they serve any other Indian." Clearly, no one description fits all. Indians differed from one place to another. Men and women in Indian society had responsibilities according to gender, but women's status in their culture was noticeably greater than Hispanic or Anglo women's status in theirs.

Historian William Macleod claimed that anthropologists believed incorrectly that Indians practiced communal ownership. His assessment agreed with Lucy Thompson. She wrote that Yurok individuals owned land, a factor in wealth and inheritance that created social classes and slavery. Her father trained her to succeed him in his leadership position. Historian Albert Hurtado writes that women chiefs often inherited their positions and that their duties covered a wide range of oversight, including handling economic affairs, assuring the fair distribution of food and other necessities, and organizing ceremonial occasions.[4]

Women's deliberately overlooked importance within Indian culture linked in one way to Juana's purchase of the ranch. Juana might have known Calistro and Gorgonio from the time that she lived at Santa Clara Mission. Gorgonio repeatedly mentioned the woman Calistro in his applications for emancipation and land. Juana knew that in most cases men would be more likely to be granted land, making it necessary that someone besides Calistro should apply. It was hard enough for a Hispanic woman to acquire property and certified ownership of that property. It was even more difficult for a male Indian and impossible for a female Indian.

The shortage of Indian women complicated their lives. Virtually no clear information remains about how Indian society dealt with this problem. Randall Milliken's analysis of Santa Clara Mission records shows that from 1790 to 1806, the period when Gorgonio's father brought him to the mission, one of thirteen female Indians and four of sixteen male Indians lived past age twenty-one, a survival rate of about 8 percent for females and 25 percent for males. The average age at death for girls was 4.7 years; for boys it was 12.8 years.[5]

There are theories about why so many girls died. Missions locked up girls in an unhealthily unclean building every night to prevent their having sexual intercourse before marriage, which might have contributed to their dying young. The skewed gender differential could have derived from that and from other demoralizing experiences so different from the equality Indian girls experienced in their own societies. Catholic European philosophy—including an interpretation of sexuality that demeaned women, rigid marriage customs that required couples to remain together even if their relationship soured, the cloistered lifestyle imposed on girls, and their lesser opportunities for education and means of making a living in the European social setting—meant that Indian mothers might have had difficulty summoning the strength to raise female children for so clouded a future. They may have been less diligent in their care of girls because they began believing the lessons of a society that put a higher value on boys.

In the early years of colonization, crowding similar to an urban environment in part accounted for Indian susceptibility to disease, but by the mid-1830s missions had become more like parish churches and were no longer operating as homes for large numbers of Indians, who had by then been largely absorbed into the lay workforce. If living conditions at missions damaged women's health more than men's, the female population should have, but seems not to have, recovered parity when missions definitely closed, roughly around 1834.

The 1852 census showed that Indians constituted only a little more than 8 percent of the total population of Santa Clara County, but with a continuing deficit of females. Enumerators were to list only "domesticated" Indians, suggesting the presence of separate communities of "wild" Indians, which might mean that they lived in the woods or remote mountainous areas. Possibly that is where the women were. Perhaps they worked in households or were absorbed by families and simply did not get counted, or at least not separately, when the census takers came asking about family members. Maybe they had become wives and mothers who took on their husbands' family names and no longer had single names as Indians. Hurtado writes that white men "kidnapped and raped native women with little fear of retribution from legal authorities," which may have led Indian women to hide when the census takers came around.[6] The 1852 county census cannot be entirely trusted for accuracy, but even factoring in distortion, we cannot entirely dismiss the fact that it listed more than twice as many Indian men as women: 388 males, 162 females. Calistro's name was not on that census list of Purísima Ranch residents.

Gorgonio's case provides a trickle of evidence about gender equity in Indian society. Gorgonio (Gregorio, José Gregorio, José Gorgonio), a high-status Indian of the mission, persisted by applying several times for the "emancipation" of his people and title to the Rancho la Purísima Concepción, where they lived. He repeatedly said he spoke for his "relatives." Each time, the government's response ignored his mention of the woman Calistro as one of the applicants. He also mentioned his daughter Paula and his son's wife, but they too were ignored, although his son Ramón was sometimes named in official responses. The repeated mention of Calistro in applications indicates that Indians had clung to their custom of women's eligibility for leadership despite the patriarchal influence of priests and Hispanic society.[7]

Gorgonio's having land at all was a rarity. Under Mexico, half of the land that missions had administered was supposed to pass legally to Indians, but the California government with few exceptions refused to certify that any Indian legally owned land. Mission Santa Clara was very different. Juana had long personal ties with the priests and residents at Santa Clara and would have known Gorgonio either personally or by reputation. As a leading citizen of the mission and of the Santa Clara Valley, Gorgonio would have been more often mentioned by historians had he been Hispanic or Anglo.

His status shows up in early mission records, where Indians almost always had only a single name. The listing of Gorgonio in one instance gives him a Spanish surname, Borgares. He must also have had a good command of Spanish and an understanding of the system to have been competent to apply and reapply to the government for emancipation and for the land. Like Juana, he understood the new and protected the old. They recognized the need to surmount obstacles by devising methods compatible with the ruling class and persisting to argue for what they wanted.

Gorgonio's life can be traced to 1790, when he was a year and a half old and his father had him baptized. Indians knew by then that their tools for defending themselves had proven less effective than those of the invaders. They also needed to access new food sources because European agriculture had diminished native foods. Cattle and horses took up space previously home only to deer and other wild animals that figured in their diets, and the plants they lived on gradually disappeared under the plow and under the hooves of domesticated animals. Spanish soldiers did not tolerate Indians' killing livestock for food unless the food was for the mission, thus culturally disorienting Indians, who considered themselves partners with animals in the natural world.

For several years, Pedro Fages, governor of Alta California at the time that Gorgonio was born, passed regulations that motivated Indians economically to join a mission or to bring their children to a mission for education. To repair and improve the fort at Monterey, he hired Spanish-speaking Indians with construction skills, offering an advance agreement about when they would be paid and what their pay would be—blankets, clothing, beads, and food. Mission training equipped Indians to do such jobs and to work for private householders and ranchers, where they had more freedom to negotiate terms and retain their own lifestyle.[8]

Tribal elders had to weigh diminishing investment in their communities against advantages of learning new methodologies. Gorgonio's father, Crisostomo, was thirty-eight when he took his son in for baptism. He himself joined the church four years later. He had the option of continuing to live in his village or moving to mission housing. He died in 1801. Gorgonio's mother, Segue, also joined the church, but her death is unrecorded.[9]

Once the missions closed, Indians had no access to the legal mechanisms by which the government granted land. One event in southern California gives a look at a dramatic scene probably similar—if not in detail, then in purport—to others that went unrecorded. Governor Juan Alvarado hired William Hartnell in 1839 to travel to missions to report on how well administrators were parceling out land to Hispanic settlers and seeing to Indian welfare. Hartnell had come originally to California in 1822 as an employee of a trading company, married a Hispanic woman, owned something of a library, and opened a school that closed for financial reasons. In his diary, in Spanish and carefully translated by Starr Gurke, Hartnell wrote that after mass at Mission San Diego, Pio Pico, one-time governor of California, distributed 168 blankets to the Indians and explained to them that the government had allocated the Temecula Ranch to him. They complained that his cattle were destroying their crops and that they needed the housing he had taken. After hearing these and other complaints about his management, Pico advised them to appoint four men to go to the capital in Monterey to represent them. They said they all would go. Pico explained that such a deployment would take on the nature of a rebellion, but they retorted that all would go or none because they had no chief. No one went. Either way, Pico won.[10]

Under the Mexican government, Governor Figueroa in 1833 made the provision explicit that former mission property, exclusive of the church itself, should be assigned half to settlers and half to Indians, which happened nowhere, but came closer to being done at Santa Clara than elsewhere. Alan Brown, an exceptionally knowledgeable historian about the Santa Clara Valley, thinks that Gorgonio wrote his own 1839 request to the governor for protection of his land from incursions by José Castro and José Peña. Gorgonio complained that Castro and Peña were supposed to be measuring and certifying his claim, but instead were trying to appropriate parts of it for themselves. If Gorgonio did write his own application, he was evidently educated far beyond other Indians of his time and place, a supposition that seems somewhat reasonable in that Gorgonio was a special assistant to Father Catala.[11]

One would assume that priests who wanted Indians to adopt their beliefs would have taken steps to educate them in seminaries and colleges in Mexico so that male Indians would enter the priesthood and females would become nuns. Instead, Indian girls' instruction in language ended at age ten. One Indian boy, Pedro, from San Luis Obispo, was considered especially precocious at translating, so at age ten he received the unusual privilege of being sent to Mexico City for two years of education. Two Indian boys, Pablo Tac and Agapito Amamix from Mission San Luis Rey, studied in Mexico and in Rome, an opportunity that did not result in any major change because neither lived past age nineteen. They were taken to Rome in 1833, the same year that Gorgonio tried to get certified emancipation for himself and his people.[12]

According to Randall Milliken, Gorgonio had three wives. This would have been impossible within the mission system, but some Indian headmen got the right to practice polygamy in their own societies. Solano, who facilitated Vallejo's Indian relations at the Northern Frontier, was said to have had eleven wives.[13]

Clerical leadership at Santa Clara Mission contributed to Indians' success in acquiring land there. Father Magín de Catala had arrived at the mission in 1794, a priest of such sanctity that he later had the signal honor, like Junipero Serra, of being nominated for sainthood. The mission owed its success in large measure to Catala and his partner, José Viader. Of the twenty missions that had been founded to 1800, theirs had the highest population.[14]

Father Francisco García Diego y Morena arrived in 1833, the priest who became a bishop and a decade later helped ameliorate Juana's marriage problems. That Padre García Diego chose Santa Clara as his first base of operations helped Juana later because it was he who parceled out mission ranches to Indians. In a letter to Governor Figueroa, Diego mentioned the wealth of Missions Santa Clara and San José, but the relative poverty of Missions San Francisco and San Rafael. His assessment of the quantity of valuable land and resources may have influenced the allocation of nearly 12,000 acres of Santa Clara land to Indians between 1839 and 1845. The last allocation, the Ulistac Ranch, 2,277 acres, was granted to Marcelo, Pio, and Cristóbal. In 1844, Los Coches, 2,219 acres, went to Roberto; Posolmi, 3,042 acres, went to Ynigo (Inigo); the first and the largest allocation at 4,436 acres went to Gorgonio. In 1839, when Gorgonio requested confirmation of his ownership, he said the land had been granted to him by Governor Figueroa and that he had lived there with his relatives for five years, which dated to the beginning of Padre Diego García's tenure at the mission.[15]

Juana's need for official recognition of her separation from Apolinario resembled Gorgonio's need for official recognition of his and his tribe's emancipation from service at the mission. In a petition to the governor in

1836, Gorgonio wrote that Señor José Peña, one of the administrators in charge of tending to buildings formerly used by the mission and with other vaguely specified duties connected to the dismantlement of the mission, had not responded to his repeated requests that his people should no longer be required to work at the mission. Peña had grand aspirations. Early on he had acquired more than 8,000 acres, Rancho Rincón de San Francisquito. When secularization made former mission buildings available, he accessed Indian housing in what is now the town of Santa Clara. Another mission administrator, José Ramón Estrada, had powerful relatives, including his brother-in-law, Governor Juan Alvarado. In the mode of the times, both Peña and Estrada favored Californios over Indians in allocating mission resources. Estrada lent cattle and sheep to Californios and allowed them to live on some of the finer pieces of mission land as a prerequisite for applying for ownership.

Gorgonio complained of "the troublesome service of the mission," but that institution in effect had been replaced. In fact, he meant service to a secular manager who, with no funding and lacking the complex mission infrastructure, had charge of preserving the buildings, orchards, and environs. Instead of working gratis at the former mission, Indians definitely preferred to take jobs at the pueblo of San José or on ranches.

Authorities often intruded on the lives of Indians. In 1844, Mexican governor Manuel Micheltorena (1843–45) ordered the alcalde of San José to pull in idle Indians and put them to work. Whether or not Gorgonio's people knew about those instructions, they would have known the conditions that made it advisable for them to be in someone's employ, a plausible reason for Gorgonio to sell the ranch to Juana that year. His people could trust her as a colleague and at the same time could demonstrate that they were indeed employed.[16]

Gorgonio added something to his application for independence and ownership of the ranch that he had no need to explain. Everyone knew about trouble being caused in the region by Tulare horse thieves. They had attacked and injured Gorgonio and some of his relatives, stolen their clothing and horses, and burned their houses. In the application, Gorgonio implied that he and his people needed to be on hand to guard their ranch instead of traveling a distance to work at the mission and leaving their own property to the depredations of Indian horse thieves.[17]

The Tulare referred to was the southern Central Valley, a stretch of land between the high, rugged mountains of the Sierra Nevada and the lower coast range, enclosing a huge, shallow lake and marshland that was said to have covered more than 700 square miles before Americans began draining the land for farming. Indians managed to continue community life there into the 1850s. They stole horses because they had developed a taste for horse meat, they needed horses for their own use, and their location had became strategic when a trading opportunity developed. Anglo trappers bought Indians' stolen horses, which were the ranchers' well-trained ones, for resale in New Mexico, rather than wild ones.[18]

Gorgonio wrote truly of the Tulare Indians. Besides their insatiable desire for good horses, they harbored animosity toward mission Indians, whose cultural agenda no longer paralleled theirs and who no longer traded with them. During the mission period, many Indians left church settlements and became part of communities where interference from Hispanic people was still minimal. At times, they left en masse. One day in 1827, nearly one-fourth of Mission San José's population of 1800 Indians moved to the Central Valley. Many of them spoke Spanish, understood mission operations, and personally knew their former fellow neophytes. This gave them a key to preying upon the missions, ranches, and towns.

Gorgonio's persistence paid off in property seldom equaled by any other California Indian. The governor could simply have neglected to respond. That Gorgonio's petition mentioned his willingness to defend against horse thieves probably helped convince a governor virtually devoid of a military force and thus unable to overcome intrusions that jeopardized the fundamental economy of the region. The government had insufficient funds to pay soldiers, and the remunerative hide-and-tallow trade depended on vaqueros equipped with well-trained, well-outfitted horses. The hard-pressed governor obviously welcomed Gorgonio's suggestion that he and his people needed to be relieved of the "troublesome service of the mission" in order to impede intrusions of the Tulare horse thieves. That was indeed a selling point.

In 1839, Indians attacked the grain storage facility at Santa Clara. In 1840, they stole a thousand head of stock at San Luis Obispo. Sherburne Cook wrote that "hardly a ranch was spared from Santa Barbara to the Strait of Carquinez." In 1843, the same Indians who had killed Juana's brother Felipe three years earlier stole several hundred horses from another East Bay ranch. That year also, Californios in the Monterey area petitioned the governor for protection, claiming that ranching had become impossible. Workers would not remain in so dangerous a situation.[19]

With remote mountain hideaways to the east of San José, in the direction of the Central Valley, horse thieves could swoop in and out to stash horses near town. Mofras wrote that in 1841, San José residents had no horses because of almost nightly raids. During the American occupation, the military governor, Colonel Richard Mason, advised the San José alcalde that an Indian caught stealing a horse should be shot, but if caught stealing a bullock, a flogging of fifty lashes would be adequate, as it would for any thief.[20]

Gorgonio and his relatives' certified emancipation, dated December 1836, was signed by Father Rafael Moreno (he who eight years later helped Juana in applying to the bishop for assistance in dissolving her marriage) and by the interim governor, José Castro, whom the dying Figueroa had appointed. Gorgonio submitted these papers to the next governor, Juan Alvarado, who declared in writing six months after receiving them that Gorgonio and his people should receive possession of the land and live on that land because they claimed that they could support themselves there. They lacked complete freedom to go where they would, being suspect in the nearby town if they could not prove themselves employed, but having the land in their names would have helped them considerably. Alvarado ordered the mission administrator to measure the grant and complete the process.[21]

The soil and climate made Santa Clara Valley highly productive, and the valley's terrain, unlike San Francisco's, was relatively accessible without interferences from sand dunes or steep hills. Santa Clara priests did not set up official asistencias like those associated with Mission Dolores, but some Indians had to work at a distance from the mission. Two items of nomenclature support the presumption that the land Gorgonio acquired had once been a mission outpost. An early map of the rancho shows a large corral next to the Arroyo de las Yeguas, Mare Creek. The dilemma that horses bred too well in the wild was handled sometimes by gathering mares in a corral, which needed to be near water. The government occasionally passed regulations requiring, as in 1807, that each settler retain only twenty-five mares and kill off the rest.[22]

The second clue that the ranch was a mission outpost is the name itself. Indians would have called that land by their own tribal name, which missionaries either did not learn or did not bother to record, although anthropologist Alfred Kroeber says that the locale was known as "Tamien." Priests would definitely have been the ones to choose the name "Rancho la Purísima Concepción." By contrast, Camilo Ynitia, an Indian who applied later in Marin County, a more secular region, obtained two square leagues that included his birthplace, which was confirmed to him by Governor Micheltorena in 1843 with its Indian name, "Olompali."[23]

Mission Dolores formalized distant sites with fairly substantial buildings because of difficulty in traveling to and from those sites, whereas

Santa Clara, just fifty miles south of San Francisco, did not. Easier travel meant that Santa Clara Indians could more readily leave their outposts to attend mass and work at the mission. Santa Clara Valley trails crisscrossed the land and in the rainy season relocated to avoid marshland along the bay. Mission president Fermín Francisco de Lasuen had made widening trails part of his plan to improve the links between missions, including a connection across the mountains of the coast range to Santa Cruz and Monterey.[24]

In his 1852 deposition regarding the authenticity of Juana's title to the rancho, Maximo Martínez, owner of an adjoining ranch, spoke of Ramón, Paula, and Calistro, and referred to Gorgonio as a "friend." Gorgonio and his family were Juana's friends, though no written document calls them that. She took on ownership of the ranch at a time when other Hispanic people were deserting theirs because they believed that Indian depredations made ranching too dangerous.

Juana had commercial contacts in San Francisco. In a time of danger, she agreed to shoulder a responsibility that had become burdensome for many. This interpretation of her purchase of the ranch fits with the conditions of the moment and with her previous willingness to accept challenges. When the United States became involved six years later, the situation worked out differently than anyone could have suspected and far worse for Indians than to that time had been the case.

Under Hispanic governance, Indians learned various occupations and became part of the society and its workforce. Confrontations, disagreements, and battles happened over the Spanish and Mexican years, but many Indians lived in Hispanic households and staffed ranches. The Anglo conquest brought in a government that passed laws so injurious to Indians that their status resembled that of slaves, but worse. Slaves were at least considered to be worth money. Some Indians, especially children, were actually sold, but slavery was outlawed in California, and thus Indians who had been purchased were in legal limbo and were somewhat like indentured servants. Some gold hunters thought Indians were better off dead. A historian of the missions, George James, wrote that within the "policies of the three governments, Spain, Mexico, and America . . . the last is by far the worst. . . . Our treatment of the Indians reads like a hideous nightmare."[25]

Complex factors accounted for the harsh treatment of Indians by Anglos. Indian vaqueros, farmers, artisans, and miners were interpreted by some immigrants to California as competitors. Some had taken pride in farming their own land but had lost that land in one way or another. Others who had worked as skilled laborers at crafts found themselves displaced by newly developing industry that used factory labor, and they wanted to retrieve their lost status.[26]

Outright killing and war caused the California Indian population to decline from an estimated 150,000 in 1848 to about 30,000 a decade later. Demoralization of Indian women and their resulting low numbers also contributed to the horrendous decline. The rape and killing of Indian women went unrecorded and unpunished. Such things had happened under Hispanic rule also and was similarly hidden, but the huge increase in population with the gold rush and the lack of respect for Indians put Indian women at unprecedented risk. One diarist told about three fellow miners who went to an Indian village for the purpose of rape, which was made easier because all the men were absent. The woman they chose to attack tried unsuccessfully to buy her freedom with roots or baskets.[27]

James Weeks, an early Anglo immigrant who very likely was acquainted with Juana and who worked in the redwoods where she acquired wood for building her house, hints at more than he tells in the following excerpt from his 1880 manuscript "Reminiscences":

> One of our men captured a young squaw, the Indians came and built fires around us, at dawn they where [sic] coming into camp, they were motioned off they kept advancing, we was ordered to open fire, our fire was effectual, brains began to fly and also it rained arrows for some time, some few passed by me, no one of us was hurt. I saw one Indian they left on the sod with the forehead blown off him . . . from thence we took into the mountains clothed with redwood timbers. The Indian girl left. I suppose returned home to her people, she was dressed in purple. She did not like Captain Young for her husband.[28]

Gorgonio and his relatives may have thought that Juana's purchasing their ranch would give them the economic advantage of selling their hides and tallow to the big traders coming in from the East Coast, as well as offer the protection they needed from the government officials who were given to jailing Indians and forcing them to work. There was little time, however, for their agreement to fulfill itself quite in the way they had intended. Invasion and discovery introduced new and unpredictable complications and dangers for every resident of Alta California.

Part Four

THE UNITED STATES, 1846

Eleven

"HORSES, CATTLE, AND EVERYTHING TO DO WITH A RANCH"

Owning and Managing a Ranch

That Apolinario Miranda, Maximo Martínez, and Gorgonio all applied for land within a year of each other in the 1830s was a sign of the times. Governors from Mexico had been distrusted wholesale, but the newly arrived governor José Figueroa seemed to come closer to speaking their language. During the twenty-four years of Mexican rule, Californios unceremoniously sent back home four of fourteen governors. Not everybody loved Figueroa, but he worked out fairly well. He helped his reputation by bringing Mexican padres to replace Spanish ones in the northern missions—that is, in Juana's neighborhood.[1]

Each of these three new landowners filled a different role in Juana's economic ventures within the decade following their successful land acquisitions. Apolinario grew fruit that she sold to incoming ship crews. Maximo arranged with lumbermen to harvest his redwood forest, which later supplied wood for Juana's ranch house in the Santa Clara Valley. Gorgonio grew wheat, corn, and beans on the land he sold to her at a time when cattle, of which Juana had an excess, made a better investment, both because of the booming ocean trade in hides for eastern U.S. manufacturers of leather goods and because the hilly terrain with sufficient water from springs and streams provided better for cattle than for crops.

Before secularization, padres had handled many categories of enterprise in developing the Santa Clara Valley into a mission farm. They arranged for purchase and sale of produce, ordered and received shipments of tools from Mexico, and constructed storage facilities. As one of their

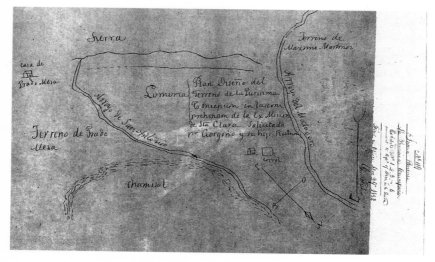

A map of Rancho la Purísima Concepción, based an oral description by its owner, an Indian named Gorgonio. It shows a house, a corral, hills, the general course of the local streams, and an adjoining ranch.

first projects at Mission Santa Clara, Fathers José Murguia and Tomás de la Peña Saravia in 1778 put up a granary approximately fifty by fifteen feet with two doors that had locks. The mission also had an enclosed threshing floor sixty feet in diameter. Missions had special ventilated spaces for storing husked corn, sometimes above the priests' quarters, which served the double purpose of providing corn for people and husks for horses. Mission tools such as chisels, files, shovels, bolts, soldering irons, and hammers would have stayed with mission administrators.[2]

When Gorgonio sought emancipation and ranch ownership, he lost access to those facilities, tools, and management. Mission administrators appointed by the governor wanted the land and economic advantages for themselves and their peers. They purposely erected barriers to diminish or eliminate Indians' profit potential. In applying to Governor Juan Alvarado for his and his relatives' emancipation, Gorgonio showed astuteness about legal matters and a highly unusual willingness to assert his and his tribe's rights.

Juan Bautista Alvarado, the first governor born in California, favored his own people, but concerns about unfriendly Indians weighed heavily on him in 1840 when he confirmed Gorgonio as the ranch owner. Yoscolo, an Indian from the San Joaquin Valley east of the coast range, had been blamed for cattle thievery and other depredations, including a major break-in at Mission Santa Clara. He had been a highly placed member of the mission community and had gathered a following, said to include five hundred Indians in his gang of robbers and fighters. A posse of Hispanic men overtook him in the Santa Cruz Mountains and returned with his head for public display. They would have been especially angry because two of their force died, Cibrian brothers, of a family long associated with Juana's, which included Juana Cibrian, the wife of Hilario Miranda, Apolinario's brother. Yoscolo had already been killed when Alvarado approved Gorgonio's land request, but the governor would have taken into account that Gorgonio and his tribe could create a kind of guard post in the eastern foothills of the Santa Cruz Mountains as a line of defense against likely Indian retribution for Yoscolo's humiliating treatment.[3]

Four years after the unforgettable Yoscolo incident, changed dynamics possibly motivated Gorgonio's sale of the Purísima Ranch to Juana, who may already have been advising him and his people. By purchasing, she could officially operate as their agent in selling produce and in dealing with men who wanted "to squeeze them out," as historian Alan Brown translated Gorgonio's complaint.[4]

Because Mexico, too busy handling its own disruptive political matters, had never integrated California into its economy, local business methods had developed in a direction compatible with those of the United States. Juana had learned that complex set of interactions in Yerba Buena among Anglo merchants, including Robert Ridley, her son-in-law; William Heath Davis, who mentioned her several times in his memoir and described calling on her daughter; William Richardson and Jacob Leese, said to be the first residents, along with Juana, of Yerba Buena Pueblo; and Charles Brown, the deserting sailor she had helped. All these Anglo men had Hispanic wives from Juana's community. She communicated so well with William Thomes, the sailor who bought milk from her, that he thought of her as a friend. She had ample opportunity to learn the English language and American business methods, to develop business contacts, and to gain political insights.[5]

In her request for permission to purchase the land, her mention of needing space for her cattle fit market conditions. Cattle had become the key commodity in the region. Her San Francisco land, sufficient for dairy operations, lacked ranch potential. In her application, she stated that her herd was growing. California had become a large-scale supplier of hides and tallow. Records from a year before Juana's purchase of the ranch note that people of San José had hides ready for shipping, a distance of about fifteen miles from the Purísima Ranch and accessible over well-traveled trails that had been developed to move lumber from the redwood forest in the mountains. Most advantageously for Juana's hide-and-tallow business, that road, the Arastradero, formed one of the borders of her ranch.

Getting hides to the bay for shipment through San José on their own account presented a difficulty for Indians. Among the innumerable impediments to normal life for Gorgonio and his people was the harsh penal system. Indians suffered lashing as punishment far more frequently than anyone else under Spanish, Mexican, or American government. In San Jose in 1847, a judge sentenced an Indian named Hopes to twenty-four lashes with a cat o' nine tails and payment of costs for stealing a hat from Juan Williams. This happened during the American occupation, but it illustrates a dangerous and demeaning attitude toward Indians. In a case between two Hispanic people before Americans invaded, a verdict simply insisted that two horses should be returned to their rightful owner, Juan Miranda, Juana's brother-in-law, without mention of punishment.[6]

Two other features that may have encouraged Gorgonio and his relatives to sell to Juana were the expectation that she would leave most details of running the operation to them and in addition would refrain from the missionary habit of attempting to alter their beliefs, ceremonies, and customs. Many Indians had become expert artisans, builders, cowboys, and farmers. The Purísima Ranch would have been in good hands with them in charge of operations and Juana in charge of finances.[7]

Navigating the murky waters of the economy took careful attention. Captain Phelps wrote that in 1842 he purchased a cow for food with six dollars worth of goods that had cost him four dollars, and that the same cow would have cost fifty or sixty dollars back home in the East. In 1849, the equivalent cow sold at five hundred dollars a head upriver in Sacramento, where cows could have been rather easily driven from the Santa Clara Valley. By 1853, a cow still got a good price, but not exorbitant, selling for fifty-five dollars in Juana's neighborhood.[8]

Besides the Indians' willingness to sell the property and Juana's to buy, their transaction was facilitated by the entry of yet another Mexican governor on the scene, Manuel Micheltorena. Land was not considered a commodity under Spain and Mexico. Government approval was required to certify ownership, and many personal considerations entered into the decision. Juana submitted to Micheltorena her request for permission to purchase. Micheltorena's status lacked security, and his welcome had been only moderately friendly and at times decidedly unfriendly. He had brought with him a nearly destitute convict army, which Mexico thought was needed because that distant government correctly feared both a California rebellion, which did occur, and attack from an outside power, which was imminent.

Californios felt insulted by these three hundred soldiers who were said to steal what they lacked in supplies or salary. Rumors of war between Mexico and the United States made Micheltorena uneasy about the large English and American population in California, but some Californios said they liked Americans better than Micheltorena's Mexican criminals posing as soldiers.

In general, Micheltorena distrusted Americans, but as a notable exception he made friends in Monterey with Thomas Larkin, who advised him on finances and lent him so much money that Larkin's biographer thought their deals "came very close to corruption." One can visualize Micheltorena handing Larkin the paper from Juana and saying, "What do you make of this?" Larkin had good reason to advise Micheltorena to respond affirmatively. He either knew Juana personally or knew of her through her adopted Indian daughter Cecilia Briones, who had married his stepbrother, John Burwood Cooper. Besides, getting land out of the hands of Indians appealed to nearly everybody but Indians.[9]

Gorgonio's decision to sell may also have been influenced by certain of Micheltorena's policies—for example, that part of the income from properties of former missions being handled by appointed administrators was to be allocated to the support of the military and the government. Appointed mission administrators could demand that Indians contribute to the economic viability of buildings and land on property adjacent to what had been mission churches and were now parish churches. Affecting Gorgonio and his clan more personally, the governor also ruled that emancipated Indians must find useful employment.[10]

Micheltorena signed other papers concerning Indian land. In the 1830s, two influential Indians became Mariano Vallejo's intermediaries with local Indians. Camilo Ynitia, who petitioned the governor, was granted Olompali in 1843, two square leagues of low-mountainous terrain. Juana's brother Gregorio helped mark the boundaries. Camilo built a one-room adobe house with walls nearly three feet thick, ceilings eight feet high, and a hole in the wall to let smoke out. He retained 1,480 acres and in 1852 sold the rest to the county assessor, James Black. Olompali is now a state park. Anglos in particular resented an Indian's owning a large ranch, and there were threats on Camilo's life.[11]

When Juana bought her big ranch in the beautiful Santa Clara Valley she knew so well, she undoubtedly thought she would follow the example of compatriots such as José Peña and Francisco Sánchez, who stayed mostly in town and left daily ranch duties to others. Some ranchers lived in town in winter and went to their country homes from spring through autumn. According to Maximo Martínez, Juana built a large dwelling house on the ranch immediately after purchase. She had known one of the sawyers from the Martínez redwoods who was said to have constructed Juan Prado Mesa's house in 1841, Charles Brown. It had been nearly a decade ago that she had helped him desert from his ship, and he was living on a ranch near her home, at a place called Searsville, close to the lumber operation that was his occupation for a time. He may have helped with the building of her house, which in part accounts for its having lasted so well so long. Redwood is long lived, even after being cut down, and recent investigations have suggested that American building practices united with Hispanic ones in the construction of her home.[12]

For the first half of her life, Juana was at heart a town person. Evidence suggests that she intended to stay that way. Proximity to friends, family members, and patients fit her lifestyle. Safety, sociability, and economic factors favored having neighbors and access to a lively mercantile establishment. San Francisco was her town, whereas San José was the pueblo of choice for her ranchero neighbor, Maximo Martínez. Maximo had twice held the position of alcalde nearly thirty years before he applied for his land grant. However, he was countrified enough to build two houses on the ranch, where his family and descendants lived.[13]

Maximo learned about the value of the property he chose from English-speaking men who worked as lumberjacks in the redwoods and went to San José for supplies and entertainment. He named his land for the lumbering operation, Rancho la Cañada del Corte de Madera. James Weeks wrote in "Reminiscences" that when the Americans needed horses for their military operations, he and Charles Brown, both onetime sawyers in the Martínez redwoods, asked "our old friend Maximo" for them, telling him that the government would pay him in the future for the two he supplied. Perhaps they actually believed that.

Maximo resembled Juana in that he was a leading citizen and an industrious landowner who maintained cordial relationships with diverse people. Besides Anglo friends such as Weeks, to whom Juana wrote when he was alcalde of San José, Maximo had ties to Indians. When he testified in Juana's land case, he referred to Gorgonio as someone he knew well.[14]

Juana retained her residence in San Francisco (Yerba Buena and Mission Dolores). Two years after purchasing the ranch, she again reported to

San Francisco authorities about her husband. She was not running from her problems there and had not opted out of that community. Tormenting the family seemed to amuse Apolinario. If she intended to move full time to the ranch, she would not have needed to ask the local authorities once again to assure her family's freedom from him. The Leidesdorff letter that included one sentence about sewing she had in process for Rosario Vallejo was dated a month after that complaint. Juana's continued involvement in financial arrangements would have been superfluous if she were planning to move away from Yerba Buena. William Davis's list of all the citizens of Yerba Buena, two years after she purchased the ranch, includes Juana, her children, and, separately, Apolinario and three servants.[15]

Other than for business and personal ties, Juana remained in Yerba Buena for family reasons. Her daughter, Presentación Miranda y Briones de Ridley, gave birth in 1845 to Clara, her first child and Juana's first grandchild. Juana became Clara's godmother at Mission Dolores, and she was godmother again that year for a child with the family name Galinda, probably descendants of her brother Felipe. On June 8, 1846, Juana served as godmother for two children of converts to Catholicism, a three-year-old boy born in the United States and his sister, recently born. On June 11, Juana and her eldest son, Tomás Miranda, were godparents to a boy born to an unmarried woman from the United States. Juana and Tomás shared that honor again in 1847 for a child of Juana's niece María Ysidora Briones, married to Francisco Peralta. When the second Ridley child, Roberto de la Cruz, was born that same year, Juana's daughter Narcisa was godmother. The family thus clearly did not immediately abandon San Francisco after Juana purchased the ranch. They continued to be active participants in the life of the Mission Dolores community and church, a neighborhood that made some attempts to form a pueblo, but without success.

Juana's frequent presence in Mission Dolores records at this time demonstrates her continued alliances not only with relatives and Hispanic people, but with Americans living there and with people whose names do not make it into history books. Class was not a consideration when she offered aid and services. Her work as a midwife and doctor gave her an entrée into the confidence of many.[16]

Beginning in 1846, there must have been much banter and wonder among the locals when a U.S. warship stood in the harbor, making no overt threats, but causing agitation. The U.S. occupation of California that began in this year only slightly ruffled the surface of daily life for Californios in the Bay Area. The military governor acting for the United States, Colonel Richard Mason, felt uncomfortable administering a civil government and did everything in his power to avoid confrontations in Monterey, which Americans took over as their capital. Not all newly arrived Americans appreciated his delicacy. They would have preferred to be definitively in charge, but for Juana the new government at first had minor impact.[17]

The trip between San Francisco and the Purísima Ranch was difficult, and more so with children. Most likely, Presentación handled Juana's business interests in San Francisco when she was away. Juana did not entirely leave behind her residences at the Ojo de Agua, Yerba Buena, and Mission Dolores, but she had a well-functioning family home at the Purísima Ranch by 1848, which was fortunate in light of the upheaval caused by the discovery of gold virtually simultaneously with the visit of surveyor Chester Lyman, who boarded at her ranch house.

Lyman, one of the better surveyors in the San Francisco Bay area, worked in San Jose and San Francisco, as well as for private clients such as English captain William Fisher, who had purchased the 20,000-acre Rancho Laguna Seca southeast of San Jose. Within several mundane pages of his published diary, Lyman recorded some tantalizing insights into a day at Juana's ranch. "Some of the family were up at half past 3 am." Family members were traveling that day, so perhaps they got up so early for a good start. Some visitors to other ranches mentioned that everyone rose at the break of dawn, welcoming the sun's return by singing a holy song. At Rancho San Bernadino in southern California, everyone got up at three o'clock, said their prayers together, and went to their various jobs. Lyman did not mention whether Juana's household rose that early every day or only that day.[18]

"Sun 23 jan 1848 Sen Pena and his wife and the oldest daughter started for the Mission." They may have been on their way to mass. Those few words explain also that the family from whom Juana would buy several rooms of their Santa Clara adobe, former mission property, stayed as her guests. She tended to do business with people she knew. On Friday of that week, Juana and her daughter, two sons (probably Tomás and José Julian because Dolores was only seven years old), "& 1 or 2 others started for San Francisco." It would be pleasant to know who the one or two others were, but we must be content to infer that Juana's San Francisco connection remained intact.

Noting the date, January 28, 1848, stimulates the imagination to wonder about whether they set off to San Francisco because they had heard about gold, the news of which historians claim was spread on January 24. The usual story is that James Marshall found gold while supervising the construction of a mill on the American River, but it seems far more likely that Indian workers found it, showed it to him, and passed the word along their many rapid information routes at the same time that John Sutter was trying to keep the matter secret. Knowing how much information flowed in Juana's direction, and considering that by summer of 1848 Indians made up about half of the mining workforce, one must be forgiven for imagining the possibility that she funded and helped manage gold mining by some Indians from her ranch in that earliest effort.[19]

Lyman found his "quarters at madam Briones quite comfortable. the family is composed of the Widow Briones [by then she actually was a widow] 3 daughters (2 grown up) 2 or 3 boys, half a dozen indians, 2 little pet pigs in the cook house & 15 or 20 dogs." That he mentions a "cook house" verifies that Juana's household was like all others in the area in that cooks worked partly outdoors and partly in attached or separate sheds. The earliest map shows two houses of equal size next to each other, labeled "casas de Juana Briones." The second house might have been entirely a residence for family and guests, a place for the workforce to live, a kitchen, or, less likely, a place where workers made riatas, saddles, and shoes, packed wool, and handled other ranch jobs.[20] Lyman also mentions his concern about the numerous bears when he was out surveying. Perhaps all those dogs, besides helping to clear out garbage, warned householders if bears approached or even convinced bears to stay away.

Lyman noted that the two older girls did the cooking. The youngest, Manuela, was nine. Narcisa and Refugio, fifteen and thirteen in 1848, were cooking for a house full of people. Lyman referred to only three daughters, probably because the eldest, Presentación, was absent. She had two children and her own home in San Francisco. Lyman said of the two daughters who cooked that "they are rather pretty looking, but like most Californians dirty and slovenly." Considering the number of people for whom they prepared food over a wood fire, one wonders at any prettiness showing through the dirt. Through Lyman we also know that, as mentioned earlier, Juana had two sick people in the house, an Indian girl with a fever and a sailor with a very bad cough. Juana's career as a doctor and manager of a small hospital went with her wherever she lived.

Lyman's diary thus reveals that Juana's home in early 1848 was large enough to put up three guests—one who stayed comfortably with room and board for two weeks and two of his assistants for at least one day—two patients, "half a dozen Indians," and Juana's numerous family. Including Señor Peña and his wife, the total comes to eighteen people being housed and fed at Juana's ranch.

Lyman had been hired by the administrator of the estate of Juan Prado Mesa, whose Rancho San Antonio bordered Juana's on the south. Two creeks ran somewhat parallel, making the land between them subject to dispute about the boundary line, at least so Juana thought. Rancho San Antonio was a mess and never had been cared for. Lyman boarded with Juana instead of staying at the dilapidated, poorly constructed Mesa ranch house. Records suggest that James Yoell, who administered the Mesa estate, was incompetent or a cheat. The heirs did not speak English, and he did not speak Spanish. Papers in the probate court records of Santa Clara County appear to support the idea that the administrator lacked positive intentions toward the heirs' interests. The tone of much of the material that remains in archives about Rancho San Antonio is like the following: "Geronomo Mesa, guardian of the minor heirs of Prado Mesa, waives all notice whatever in the delivery of letters of administration to J. A. Yoell on the estate, by and with his advice . . . certified paper showing debt of Juan Prado Mesa to Joseph Thompson in amount of $800." This may have given Juana advance warning about the difficulties to expect when speculators, some honest and some dishonest, came into California and overturned many of the previous understandings about law and land.[21]

Having Lyman board with her probably gave Juana the idea that some of the suspect dealings at the Rancho San Antonio could be washing over to her ranch and that the administrator had in mind taking some of the property she believed was hers. This was during the American occupation, before California had become a state and the U.S. Land Commission had started sorting out titles, so Juana wrote to the mayor of San José, James Weeks. Alcaldes under the American occupation had comprehensive jurisdiction in every kind of matter, and he was the closest authority she could reach promptly. She may also have known him personally as a friend of Charles Brown and Maximo Martínez:

> To the Justice of the Peace of the Pueblo of San Jose,
>
> I Juana Briones of this jurisdiction before your honor appear and say: that a surveyor and other persons have presented themselves on my land, measuring the same in favor of the heirs of Don Prado Mesa, I claim the said land to be my property, by the [document?] which is in my possession, and other testimony if it should be necessary for which reason I pray you to be pleased to protect my rights from being disturbed; making the necessary oath; not signing because I cannot write, Don Antonio Inojosa signing at my request, Antonio Inojosa

James Weeks responded, "Not to worry, I will see to it that your rights are protected."[22]

Encajonado, Juana's ranch house, had wooden laths nailed to vertical posts to form a crib filled with mud. The walls were revealed when Charles Nott removed the exterior siding in about 1900.

When Charles Palmer Nott purchased Juana's house in 1900, he wrote in a letter to his fiancée that he would tear down most of the rooms and retain only three, which remain to this day. The house must have been fairly large. Having expert Indian builders on staff, having a long acquaintance with sawyers in the redwoods, and owning a property bordered by the Arastradero, the route for hauling lumber, gave Juana valuable construction resources. The earliest extant surveyor's map shows a section marked "lime kilns" on the ranch, which probably supplied the material for the "beautiful smooth plaster" that the Notts found when they removed boards, inside and out, that had been protecting the house.[23]

Juana had apparently built a comfortable house in the style of her people at the time: a series of rooms, each more than fifteen feet square, opening onto each other and onto covered porches on both sides. The porches served both as hallways and as extra rooms for a people accustomed to living outdoors. One could sit and sew, cut vegetables, and make riatas on the roofed-over porch. One of Juana's grandsons recalled grinding coffee beans on the porch as his childhood daily duty.[24]

Given evidence of Juana's alert activity at the ranch, it is surprising that her brother Gregorio, testifying in a land case six years after Lyman's visit to her home, mentioned that his sister Juana "still resides here," meaning in San Francisco. In order to leave her children in one place or the other, she needed reliable workers at both who could be trusted to oversee the household, the children, and the farm. It was a full, active, responsible life.[25]

Although Juana had essentially grown up in San Francisco, considered as the presidio, the mission, and Yerba Buena, she knew the rest of the peninsula well, in part because of the people living around her. Owners of all the ranch properties contiguous to the Rancho Purísima had been connected with her or her family over many years. Maximo Martínez's family included Antonia Richardson—Juana's neighbor at Yerba Buena— and Ignacio Martínez of the Pinole grant where Juana's brother Felipe settled. Her cousin Antonio Buelna was of a prominent family among the early settlers of Branciforte; and two Robles brothers, also of Branci-forte, bought Peña's ranch in 1847. Juan Prado Mesa's parents, like Juana's mother, had arrived with the Anza party. Long after Mesa's death, two of his sons married Juana's daughters Manuela and Refugio. She knew all her neighbors—if not personally from her childhood on, then at least tangentially.

The way that Juana managed her ranch has never been described in print, so whether the experience of an older woman, María Ignacia López de Carrillo, can be transferred to hers is a guess. Manuel Vallejo's mother-in-law was a widow when she applied to him and he conveyed a ranch to her, now roughly the town of Santa Rosa. Her sons handled the cattle, and she rode a horse they tamed for her. She spoke Spanish and the local Indian language, in which she supervised sowing and harvest-ing. She was illiterate like Juana, but unlike her in that she refused to have anything to do with Anglos. She detested them, it was said, because two members of the Bear Flag Revolt party had raped and killed her daughter-in-law.[26]

During the first decade after Juana joined the company of ranchers in the Santa Clara Valley, she became convinced of the relative safety and potential for making a living in the country compared to the danger of San Francisco. One historian referred to San Francisco during that time of upheaval as a "cesspool," in part due to "the reign of crime." Many His-panic people fled the city, especially because criminals often targeted them. Juana stayed connected in San Francisco while bowing to the necessity of settling her family in the country.[27]

Presentación's residence closer to San Francisco gave Juana a comfortable place to stay and relieved her of the need to maintain a residence there. Juana and Presentación were probably more like sisters than mother-daughter. There was a ten-year gap between Presentación and the next Miranda child who lived past early childhood. Girl children were expected to share child care and household duties, so mother and daughter would have worked together on many tasks, and the eldest especially learned from her mother about business and owning property. A receipt dated 1852 and signed by Presentación has miraculously survived: "I have received from Father Flavian Fontaine ninety dollars ($90) for the rent of my house for three months, beginning January 1st and ending April 1st of the same year." Presentación, the only child of Juana's who married an Anglo, did so twice, Ridley in 1844 and, ten years after he died, Henry Witcomb at the Church of the Nativity in Menlo Park. Her sharing in Ridley's insider status would have given her the insight that the best attorney in California for pursuing land cases was Henry Wager Halleck. She hired him herself and would have recommended him to her mother.[28]

The difference in legal systems affected everyone. Juana had needed government approval to purchase her ranch, a feature of a policy by which the government assumed prior ownership of land, similar to U.S. policy that whatever appeared unencumbered could be considered public land. Spanish legal policy especially saw land as, in most cases, inheritable but not saleable. Under the U.S. system, land became a commodity, carefully measured and kept track of by government, but purchasable nonetheless. Using land as payment for services was featured under both Mexico and the United States.

In Juana's application to purchase, the mention that she needed land for her growing herd of cattle was common in land-grant requests. A researcher who interviewed local people in the 1890s noted that Juana's employees had joined in roundups on the Robles-Seale ranch, Henry Seale being the man who had acquired the ranch from Robles. That would have been the better location of the two for roundups. Seale had flatland; Juana had gently rolling hills.

Juana's many connections in the business world would have facilitated her profitable engagement in the hide-and-tallow trade, although that trade collapsed six years after her ranch purchase, never to return. That market's disappearance can be attributed in part to sailors' abandoning ship for the gold fields. Because workers received only peasant wages, none would load hides and raise sails for the return voyage to the northeastern shoe factories. No one could be found in San Francisco to carry luggage because everyone could find better jobs than that. Around 148 ships sank slowly into the sand and mud. Not even the U.S. military had a cure for desertion. Officers had to admit that soldiers would desert and easily give up the pittance they received from the government for the alleged wealth awaiting them just upriver.[29] Beef sales more than made up for the loss in sales of hide and tallow, though, and payment was in cash. Before this time, negotiations in deals had stretched over a year or more. The inflated market enticed southern California ranchers, who herded beef cattle four hundred miles or more up to the mining region.[30]

The relatively friendly American occupation was built on the presence of about four hundred foreigners, mostly American and British, in the Monterey and San Francisco districts. Some had lived twenty years or more in the area, held responsible and respected positions, and enlivened the economy. English-speaking people's influence was considerable, but the common language had remained Spanish, and the law continued to be Spanish derived. Many resident Anglos fit a niche by understanding both systems and mediating between the two.[31] Because U.S. military governors adapted to existing regulations, most of the populace reacted complacently to the U.S. occupation, but a few retaliated when some of their horses, cattle, and equipment were appropriated.

Largely due to news of riches for all, California never held territorial status or experienced the hesitant admission process. When Californians learned in 1850 that they now lived in the thirty-first state and that the region would transfer to civilian management, Anglo politicians in all due haste inserted laws and customs that ironically jolted non-Anglo populations more than the military had.

Pursuant to all this came the land imbroglio. The Treaty of Guadalupe Hidalgo that settled the Mexican-American War asserted the validity of certified land ownership. The trick was to prove certification and at the same time to discourage squatters while one's ownership was in the long process of being approved. These challenges made Juana's previous problems seem like child's play and introduced her to a world where lawyers took over as captains of the ship.[32]

The necessity of adjusting to new conditions brought by the gold rush and California's new statehood influenced Juana's decision to live full time on her ranch. One of her grandsons, Tomás Dimas Mesa, recalled after her death that she loved horses, cattle, and everything to do with a ranch. So she did by the time he was born in 1867, when many more people lived in the environs and the isolated ranch she had purchased twenty-three years earlier had evolved into quite a center of activity.[33]

Americans brought trouble aplenty, but they also hastened the advent of amenities, such as better methods of travel. A person who had never flinched at traveling to patients, family, and church or for business, Juana could well appreciate improved roads, stagecoaches, boats, even trains, especially gratifying as one aged and mounting a horse became less exhilarating.

Twelve

FIRST GOLD, THEN LAND

Coping in a Populous Valley

Inventive swindlers ranked high among the many dangers to miners and everyone else during the gold rush. It was all so unreal anyway. Historian Rodman Paul studied two years of blatantly false letters in San Francisco newspapers starting in 1854. They trumpeted cheap, easy, fabulous wealth on the Kern River. Such reportage, widely duplicated in person and in print, led the cognoscenti to bet on water companies instead. Paul wrote that anyone who invested in mining lost "caste." San Franciscan John Henry Brown, who bought one of Ridley's saloons from him, wrote about a man who mixed a couple of ounces of gold dust into dirt in the street and showed people how to pan for it. His partner quickly sold his entire stock of pans. Such inventive swindling moved along to include the area of land acquisition when that seemed less physically harmful than standing in cold water all day wielding a pick and shovel.[1]

The land grab, gold rush, and King Cotton deeply harmed the lowest echelon of their respective societies even as they enriched many. California Indians suffered death and devastation. In the South, slavery became more entrenched when cotton rose to prominence as a wealth-producing commodity. Although the toll of death and maiming in the Civil War has been documented, the Indian death toll in California has not because the war against them was fragmented and widespread and usually not called a war at all. Historian Lisbeth Haas writes that under the U.S. occupation of California, the Indians became wards of the government, were required to carry a passport or permission from an employer to travel, and were prohibited from gathering in crowds. The law also stipulated that Indian land belonged to the government, and therefore heads of village groups had no authority to cede land. Gorgonio was fortunate that Juana had purchased his land.[2]

Independent miners questioned whether Indians working for an employer should be allowed because they trespassed on claims that persons working for themselves thought should belong to them. Permutations of the status of laborers created complexities that baffled state legislators because the United States had no mining laws until 1866, by which time small-enterprise gold mining had been transformed into big business. In the early years of the gold rush, independent miners made their own laws and often managed to prevail by intimidating competitors with the rhetoric of freedom in an environment where slavery, peonage, contract labor, and indentured servitude were widespread. The system, or lack of it, complicated life mainly in the mines, but also elsewhere, for everyone.[3]

Contention about slavery crossed the seas, mountains, and deserts, making its way to California in several guises. Owners enticed their slaves with various ingenious arrangements. California had outlawed slavery, but a case could be made that contracts drawn up in a slave state were legal. Another practice in the scramble for cheap labor related to miners from China, some of whom agreed to repay their passage and other expenses with labor.

Both slavery and gold rushed California into the union. The government wanted money, and the North wanted another free state, but slavery had many supporters within California. As late as 1865, Thomas Fallon, a resident of San Jose, wrote in his journal that "Confederates in this county have been stealing horses and chickens 'for Jeff Davis.'"[4]

In its constitution, California rejected slavery from the beginning, but it has been said that a majority of state representatives favored Southern causes. It has also been said that a young Unitarian minister from Boston, Starr King, helped save California for the Union. He spoke convincingly to many hostile audiences and had a seminal role in funding the Sanitary Commission. California's contribution of more than a million dollars made up one-quarter of all the money raised for the commission, a project to feed, clothe, and nurse Union soldiers that contributed mightily to the Union victory.[5]

California's becoming a state at the time was in doubt because territorial status usually came first. A territory, so-called because the area's sparse non-Indian population did not meet statehood requirements, had representatives in Congress who could speak but not vote. Californios had long chatted about the future of California over their tea and aguardiente, and if lore about Juana is accurate, some of that chatting went on in her parlor. They talked about three options for California—forming its own republic, inviting England or the United States in to replace Mexico to head the government, or being divided into two regions, north and south, so that each could make its own arrangements. Even after California had become the thirty-first state, discussion did not die about either dividing the state or forming a West Coast republic.

If California and Oregon had set up a republic, contiguous territories would probably have joined them. The railroad terminated in mid-Missouri, increasing the sense of the Far West's isolation. Historian Patricia Limerick writes of westerners who thought of themselves as in federal captivity, unable to access fully the land and resources. They sometimes compared themselves to the original thirteen colonies, for whom revolution was the only cure.[6]

In some ways, California acted like its own boss, with two undeclared internal wars going on in the 1850s—one intended to eradicate Indians and the other to move as much land as possible into the possession of Anglo newcomers. Both of these pseudowars seriously affected Juana, one in depriving her of her workforce and the other in creating a situation where she had to invest considerable time and money just to hold onto her property.

For Juana, the changeover to U.S. government at first impinged on her lifestyle only minimally. She had known Americans since her young womanhood, when mostly men integrated into the society by marrying Hispanic women. Foreigners made up nearly 10 percent of the non-Indian population of California when the first U.S. naval vessels arrived in Monterey and San Francisco bays in 1846. Even before the arrival of the military, a scattering of Americans had come overland and been introduced to the country by John Sutter, who acted like a potentate in dealing out land without consulting the governor.[7]

A few more immigrants at first seemed fairly normal, but as Americans arrived in gradually increasing numbers, they felt more independent, less indebted to Californios, and less friendly toward Spanish speakers. In itself, Mexico's loss of the war with the United States would have hatched a changing demographic anyway, but the nearly simultaneous gold discovery added extreme turmoil into the mix. The mining craze enveloped much of the land mass of California in one way or another, involving housing, transport routes, supply stations, food production and delivery, and the many services and products needed by a ballooning population.[8]

The myth of Anglo-Saxon superiority became a useful tool for domination. Racism made life difficult for Hispanic, Chinese, and African

American people, and nearly fatal for Indians. The sense of innate superiority abetted unconscionable Anglo acts. Historian Douglas Monroy writes that a general belief prevailed among Anglos that the United States owned the gold because the government had paid Mexico fifteen million dollars for California, Arizona, New Mexico, and adjoining territory. In several gold-mining locales, Americans put up signs stating that persons other than U.S. citizens would be exiled by force if they refused to leave willingly. Of course, by law, Californios were American citizens, and so were blacks because California had outlawed slavery, but race, not citizenship, drove exclusion.[9]

Indians were a separate category. Sherburne Cook explains that the Spanish "had systematically availed themselves of human resources, whereas the English had tapped only material wealth." In other words, according to Cook, the "Ibero-Americans" incorporated the Indians into their society and economy, whereas the "Anglo-Americans rigidly excluded them from their own social order." Indians were almost entirely excluded from the mines within two years. California governor Peter Burnett, in his annual message to the state legislature in 1851, explicitly set forth a "war of extermination" until Indians should "become extinct." Those words seem devastating beside Louise Clappe's writing to her sister that same year that she saw near the road on the way to mining country "a number of Indian women" gathering seeds, naked except for grass skirts. Clappe observed normal Indian life the same year that the governor issued carte blanche to kill them off.[10]

Some Californios, especially those with Indian employees, mined before the mobs poured in, and Juana herself may have done so. Chinese immigrants, said to number twenty-five thousand by 1852, had to work in the less-productive, already-mined region in the north. About fifty thousand Mexicans, many of whom traveled north from Sonora with their families, gathered in the more southern portion. Others arrived from virtually everywhere. Within three years, one hundred thousand miners harvested more than eighty million dollars, but their money went fast as they paid a dollar per egg and comparable prices for other foods and products. Juana's business savvy, honed over many years, would have made her ranch and city property pay off, regardless of the myriad difficulties that accompanied the influx of miners.[11]

As exciting as the rush was for other quarters of the globe, ordinary people in California had an unaccustomed range of problems to solve. The market for food enlivened the economy, but danger made San Francisco unendurable for Juana, who had children to care for, and made operating a dairy impractical with thieves rampant and no effective police force. One San Francisco group that pretended to substitute for the absent police aptly called itself the Hounds, a name they undoubtedly considered humorous as they terrorized the city or, more exactly, terrorized persons with any hint of racial difference from themselves. Their amusements included lynching and rape.[12]

Juana's previous gender and family hurdles prepared her to cope with a new set of rules that were more discriminatory toward women and with the added difficulty of discrimination against Hispanic people. She probably found conditions in the Mission Dolores neighborhood slightly better than those at North Beach, but a definitive move to the country made better sense. By the time the search for gold had turned into mania, she and her children lived primarily at the Purísima Ranch.

Retreat, however, did not of itself solve the major problem of holding onto her land and using it profitably. Many people attracted by gold stayed to gather other riches, or at least a living, from land, and such people were seemingly looking everywhere. In her request to purchase the ranch, Juana had written that she needed room for her cattle, a good source of income for a time, but developing the land and acquiring a labor force became two intertwined challenges. Indian workers at first had other options. They could join their trade partners in the Central Valley who were doing well in the horse business, and mining opportunities beckoned until Indians were excluded from them. Juana needed workers. By 1848, excluding Presentación, who had a family and ranch of her own by then, Juana's eldest child at home was seventeen, the youngest seven—a family not yet old enough to replace a dispersed workforce.

After the early 1850s, Santa Clara Valley Indians became more and more invisible. Honest census records from 1852 would have indicated how many remained with Juana, but generally Indians "not taxed" were not listed. Even that basic information about them diminished after that census, so how soon Juana's staff dispersed is uncertain, but they definitely at some point had to run for safety, except for a few who managed to find a niche. Delfina Cuero, a Diegueño Indian, said that the Indians went farther and farther away from their homeland, looking for some corner where they would not be chased away. Most of Juana's Indian employees probably had to do the same.

Kent Lightfoot attributes to Alfred Kroeber and his research team at the University of California, Berkeley, the idea that Indians like Gorgonio were "extinct" or had "melted" away. In the East Bay, where Santa Clara Valley Indians would have been most likely to take refuge, at least five different Bay Area tribes moved to Alisal in the Coast Range near Pleasanton and to other places nearby, such as a section of Agustín Bernal's ranch, the hilly edges of the Livermore Valley, and similarly difficult-of-access areas such as Niles Canyon and Sunol. Tribal identity merged in these communities, making them less interesting to anthropologists, who preferred to study Indians who had stayed closer to their original cultural ways. In the 1840s, at least a thousand former neophytes from Mission San José and possibly more from Mission Santa Clara fled to nearby hiding places.[13]

Gorgonio and some of his clan might have held out at Juana's ranch as late as 1858. That year, Juana and her children brought suit against local landowners who, they said, were overstepping the boundaries of the Briones Ranch. In this instance, many persons testified about their years-long knowledge of the road called Arastradero that Juana claimed as one of her ranch boundaries. Sebastian Peralta said that "he knows Gorgonio and has heard him say that the Arastradero the affiant described was the boundary of that ranch." Peralta's use of the present-tense "knows" presumably indicates that Gorgonio still lived there. One person testified that Gorgonio's house was about a mile and a half from Juana's, which means that their home probably was the flat place where Adobe Creek banks are unusually low and where the impressive Indian artifacts of the Florence Fava excavation were found, off the present El Monte Road in Los Altos.[14]

Although Gorgonio, his son Ramón, his daughter Paula, and Calistro, the Indian woman whom Gorgonio repeatedly mentioned in legal documents over eleven years, seem to have stayed longer in Santa Clara County than most other local Indians, they eventually must have escaped to a safer place, the most likely being to property owned by Phoebe Apperson Hearst, a renowned philanthropist who owned a ranch that is now the Castlewood Country Club near Pleasanton. She became a supporter of Indian culture and helped found the anthropology museum at the University of California at Berkeley. She provided local Indians with work and living space. Andrew Galvan, now the curator at Mission Dolores, said that his grandmother, Dolores Marine Galvan, was born at Mission San José in 1890. She thus was a contemporary of Gorgonio's. She worked along with several of her siblings for "Aunt Phoebe" and lived in Alisal among a group called the Verona Band.[15]

When the U.S. Land Commission entered the mix to verify ownership of land throughout California, persons who testified about Juana's legal right to the ranch said that Indians worked on the ranch after she purchased it. In 1852, Maximo Martínez of the adjoining Rancho Corte de Madera, said that Gorgonio, his son Ramón, his daughter Paula, and his relative Calistro had lived there; that they and other Indians of their community raised vegetables including wheat, corn, and beans; and that they had cattle, horses, and oxen, and had built two or three small wooden houses before 1840. He said that at the time of his testimony Juana managed the ranch with Indians and other workers.[16]

When Juana purchased one square league, she knew that the boundaries were somewhat vague. She later hired a surveyor to help clear up discrepancies. Even with that expert study, over a period of twenty years the ranch would be figured either at 4,496.36 acres or at 4,338.19 acres when using the Spanish vara as the measure or at 4,442.238 acres according to the Bureau of Land Management's determination dated August 1871. There seemed no end to the people who would argue over an acre or two, but the Purísima Ranch presented fewer problems than most. Gone were the days when someone like Juana's sister Guadalupe Briones de Miramontes could be so explicitly assumed to have rights to land that her name would appear in the center of a diseño without boundary lines. José Peña even used that vague, uncertified gift of land to allege that Maximo Martínez did not need more land than he already had because "he has ceded the addition he obtained to Guadalupe Briones." Reasons to argue seemed endless.[17]

Many diverse happenings affected the decline of cattle ranching on Juana's land. A drought in 1856, the introduction of American cattle breeds, and the Anglo habit of putting up fences along what they thought were their boundaries began to diminish profit in the cattle business, which also depended on horses for all phases of the operation. Although good horses were highly prized, they were so plentiful in the 1840s that one could be purchased for about three dollars, less than the cost of the saddle and bridle. One visitor explained with considerable insight the centrality of cattle raising in 1849 by saying that a Californian could describe in detail each of the hundred or more domesticated animals, horses, mules, and oxen he saw that day. Less-populated land suited cattle, but once fences and smaller properties increased, the Santa Clara Valley evolved into one massive orchard by the 1920s; nevertheless, cattle did so well that the last cattle ranch in Juana's neighborhood closed in 2005, and horses and cows can still be seen on nearby hills.[18]

The breakup of ranches and the many fences that diminished the open-range style of cattle raising changed the dynamics of Juana's life. Squatters constituted a serious hazard for landowners. A professional but undated survey of Juana's ranch, most likely of the mid-1850s, already shows names of people who may have purchased plots, but more likely were, or started out as, squatters in the same area where archaeologists have found extensive

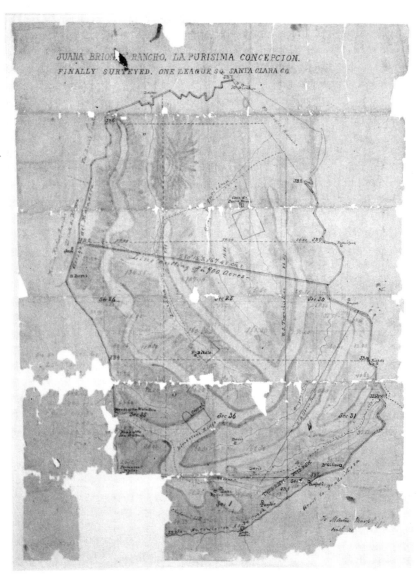

A Rancho la Purísima Concepción survey, ca. 1855. The dotted line is the boundary of the land Murphy first leased and then purchased from Juana. Don Nielson recently compared the survey with current maps and found that the existing house is precisely where "casas de Juana Briones" is shown in the upper right third of this survey map.

Indian burial remains and artifacts. As clearly as the handwriting can be deciphered on the map, persons named Taylor, Davis, Keefer, Danfield, D. Gilberto, Ricket, Bryant, and Rutherford had houses near that site. It would not have been unusual for them to push the Indians off, threaten them, and appropriate their resources, although the Indians may already have found, even before these householders arrived, that leaving was the healthiest course for them.[19]

Some of the goings-on in the area validate the opinion that squatters were vicious, scheming thieves, but many people honestly believed three related concepts: there was plenty of vacant land, the place now belonged to the United States, and Americans thus had the right to homestead land not visibly in use. In one of the more prominent examples of the uproar squatters caused, John Sutter's holdings at Sacramento evaporated. Eight people died there in a two-day land riot in 1850. Historian Andrew Rolle refers to the questionable honesty of a system that appointed judges, juries, and sheriffs who were squatters. It was said that in the vicinity of San Francisco Bay there was not a single ranch without squatters.[20]

Next door to Juana, three men died on Henry Seale's land, formerly the Robles ranch. Details of the tragedy varied from one telling to another, but all indications are that Seale's brother Thomas tried to eject a squatter named Paul Shore. In another version, a neighbor, S. J. Crosby, urged his dog to attack Shore, resulting in his death. Thomas Seale turned himself in to Sheriff John Murphy, claiming to have acted in self-defense. When Crosby came to testify, the brother of the deceased murdered him, and a bystander died accidentally.

Recalling the difficulties of this period, a former judge said that the courts and police could not clear squatters off the Murphy land, part of which the Murphy family had purchased from Juana. He said that Mrs. Murphy had treated them with such kindness that they left voluntarily. This account had to be an idealized version. By law, squatters who were forced to leave had to be compensated for their improvements, the value of which offered another area for dissension. No records explain why Juana first leased in 1855 and then sold half her ranch to the Murphys, but one reasonable surmise could be the squatter problem; another could be her need for cash to pay her legal expenses when she had to prove her claim to the land.[21]

Sandy Wilson, a squatter, took over the home of Juana's Buelna relatives, which its owners had temporarily vacated. The owner of the land would come occasionally with other Californians on horseback and, without dismounting, would run chains along the boundaries to validate pos-

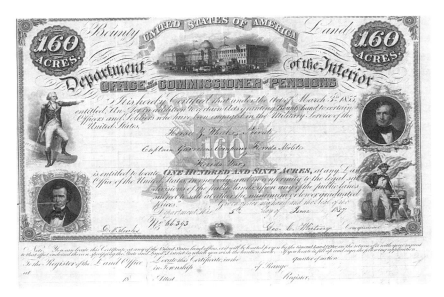

Military bounty land warrants are certificates for allotments of public land that were issued to former soldiers as a reward for service. They could be bought and sold, and came to be used as scrip. They further complicated legal cases that sought to prove land ownership.

session, even though someone else was using the property. Wilson, neglecting to consider that he did not own the land, complained that their chains damaged his wheat. The next time they did this, he pulled one man from his horse and thrashed him. When Sheriff Murphy came looking for him in response to a complaint, Wilson met Murphy along the trail, responded to his inquiry about whether Wilson was at home with, "Yes, Wilson was there, at least he had been ten minutes earlier." In a curious modern resonance to this story, Tom Hunt, who lived for fifty years in a cottage next to the Juana Briones house and inherited a life interest in the cottage and land around it, would once a year confirm private ownership of the land by chaining off the rarely used track that led from Arastradero Road into the property.[22]

Most researchers blame the Land Commission for the devastating loss of property by people who owned land before the U.S. takeover, but many unaccustomed practices, most of them conducted in English, introduced other imperfectly understood problems, such as formerly unknown property taxes. In 1851, the new state imposed taxes on the value of property at sixty to seventy cents per hundred dollars of valuation, plus a county tax of a dollar to a dollar fifty. The unfamiliarity of taxing land or chattels caused many properties to be sold at auction to pay government debts. Juana's children had her example of managing property to the minutest detail before them, but as late as 1904 a controller's receipt states that "all of lot 9 B1 N.R. 4 E., said land was sold to the state . . . for delinquent taxes. . . . J. D. Miranda . . . properly indorsed . . . receipt . . . to wit: $2.15." "J. D." was Joseph Dolores, Juana's youngest son, whose estate was being sold for taxes.[23]

Land endured longest as the basic economic reality, but people just could not put exotic mining out of their minds. In Mayfield in 1870, people went berserk over rumors that gold had been found at Stevens Creek in the foothills ten miles away. The *Sacramento Daily Union* on July 30, 1870, described Mayfield as "deserted." Every pick and shovel in town had been sold, and residents had frantically dashed off to the alleged mines. The *Mayfield Enterprise* said in its July 30 issue of that year that 150 miners were at the creek, and a daily stagecoach went between town and the mine. The newspaper never mentioned that gold was ever found there.[24]

In a letter written about a month after her brother Gregorio died, Juana told her dear nephew Pablo that she had arrived safely home from Bolinas. Almost certainly she was returning from Gregorio's funeral, and, as certainly, she must have been nursing him in his last illness. She told Pablo that she wanted to inform him of a conversation she had overheard by some men who wanted to get Pablo involved in a mining project. She wanted him to know that these men were strangers to her, perhaps because she suspected that they might suggest to him that she was interested. She warned him to be careful:

Sr. Don Pablo Briones

Rancho de la Parisima [*sic*] June 13, 1863

Dear Nephew,

It has been three days since I took the coast road home, the return to San Francisco seeming much shorter than the last time. This explains the delay in writing you and now I write you from San Francisco where I am very comfortable.

The other day I heard a conversation about some mines (which I think you know about) or which ones they are. These men are talking about getting you in the business with them. I'm writing you this to warn you to be careful with these men. I do not know them.

Here we are all fine and I hope that all at your house are also well. Say hello to my *comadre* Ramona and all the *familia* and you please know I send you my respect and appreciation. Wishes for your happiness.

Your aunt,

Juana Briones

However much Pablo admired Aunt Juana for her vast knowledge of medicine, he must have thought he knew more about mining than she did and about the land where he had lived since his youth. He wasn't worried about "caste." The year she sent him that letter, he went in with two men on copper mining near his home. All the excitement, work, and investment may have profited someone, but most investors lost more than they could afford. The mine was not a total sham, though; it yielded copper fifty years later. Jack Mason, author of a history of the area, comments that "[h]itherto level-headed Bolinas boys quit their ranch jobs to join the get-rich-quick operation." Copper had taken over the speculative mentality that year as gold had earlier. Nearly four hundred copper companies developed and failed in California, their failure due in part to the absence of adequate smelters.

That letter to Pablo gives evidence of much change since Juana had purchased the ranch nearly twenty years earlier, when there were no stage-coaches. Even taking the "coast road" was an adventure. From Bolinas, the driver had to know the tides to get around the steep rocks that ocean waves attack daily.[25]

Little remains today to suggest that speculators, miners, squatters, and their ilk ever lived in the area of Juana's ranch, although one place at the ranch house retains an intriguing relationship to Gorgonio and his people. Priests had tried to train Indians away from their beliefs, but the Indians simply hid their ceremonial sites and, according to Kent Lightfoot, "an underground world of Indian daily practices" prevailed even in the missions.

A photograph taken in the 1880s or 1890s at the back of Juana's house shows a pile of stones. The man and children are probably Juana's grandson and great-grandchildren. That there is a small stream close to the house, Purísima Creek, which shows on old maps, makes Indian use of the rock pile in the picture a possibility. Water is still pumped to Tom Hunt's cottage on the property from the spring where the creek originates. Testimony in 1854 about the ranch boundary mentioned a nearby waterhole with three springs, a locale that cannot be positively located now because depletion of the aquifer has diminished surface water. However, the presence of water and the location of the rocks on a hill suggest two potential uses of the rock pile by Indians, a place of worship or a sweat house.

The story that Indians collected and piled those stones passed from one of Juana's daughters, born in 1835, through a relay of seven persons to me in 2003. Gorgonio or his relatives told Juana's daughter, Refugio Miranda, about the stones. She was nine years old when Juana bought the ranch and sixty-five in 1900 when she sold her mother's house and land around it to Charles Palmer Nott. Refugio told Nott, and he told Edith Cox Eaton, to whom he sold the property in 1925. Eaton told Tom Hunt. In the 1970s, Monajo Ellsworth, who says she is part Cherokee, passed the house as she was walking her child in a stroller. She told Tom as he worked in the garden that she had always been curious about the place. He showed her around the house and told her that Indians had collected the stones that now form the fourth wall of an enclosed patio. Monajo told me about the stones at a public meeting sponsored by the Palo Alto Historical Association at which the Juana Briones Heritage Foundation was explaining the history of Juana's house. My husband and I went with Monajo and her husband to the house, examined a rock wall that now encloses one side of a patio, and agreed that they were the same rocks as the ones in a pile in the photograph more than a century old.

An author writing local history in the 1890s interviewed people of the area who told her that Indians built altars of piles of stones, threw on them various items they called "pooish," composed of shells, feathers, food, and trinkets, and set them on fire. They danced around this fire to their god "Cookany," of whom visions in the form of animals would rise up in the smoke. The rocks might also have been used for sweat houses. When the celebrants were covered with sweat, they would run out and immerse themselves in cool water. Either the stream or the three springs near Juana's house would have served that purpose. Gorgonio's people could have practiced their traditional ceremonies there when they were working for the mission in managing that land.[26]

Perplexing circumstances with no single solution drastically affected Gorgonio and his kin. They had reached a kind of relationship with Hispanic people that, although hardly ideal, nevertheless gave them a place in the delicate balance of the government, church, economy, and culture. When Anglos took over, even tentative solutions seldom applied. The question that may never be answered satisfactorily is, What happened to the Indians who lived and worked on Juana's ranch—Gorgonio, Ramón,

The stones in this pile at Juana's house, ca. 1890, were later used to enclose a courtyard. Oral tradition claims the rocks were gathered by Indians to build a kind of altar.

Paula, Calistro, and their relatives—and how long did they remain as Juana's ranch hands?

If Gorgonio was still alive in 1860, he would have been seventy-two years old. Two other Indians did remain in the area and were written about. Ynigo spoke to historians and even had his picture taken. In 1920, so did James Boholi, said to be the last Santa Clara Mission Indian. Juana's children surely had an opportunity to know and learn from the Indians on the ranch. Perhaps some of the men among them, especially Gorgonio, became the male mentors that the Miranda children lacked when parental discord deprived them of a father.

Gorgonio and his relatives tried hard and for a time succeeded in providing a good home for their people. Several miles from where they and Juana Briones lived and worked, the Dumbarton Bridge now crosses the bay, with a clear view, on the bay's eastern shore, of a hill that could have been their final resting place, and in some people's minds remains a memorial to them.

Thirteen

THE LAWYER'S OFFICE

Some Prospered, Some Failed

Acquiring land had to be high on Juana's agenda in the 1840s, but a decade later, soon after the United States took over, her priority became retaining property while her contemporaries on every side were losing theirs. She had at the same time to exercise diligence in managing her assets. Some California residents gave in to the mind-set of easy riches. Persistence in retaining one's rightful property was one side of the equation, but making the land pay involved the hard work of staffing, understanding the changing market, and sidestepping the imponderables. Land became something like currency; you could trade it for a horse or some hardware. One of Juana's relatives, Luisa Soto y Mesa, and her husband, John Greer, had a son who claimed that his mother had exchanged 1,000 acres for some hardware worth about ten dollars. Perhaps everyone at a certain age can look back on stupid financial errors they have made, but there are many stories about many people, like the one about Luisa Soto from the very era when Juana was striving to hold things together.[1]

As long as Indians could survive in the Santa Clara Valley, Juana had ranch hands who knew her and knew the land. When they had been almost entirely driven out, she hired Chinese agricultural workers. The 1870 census lists four male farm laborers on the Purísima Ranch, ages nineteen to twenty-seven, born in China. Their names appear between those of Juana's family members on the ranch, written as Ah Kim, Ah Moe, Ah Jim, and Ah Kang, leaving out family reference and starting them all with the diminutive "Ah," as if to say "Little Pete" or "Little Tom." Kim, Moe, Jim, and Kang were given names.[2]

A Murphy family biographer explains that "[t]he procedure, if one wanted to hire Chinese laborers, was to write a letter to governor Stanford at Mayfield." A branch of the rail line that went down the peninsula had a flag stop on the Murphy property, a great convenience for people and produce, obtained because the Murphys ceded land to the railroad for a dollar a year.[3] The story of railroads captured the national imagination when they were completed across the Sierra Nevada Mountains in 1869, giving the top leaders of the endeavor, including Leland Stanford, lasting honor and wealth. Their accomplishment was completed precisely one century after Spanish Mexicans' first entrance into Alta California by land from the south. Both endeavors succeeded in their way. The Spanish occupation succeeded in protecting for a time Spain's Pacific commercial interests. The intercontinental railroad contributed greatly to solidifying the West Coast's commitment to continuing as part of the United States. Less dramatic but more important for locals, railroads operated within compact areas well before the grand achievement over the tall mountains.

Chinese laborers had made up nearly the entire Sierra workforce to complete the railroad. Other categories of workers departed fairly rapidly once they comprehended the job's danger and difficulty. The Chinese laborers' remarkable duty and commitment rarely received mention or praise, although one speaker at a banquet celebrating the nearly finished railroad referred to their "fidelity and industry."[4]

When the railroad was finished, the Chinese construction workers had to find other jobs. Many went into agriculture and soon replaced Indians as scapegoats. In July 1870, the *Mayfield Enterprise,* the short-lived newspaper in the town Juana would move to fifteen years later, disparaged Santa Clara County ranchers for hiring "foul pagans" who took jobs away from "starving white men." The reporter used Dan Murphy as an example of employers who were "enriching the Chinamen at the expense of our citizens." Cecilia Tsu writes in a 2006 article about Chinese farmworkers in the Santa Clara Valley that promoters attempted to portray the agricultural labor there as evidence of the manly superiority of white men in "the contest over constructing and reconstructing racial ideology in California agriculture." Chinese workers were particularly sought out for orchard, berry, and vegetable agricultural labor, and by the 1880s they constituted 7 percent of the county population in an area that had evolved from raising cattle to growing wheat and then to producing fruit in massive quantities.[5]

By 1860, Martin Murphy, who first leased then purchased half of Juana's Purísima Ranch, thought that cattle no longer constituted the best investment on that piece of land. The beef bonanza of the early gold rush days became less lucrative in part because supply grew exponentially when cattle were driven in from southern California, Texas, the Middle West, and Mexico to feed the dramatically increased population of California. Within five years, Murphy purchased ranches that totaled 72,000 acres, giving him the opportunity to move cattle to less-populated areas and to take advantage of the rich Santa Clara Valley soil for agriculture.

A Murphy family biographer wrote that Martin marveled at Juana's energy and ability. She would have clarified for him some of the intricacies of agriculture in a semiarid climate. Spectacular results could be obtained by those who knew what they were doing. Juana and her people were second-and third-generation farmers in the region and had learned about the ecology from missionaries, from their own parents and grandparents, and from the Indians. Juana's grandfather and her mother as a child had farmed the valley land as early as the 1770s at the pueblo of San Jose. Missionaries became extremely knowledgeable about the terrain they had access to, in part because they were free to ascertain what grew best in their area. Missions exchanged produce with each other so that they could exploit the best potential of their own region and still have access to foods they needed. The missionaries made mistakes at first, however. Even though they had books on agriculture, none as yet had been written about California. At the first mission, San Diego, they finally managed to grow wheat the third year. The first planting in the lowlands was washed away; the second on the hot, dry mesa died. Finally, in the right environment, the mission harvested a good crop. At Pueblo San José, originated explicitly to produce food, the people lost their first wheat crop after having planted in the wrong season. Murphy thus had a mentor in Juana, whose knowledge was based on generations of experience on the best use of the 3,000 acres he purchased from her. For people brought up in the Northeast or the Midwest, like the elder Murphys, wondrously fertile soil and gentle weather seemed a reward for their diligence in pursuing their beliefs and their family's well-being.[6]

After interviewing people who had lived in the area during Juana's lifetime, a later resident thought that Martin planted the first orchard in the area. It is more likely that he followed Juana's example. As noted above, his biographer respected Juana's ability at raising cattle for the hide-and-tallow business, so his realization that the land would be put to better use for something other than cattle undoubtedly owed something to Juana's insights. Her sister-in-law Juana Cibrian testified in the Ojo de Agua case that Apolinario planted trees, one of numerous opportunities for Juana to learn about orchards. Her Santa Clara Valley property and adjacent lands became famous in later years for fruit such as apricots and plums.

Tom Hunt, who moved onto a small portion of Juana's land in 1956 and resided for a time in the *casa de Juana Briones* designated on early maps and photographs, said that orchards flourished there almost beyond belief. That apricots grew fantastically well on the part of the ranch Juana retained was recognized very early due to the soil and drainage on the foothill slopes. In the 1970s, when the cash crop had become computers and developers replaced orchards with houses, old-timers often told newcomers how they used to go to the hills every spring to gaze down in wonder upon a valley that resembled a glorious, gigantic bowl of blossoms—the Valley of Heart's Delight, promoters called it.[7]

Not only history tells of the area's agricultural potential. A newspaper reporter in 2004 interviewed Vince Junio about his 933-pound pumpkin that won a contest at the town of Salinas, which grows and distributes nationwide food such as spinach and lettuce. During its peak growth period, Vince's pumpkin gained about thirty pounds a day on land in Los Altos Hills, a town incorporated in the 1950s on Briones ranchland. In 1957, the Santa Clara Valley produced millions of dollars of income from prunes, apricots, strawberries, cherries, walnuts, grapes, and pears on about 60,000 acres. Part of this commercialization has been said to have originated in 1856 by French brothers who imported prune trees, but the much earlier Santa Clara and San José missions had orchards and vineyards. In 1778, Santa Clara Mission grew pears, apples, peaches, quinces, and pomegranates. Mission San José a few years later produced apples, pears, peaches, apricots, plums, cherries, figs, olives, oranges, pomegranates, and grapes.[8]

Nineteenth-century observers familiar with other agricultural areas enjoyed telling anecdotes about valley productivity. Alfred Doten wrote in his journal that in a San Francisco market in 1857 he saw three squashes that together weighed 800 pounds and in San Jose a 264-pound squash. John Hittell's 1878 catalogue of agricultural wonders included potatoes that weighed as much as seven pounds each, cabbages seven feet wide, a red beet five feet long.[9]

During Juana's lifetime, no definite statements told of Briones Ranch production other than cattle, sheep, and grain, but many indicators, including the presence of Chinese laborers, point to the probability that the family planted orchards and other fruits and vegetables. By 1880, nearly half of the agricultural workers in the county were Chinese. They were not specialists in cattle management. They cleared chaparral that households and trains used for fuel, planted and tended orchards, and picked and packed fruit to ship to markets and to the emerging canning industry.[10]

Californios have been described as entirely devoted to cattle, but they learned many farming techniques at missions by necessity. For a long time, starvation and scarcity hung as a backdrop to every other consideration. They depended almost entirely on what they grew themselves, and they frequently would plant a small garden for their household needs and dedicate the agricultural lands to their best use, which in Juana's case was probably orchards. Others in the family two generations hence had orchards. Frank Briones, Juana's grandnephew in Bolinas, "devoted his time to ranching and his hobby, raising and experimenting with fruit trees . . . he grafted trees and they'd grow beautifully for him," according to his sister Rose.[11]

Clues from present land use also point to the probability that Juana grew fruit. In an area of real estate now valued at as much as a million dollars an acre, apricot orchards still grace some former Briones Ranch land. One orchard is on the property of a meeting center of the Packard Foundation, the Taaffe House, named for the man a Murphy daughter married. Her father gave to her as a wedding gift most of the land he had purchased from Juana. Another apricot orchard is on part of the land of Alta Mesa Cemetery, which was purchased from Juana's son, Tomás Miranda. Another tantalizing clue to Juana's land use, although less conclusive, is a large clump of prickly pear cactus in the yard of the Juana Briones house, an import that is now uncommon in the region. Hispanic people often hedged a small cultivated space with such cacti and used parts of the plant for food and medicine, both of which would have been added chores in the daily life of the Briones household.[12]

Bank manager Joseph Mesa, son of Refugio and the grandson who most resembled Juana, wrote a railroad promotional piece recommending the locale as a real estate investment. Without mentioning his grandmother, he wrote about a section of land on the former Briones Ranch that had "one of the nicest and healthiest orchards . . . of peaches, apricots, and prunes. . . . [B]etween the trees are pumpkins besides different varieties of vegetables." Five years earlier, his mother, Refugio Miranda de Mesa, had sold Juana's house on 40 acres that Mesa also described, suggesting that at least part of it was already in crops before Nott's purchase. Mesa continued:

> A little farther up the Arastradero road is another fine orchard owned by Chas. P. Nott; it is set out to pears and apples and a few fig trees; also, about six acres in Logan berries, and about two acres in blackberries. The berries paid over $600 last summer, the vines, too,

being only two years old. There was also raised about seventeen tons of hay on about five and one-half acres of land, and a small piece of land planted to corn. Some of the corn stalks grew to the height of eight feet. There are forty acres in this little ranch, most all rolling land. Frost is almost unknown in that locality.[13]

One of Mesa's advertising sheets gives his address at a property owned by the family during Juana and her daughters' time, on Mayfield's main business neighborhood, Washington Street. Joseph Mesa also ran a hardware store on another of the family properties and advertised with big businesses in Mayfield and Palo Alto on two screens painted by a local artist, Otto Schroeder, large enough to fit as stage backdrops, both still preserved in Palo Alto, one in a bank, the other in the Women's Club.

Before Anglos took virtually full control and while Juana's folk held onto shreds of their former status, some immigrants exhibited more friendliness than most who came later. The Murphy family had entered California overland the year Juana purchased her ranch. They came with the trickle that developed into a torrent of settlers traveling in covered wagons over the prairies and mountains. The Truckee Route that the Stephens-Murphy party pioneered became standard across the mountains, and their party was said to have been the first that managed to bring its wagons intact across the Sierra. The presence of families in that party of 1843 and the Murphys' wish to live in Catholic country gave them something of a bond with Californios.[14]

The Murphys also helped to found Catholic institutions, creating a further bond. They assisted Jesuit father John Nobili, who set up Santa Clara College, a boys' school, on the old mission site. In 1851, of forty-four students, among the half who boarded were three Murphy sons. Juana's youngest son, Dolores, age ten, and his cousin, José Miramontes, were day students, among only seven with Hispanic surnames in the entire student body. That the Murphys were Catholic did not necessarily unite them culturally with Californios. The college required all boys to study in English. In 1859, American boys broke up a student military organization because they refused to march with what they called *greasers*, a disparaging term then in use for Hispanic people.

In the field of education, the Murphys also deserve credit for starting Notre Dame College for girls, which created a separate Spanish-speaking division but expelled Sarah Winnemucca, an Indian girl who later became famous as a spokesperson for the Paiutes. Parents objected to having their daughters associate with an Indian. Even her ancestral credentials did not protect her from the disdain held for her people. Winnemucca's grandfather, whose name translated for the travelers as "Truckee," had helped the Stephens-Murphy party get safely across the mountains.[15]

Father Nobili witnessed the leasing document between Murphy and Juana. Having a priest as a friend would have been an advantage for Martin Murphy in the negotiations. Another would have been the character of Martin's wife, whose son described her as economical, honest, deeply religious, and possessing business savvy. Nevertheless, good credentials and a priest as witness did not override Juana's idea of proper business negotiations.[16]

A corral illegally constructed by Martin on Juana's land probably initiated the negotiations for the Murphy rental of about half of Juana's ranch. Their agreement stipulated that he must divide that corral in half, removing the present fence and replacing it along the line of the boundary of the land he proposed to lease. He could use the land only for grazing eight hundred head of cattle, none to cross onto Juana's land. He could not sublease any portion. Any structures would remain at no cost to Juana when the agreement terminated. Juana obviously had good advice on putting together that lease, and she inserted her own wisdom into the wording, which was in Spanish.

One can readily imagine Juana with an escort of her sons and her lawyer, descending on Murphy at his home to explain the situation, gently but firmly saying that very likely he did not realize that he had trespassed, but of course such an action must be corrected, deliberate or not. Or perhaps her lawyer hosted the meeting in his office, more neutral territory. She took every detail into account. The rent of fifty dollars per month had to be paid promptly every three months to Juana or her representative. At the time of the lease, Martin may have tried unsuccessfully to buy land from her. An unsigned paper with wording very like the final purchase agreement is dated a year earlier than the actual 1856 title transfer, at which time Juana accepted seven thousand dollars cash in hand for the parcel.[17]

Juana had every reason to feel confident that her title was secure when she leased and then sold the land. Henry Wager Halleck's defense of her property illustrates his consummate skill as a lawyer, for which he was adequately compensated with fees substantially higher than received by other land case attorneys. The April 1854 Land Commission proceedings established Juana's ownership of the ranch with the statement that the case presented "no point of doubt or difficulty" and was certified with "the seal of the Office of the Board of Commissioners to ascertain and settle the private land claims." With that certification in hand, Juana would have felt secure in her ownership. Two years later, November 1856, the attorney general's notice again sounded conclusive: an appeal would "not be prosecuted by the United States."[18]

As it turned out, though, unquestioned ranch boundaries could be questioned. Waterways made a convenient point of contention. Creeks were given various names over time and changed their courses. Identifying their sources was a business fraught with ambivalence. Attempting to locate the headwaters of these creeks brought into question which part should be considered a tributary or a main stream. The 1854 document mentioned that San Antonio Creek bordered Juana's land on the south and east and that Matadero Creek bordered it on the north and northwest. In 1860, attorney Jeremiah Clarke had his objections added to the original case documents. In an inverted way difficult to decipher even if one heads out into the present nature preserve to pinpoint his allegation, he used creek identity and origin as the bases for his claim.

Juana and her children had gone to court saying that the Teodoro Robles family was trespassing on their land, giving Clarke an opportunity to insert doubt into the equation and perhaps gain property thereby. He alleged that a surveyor had drawn a straight line between the creeks, San Antonio and Matadero, falsely claiming that they connected as a genuine border. Two "professional surveyors" hired by Clarke found that "in the original survey done by the deputy he substituted a small tributary for the main stream." In harmony with other of Clarke's statements, his surveyors were "professional," whereas Juana's was a "deputy." Clarke later made the statement that patents should not be issued based on surveyors paid for by interested parties, thus overlooking that his own suit was based on the work of surveyors he hired.

Clarke was not entirely a neighbor. He lived in San Francisco and delved into similarly questionable land negotiations in Marin County. Juana's neighbor Secundino Robles once traded 500 acres to him for a span of horses and for a buggy that lasted one trip before its axle broke. When Clarke donated land for a Catholic Church in Mayfield, he may have been hoping to redeem his reputation with locals.[19]

His contention in the Briones lawsuit was that because there was not enough land on the west to make the full league, the surveyors impinged on land that rightfully belonged to his client on the east—that is, in order to make up for acreage said to be, but not actually, Juana's. Referring to the new survey Juana had commissioned, Clarke used phrases such as "wanton disregard" and "grossly partial and unfair character of the survey" to allege that his client, Teodoro Robles, brother of Secundino and owner of the Rancho Rinconada de San Francisquito, was legally using land that was his, but that Juana claimed as hers.

That Juana's title could still be open to question despite Land Commission wording that there was "no point of doubt" shows one reason why so many people lost all or most of their land. If one happened to be sick, dealing with personal problems, or away from home, taking poor advice became an interim solution. Searching for an upside to this situation, one can posit that lawyers and surveyors thereby got work and land got redistributed.

In 1858, a surveyor named Mr. Tracy said he had spent four or five days with his assistant, Mr. Van Dorn, double-checking his preliminary survey at Jeremiah Clarke's request. He testified in November 1859. Although Clarke in other such actions acquired a considerable amount of land, he failed to reshape the Briones ranch. Juana's motivation most likely went beyond the economic. It might have seemed easier and less costly to give in on the case, but she staunchly defended her claim with her deep and abiding commitment to justice.[20]

Many Anglos lost their land, too, but Hispanic people made an easier target. The following notice sent to neighbors whom Juana had known since childhood shows how traumatic fraudulent legal assays could be:

STATE OF CALIFORNIA, COUNTY OF SANTA CLARA

To Secundino Robles and Teodoro Robles

You are hereby notified to immediately quit the possession of the ranch on which you now reside, known by the name of Santa Rita, being bounded on the North by the land of Antonia Mesa, on the South by Juana Briones, on the East by Francisco Estrada and on the West by the low hills containing six thousand acres, more or less, as I am the lawful owner of said Rancho, and if you fail to quit possession forthwith I shall institute legal proceedings to recover the same. The Sheriff is authorized to receive possession for me or my agent.

Signed Geo B. Tingley

Nov 19, 1852 delivered . . .

both of them refused to surrender to me.

W. Johnson, Sheriff[21]

Such a notice seems intended more to frighten a resident, who would be unlikely to move on without further ado, even when the notice was delivered by the sheriff. Because the Robles brothers' English would have been slightly inferior to their Spanish, perhaps the notice had less impact on first reading than one might imagine.

By 1870, in such a convoluted economic environment, Juana was requiring payment in advance. Martin Murphy that year paid $316 in gold coin in advance for one year's rent for 108 acres of the Briones Ranch, roughly $2.00 an acre as opposed to the twenty cents an acre he had paid fifteen years earlier. Murphy had once again put up a fence enclosing acreage that did not belong to him, "a narrow strip of land" for which Juana and her son Jesús (José Jesús) were requiring Martin to pay rent. Once again, details protective of the Briones Ranch integrity abounded in their agreement—no subletting without the owner's permission, no cutting or injuring of trees or of standing timber, replacement of the fence to the actual boundary after one year, and, the clincher, payment in advance. If the participants in the agreement were to be judged on the basis of class, Murphy had it all—wealth, position, the right skin color. If judged on thoroughness, Juana would win, no doubt about it. No wonder the Murphys admired her. She was sixty-eight at the time and had not allowed the lessons of her life to dim in her memory.[22]

By 1870, the Murphys had plenty of money, or at least they were spending in grand style. A collection of family financial records dated as early as 1856 includes receipts for "buggy harness, bull patent leather collar, best steel bit," $75; "one set finest-quality silver mounted buggy harness with russet reins"; wagon $300; in 1877, $529.50 to ship a stallion from New York to San José; a $221.85 bill from the French San Francisco dressmaker for an evening dress, skirt, and black dress with jacket. Think of $200 at that time and place as about $4,000 now.

Not everyone fared so well. Some other people who figure in Juana's story experienced economic disaster. Mariano Vallejo died without enough money in his estate to pay funeral expenses. William Richardson, one of the founders of San Francisco, wrote innumerable receipts for cash borrowed with his ranch as collateral. Former California governor Pio Pico relied in old age on friends' charity and died owing two years' rent. John Gilroy married an Ortega, lost the family's Rancho San Isidro, and died penniless. Secundino Robles's property diminished from about 4,000 acres to the lot his house stood on. Elisha Oscar Crosby—attorney for many who were verifying their land titles, judge, and member of the first California constitutional convention—owned 250 acres contiguous with Juana's, but went bankrupt in 1856. Most of Juan Prado Mesa's Rancho San Antonio sold for a dollar an acre on behalf of his heirs to pay his debts. Rafael García, sister Luz's stepson, lost the Tomales Ranch and lived in poverty.[23]

In their earlier big-spending years, the brothers Teodoro and Secundino Robles purchased Rancho Santa Rita, nearly 9,000 acres, in 1847 for $3,500. After a divorce in 1855 blamed on an extramarital affair, Teodoro had to hand over half of his parcel to his former wife. Secundino's house was said to have cost $13,000 when it was completed, a fortune in 1851. The Robles brothers interpreted land as currency, but Juana, who later divided up her land among her children, saw it as patrimony.[24]

State Senator Pablo de la Guerra tried to help such people who had formerly enjoyed a comfortable lifestyle. As one of the few Hispanic men who gained prominence in politics, he said that he had "seen old people, sixty and seventy years old, crying like children because they had been cast out from the hearths of their ancestors," a statement that also could have applied to Indians.[25]

Juana took the time, care, and expense to wage legal battles necessary to retain all of her property, starting in 1851 and concluding definitively, so far as the U.S. government was directly concerned, in 1877 with a piece of paper signed by President Rutherford B. Hayes affirming a U.S. Supreme Court mandate regarding the 1.77 acres of the Ojo de Agua de Figueroa, a suit that had been filed with the District Court in 1864. The lapse between decisions and official documents seems unconscionable, but owners like Juana had earlier received binding notice in a lesser format and perhaps used the elaborate confirmation with the president's signature for a wall decoration.

The Ojo de Agua was more familiarly called the Miranda grant. To prove her claim as Apolinario's widow, Juana had hired the best attorney in California, Henry Wager Halleck—a former West Point professor, author of military texts, and secretary of state in California's military government. Halleck left his imprint on California in ways physical and intellectual: he significantly influenced the first state constitution as secretary of the convention, was the first general manager of the New Almaden mine that produced the mercury used to extract gold from ore, designed and financed the construction of the largest office building west of the Rockies and the most resistant to earthquake and fire damage, and acquired about 30,000 acres in Marin County.[26]

In a letter in Spanish to Halleck, Juana indicated that she urgently needed him to send her an exact copy of her Purísima Ranch map so she could legally lease part of it. In the second paragraph, she asked him to rent out the Ojo de Agua and visit the property to request the tenant to repair the fence and construct some little dwelling. It is amazing that Juana had to tell one who has been called the premiere lawyer in California not only what to do to protect her rights, but to do so quickly. Refreshingly direct, she also asked Halleck to tell her how much she owed him and told him that her daughter would convey his reply, making the convenience of another of his clients, in this case Presentación, an encouragement for haste so that she would not be kept waiting.[27]

Juana had worked hard to hang onto her "property south of Mayfield." The Purísima Ranch title was validated from its first run through the Land Commission and the District Court in part because Halleck knew both how to make the case and at the same time how to put it simply: "The genuineness of the original grant is fully established . . . the boundaries are indicated with much precision." Commissioners admitted that a minor adjustment could occur if surveyors discovered a discrepancy. Maximo Martínez made a good witness on Juana's behalf, saying that he and Juana had no dispute about the boundary between their properties. Maximo said she kept cattle, horses, and sheep; had cattle yards; had fenced in and culti-vated several fields; and had built a large dwelling and several "outhouses" (by which he meant small structures, not toilets) immediately after purchas-ing the property. The "large dwelling" might account for her having room to accommodate comfortably overnight all the people the surveyor Lyman mentioned. When the house went out of family ownership more than fifty years later, in 1900, the purchaser, Charles Nott, tore down the dilapidated part and preserved the three main rooms, which remain to this day.[28]

The smaller Ojo de Agua case took more arguing than the case for the grand Briones Ranch. If anyone could win such a suit, it would be Halleck. The term *brilliant* does not seem too strong to describe Halleck's brief for the Ojo de Agua. He wrote that the commissioners would certainly consider so small a claim too inconsequential to bother with—leaving one to wonder why he was bothering. He wrote that because the case was "the only one of its kind ever presented to the board," it fell into an unfamiliar category. He meant by this statement that the land had been granted to Apolinario by the presidio commander and not by the governor, as was customary.

Halleck explained that the disposition of the case "is a matter of little moment to the government whether it is rejected or confirmed" because it was "a mere house lot and garden, of very small extent and very little value." He said that the claimants had no means to appeal to the U.S. Supreme Court, but, in fact, they did appeal. He tried to lay a guilt trip on the United States. He wrote that surely no one in his right mind could believe that the Mexican government would show more honor and integrity than the United States in caring about the welfare of this poor widow trying to support her children. Perhaps Halleck was expressing ideas he received from Juana. A kind of legal genius seemed to come naturally to her, as well as strong opinions about righteousness. Although part of Juana's interest to posterity is her financial savvy, the reference to "poor widow" can be interpreted as an honest statement because she thought of all she owned as divided by seven; that is, her estate mattered because it was intended to support her children when they had families of their own.

Not relying entirely on activating sympathy, Halleck then discussed the colonization law of 1824 and the Regulations of 1828 and retreated further into history to mention the "Royal ordinance of 1784" and other directives by which captains of that era should distribute lands, giving preference to soldiers who had served the ten years that constituted the basic enlistment period, which Apolinario had done. Halleck explained all this because the commission had doubted presidio commander José Sánchez's right to bestow land on Apolinario. In *Heirs of Apolinario Miranda vs. the United States,* the document dated September 16, 1833, and signed by Comandante José Sánchez, was contested with the statement that "[w]e know of no authority existing in the comandante to dispose of the national domain at the time this instrument bears date." Despite Halleck's thoroughness, so serious a case had to be submitted to a higher jurisdiction. Most landowners would have tired of the whole thing and agreed with the opinion Halleck expressed that the land was hardly worth the trouble.[29]

When the Civil War broke out, Halleck left California to take a top job in the military. When he was general-in-chief of all the Union armies, the North won at Vicksburg and Gettysburg, battles that have gone down in history as moments in which the tide turned. John Dwinelle took over Juana's case and filed the legal brief for the Ojo de Agua to the Supreme Court in 1864. He would have needed to consult with Juana and inevitably would have gained some details for his book *Colonial History of San Francisco,* which is necessary reading for anyone studying that era at that place.[30]

The Ojo de Agua was relatively tiny in terms of ranchland. A property the size of the Purísima Ranch had the potential for division and subdivisions. Court assurance of the firmness of Juana's claim did not remove the temptation for other persons to insinuate themselves onto the land. Discomfort and expense for owners led many of them either to sell property or to abandon it instead of dealing with a long, drawn-out, expensive legal nuisance.

This undated photograph shows oxen pulling logs out of the redwoods on the eastern slope of the Santa Cruz Mountains.

By the time of the Jeremiah Clarke case, Juana had learned not to stint on using her connections to get a proper opinion from the court. She got together nearly twenty witnesses (Clarke said there were fourteen, but even that claim seems to be inaccurate) to confirm the location of the Arastradero in order to force Clarke, or his client, to remove from her land. Each person said the road was where it had always been, but Clarke wrote that regardless of all they said, a second route showed on a Robles map.

Juana gathered people with intimate knowledge of the terrain, some of whom had lived nearby for fifty years or more: Pedro Chabolla, fifty-year resident of the neighborhood; José Felíz, a forty-year resident; Bruno Bernal, a fifty-six-year resident; Francisco Arce, a twenty-five-year resident; Antonio Bernal, a forty-year resident; Henry Bee, a twenty-four-year resident; Antonio Suñol, a forty-two-year resident; and others of equivalent experience—Pedro Mesa, Peter Davidson, Juan Galindo Sr., José Noriega, José Sepulveda, Pedro Hernández, Maximo Martínez, Antonio María Pico, Sebastian Peralta, José Antonio Alviso.

As Pedro Mesa said, the Arastradero "passed about four or five hundred yards to the north of the house of Juana Briones at a place where there were some water holes." Pedro was the brother of Juan Prado Mesa, deceased owner of Rancho San Antonio, adjacent to Juana's on the south. Pedro said that thirty years earlier he had helped his father bring timber out of the redwoods over this road—around 1828, the year Juana and her husband took three of their deceased infants to Mission Dolores for burial. She was thinking of other things than the Arastradero that year.

Clarke implied that Juana cheated about a survey, saying that it was made more than a year ago and that no survey had been made by the surveyor general. He imputed dishonesty to Juana in his letter: "Still this will be so dated I suppose as to make it appear to have been recently done and so apparently to bring it within the provisions of the appropriation bill of last session. . . . I only mention it to account for the grossly partial and unfair character of the survey."[31]

After a lengthy hearing, the land was resurveyed and approved by the District Court in February 1863, seven years after the legal turmoil began. Twenty-six years after Juana purchased the ranch, she appears to have been clear of all further land ownership issues. After final confirmation dated January 31, 1870, she began deeding parcels to six of her children, excluding Presentación, who was at this time nearly fifty and owned property closer to San Francisco.

Know all men by these presents, that I, Juana Briones de Miranda . . . for and in consideration of the natural love and affection that I have and bear for my daughter, Maria Narcisa Miranda and for her better support, maintenance and livelihood . . . I do hereby give, grant and confirm unto my said daughter . . . as her own separate property for her own sole use, and benefit, and for her heirs and assigns forever, all that center portion of land being a part of the land known as the Rancho de la Purissima [sic] Concepcion, or Rancho de Briones.[32]

The words "as her own separate property for her own sole use" stand out. Like her brother Gregorio in Bolinas, Juana attempted to assure her daughter's ownership regardless of any marital arrangements, wording supplied by the lawyer, Joseph Wallis, who had replaced Halleck in handling the case for the Purísima property. Not coincidentally, Wallis's wife, Sarah, made a life's work of trying to establish women's property rights. The document also shows also that Juana and her lawyer knew enough by then to supply exact surveying information.

Juana began making gifts of 50-acre parcels beginning with Manuela Miranda, married to Agustín Mesa, both twenty-nine and with two children—Tomás Dimas, age three, and María, age six months. Refugio Miranda, married to Ramón Mesa, received the second parcel. Maps show a 10-acre parcel that belonged to Antonio Romero, possibly a stepson of Juana's sister Luz. A map also shows that Tomás was given 25 instead of 50 acres, a difference that might be explained in two ways—either he did not need the land or he had not met Juana's expectations. On the one hand, he has been said to have married a Bojorques, one of the founding Californio families, and perhaps she had land, so he did not need more. On the other hand, some receipts show that he borrowed small amounts of money— small from our view now, but not at the time, twenty-five dollars—from Martin Murphy, not an overly damning move, but a possible reason for Juana to worry about his standards of financial management.[33]

The 1860 census lists eleven people between ages four and fifty-six living at Juana's house. Isidora Soto was probably the daughter of Juana's sister Epiciaca, but identifying Ellen Briones, age fifteen, and Soledad Briones, age four, is more difficult. The surname Briones suggests that they may have been children of Juana's brothers' sons or Juana's foster children.

The papers for the Ojo de Agua list as Apolinario's heirs eight Miranda children, by name, and the widow Juana Briones, but Juana's adopted Indian daughter had died in 1853, and seven living children remained. The list also includes a "María," certainly referring to María Narcisa, whose two names came to appear as two separate people. Halleck referred to "seven children," another clue that the name "María" was entered incorrectly. Many of the heirs' names were wrong in the beginning of the Ojo de Agua brief and were subsequently corrected, including the curious "Petronillo," what an English-speaking scribe heard in 1852 when a Spanish-speaker said "Refugio."[34]

Some cross-language oddities are strange. The listing of occupants of Juana's ranch house in the 1880 census includes her sister Epiciaca, a widow, age seventy-six, whose name is written as "Kiriocca Briones." Such errors also involved more practical issues, however. The letter from Juana to Halleck was addressed to "Jalike" on the envelope. Presentación delivered the letter for her mother, so the transliterated name would not have hampered delivery, but such slips even in the high-cost world of land and law created misunderstandings that proliferated through language, social custom, and interaction among people of diverse heritage and belief.

The Miranda children's names found on most census, probate, and land records are Presentación, Tomás, Narcisa, Refugio, José de Jesús (later, José Julian), Manuela, and José Dolores—four daughters and three sons. The 1870 census at the Purísima Ranch lists six offspring who lived on the ranch, excluding Presentación, as well as Narcisa's husband, Jesús García, and their three children, Thomas, Jesús, and Clara. If missions records are used as the sole source, a discrepancy regarding the number and names of Juana's children crops up. Priests at Missions Dolores and Santa Clara entered in their meticulously kept logs the baptisms of all of Juana and Apolinario's children except Tomás and Narcisa, and those two do not appear in the Huntington Library database of baptismal records of all the California missions. They might have been baptized at some distant location and might have had different names at birth. If they were not born to Juana and Apolinario, they had to have been brought into the family very young. Their being the children of Juana and Apolinario was never a legal issue, but sometimes they are referred to as "María" instead of "Narcisa" and "José" instead of "Tomás," name changes that happened regularly in that society. Records other than mission documents give Tomás's birth date as 1831 and Narcisa's as 1833.

Church records often tell more than bare facts. One record that uncovers a few fine points about a family and a culture concerns Narcisa's son, Thomas García. At the Church of the Nativity in Menlo Park, he married a woman from Mexico whose name is given in nearly indecipherable handwriting as "Carolinam Olachea." Anglo priests hoped to Anglicize Hispanic people, which accounts for their making little effort to understand Spanish names properly. This laxness may also account for Narcisa's name being written on that occasion and others simply as "María."[35]

After Narcisa died, Juana raised Thomas. He remained long connected to her family. Two of his first cousins were witnesses at his marriage, Dimas (Tomás Dimas) Mesa and María Julia Mesa, Juana's grandchildren who lived in Mayfield. Juana's son Joseph D. Miranda, age eighty-nine, died at his nephew Thomas García's home in South San Francisco—a nice footnote showing that Thomas repaid his grandmother for raising him from early childhood. Perhaps such appreciation helps account for the García family's protecting a portrait of Juana through many generations, though whether Narcisa's husband was their close relative is unclear.

Hispanic people's names often changed to more Anglicized forms, so that "Joseph D." was the "Tomás" of earlier records, Juana and Apolinario's first son, born in 1831. The newspaper said of him that he was "an old settler of Mayfield," that he "owned a large amount of property south of Mayfield," and that services would be held at St. Thomas Aquinas Church in Palo Alto. Like his mother, he knew where he came from.[36]

Another story connected with the family that arises from time to time involves buried treasure. Before banks, police forces, and safes, people often buried valuables or otherwise arranged to hide them in secure places. At Juana's house, the clay soil that filled the redwood crib for the walls came out of a room we would call a basement, a deep excavated space under one of the three rooms that remain. Such a space could have served as a hiding place under the floor. Susan Cox Berthiaume Kirk, who lived in the house off and on as a child and young woman until about 1990, said that a favorite game for her and her brothers had been searching for buried treasure.

This story is bolstered by earlier ones. In 1937, a newspaper reporter interviewed Alvino "Al" Mesa, a bartender, one of Juana's grandsons, known as "the big Spaniard." He told about his grandmother, whom the reporter incorrectly called "doña Mesa," incorrect because his Mesa grandmother's name was Higuera, and she had predeceased her husband, Juan Prado Mesa. The story fits Juana, the grandmother Alvino knew, his neighbor at Mayfield, who died when he was seven and who could have told him about "treasure buried deep in the Stanford hills." Al said that his grandmother, who owned "Alta Mesa ranch west of Mayfield," treated wounded desperadoes who sought her out because of her reputation as a healer—both details firm connections to Juana. He said that sometimes her Indian servants would bury patients who died and that his grandmother buried the patients' loot in a corner of the same cemetery. This story of hidden treasure is one among many from the California of this period,

*The Miramontes family of Half Moon Bay
became known for their musical talent.*

involving such persons as bandit Joaquin Murieta, settler John Marsh, and Isaac Graham, a notorious character who set up a distillery and a lumbering operation in the Santa Cruz mountains. Geologist William Brewer wrote that hidden treasure "inflamed the public mind" in California in the 1860s.

Life on the ranch had enjoyable aspects, a sociable, gregarious, happy side that did not endlessly focus on business and farmwork. Music always figured large in tales of early Hispanic life in California, but other than a grandson who played the trombone, music was never actually mentioned in connection with Juana's immediate family. It was said that big family gatherings at the Briones Ranch included Juana's sister Guadalupe and her Miramontes family, who formed among themselves an entire band. Clan assemblages that lasted for days or weeks usually had plenty of music and dancing.[37]

Charles Palmer Nott purchased Juana's house and 40 acres from Refugio in 1900. The family usually did business with people they knew. Perhaps they believed Charles to be related to the Hiram (Hirum, Herman) Nott who had married Gregorio's daughter Rosita (Rosario). If he was not, he probably did not admit to it. After Hiram died, Rosita stayed in Mayfield for a time, possibly in a house owned by Juana on the same block—Juana at Washington and Second, Rosita at Grant and Second. She married Francisco Mesa, a brother of the two Mesas who married Juana's daughters, and they moved back to Marin County.

Eighteen years later, Sarah Byxbee Nott, Charles's wife, told a newspaper reporter, Cora Fremont Older, that Juana's ranch house had been boarded over when they bought it. When they removed the boards, they found beautiful plaster underneath. Sarah said that "roughly split redwood boards" were used to make the wooden crib that formed the walls, and that the "adobe in large chunks" had apparently been taken from under the house. All these features match known items on the early landscape— redwood lumbering, the Arastradero, and lime kilns that appear on an early survey map, where the beautiful plaster might have been produced.[38]

The part of the ranch owned by Juana had been legally divided up by 1878 so that each owner was taxed separately, but the total parcel would have been assessed at nearly sixty thousand dollars, which was the tax assessment for the "Briones tract" that Murphy had purchased from her.[39] Juana had protected the Rancho la Purísima Concepción wisely, had various descendants and relatives about her at all times, and was known to many people who lived in rather a wide section of the San Francisco Bay Area. One reason for her success was that she dealt with people she respected and believed would be honest, but, of course, such honest people would want to be assured just as she did that all was as it should be. Everything would be spelled out according to proper form and the highest standards of law and integrity.

Many of Juana's compatriots resembled María de los Angeles Castro Majors of Juana's birthplace, the town of Santa Cruz, who explained an opposite approach and whose life could be described as opposite to Juana's:

> Some of those who were young and very poor said they were my friends. They would make the papers for me so that nobody ever could take my property away from me, and they made the papers and I made my name on them as they told me, and I thought it was all right. But I did not know the language of the Americano, I did not know his laws. Today I am old and poor; the young lawyers who were

my friends, who made the papers for me, are all very rich. They are judges and bankers and have beautiful homes. They have hundreds of acres of land and much money, and when I sit here like an old owl in a dark corner and tell the few who ask that these men have robbed me of all that was mine by their crooked language and their crooked laws, they smile and tap their heads, so, and say "dreaming dreaming."

She could have mentioned that her problem had been "trusting trusting."[40]

*F*ourteen

CARING FOR A GRANDSON, REMEMBERING A PRIEST

Town Life in 1880s Mayfield

Juana moved to Mayfield around 1884 to be near two of her daughters, Refugio and Manuela. They had wanted to be closer to a school for their children. One school opened in a small cabin in 1856, a year after Mayfield's origin with Uncle Jim's stage stop and post office. Juana's daughters, who signed their legal papers with an X, must have understood the lessons of their generation, that their children's lives would benefit from at least knowing how to read and write. Few of Juana's cohorts had any education at all. Her brother Gregorio's handwriting revealed that he did not often have occasion to write. Having a school building right down the street in Mayfield and expecting most, if not all, of the children to attend at least for five or six years were evidence of a radical turnaround since Juana's childhood.

Nine years after that little school opened, the town became the last stop on the train from San Francisco, nice for travelers and revolutionary for farmers, whose crops arrived in San Francisco in eighty minutes. Stagecoaches were notoriously uncomfortable, but they had been an improvement over the two- or three-day trip to San Francisco by horseback. The preferred horse route that was closer to the bay turned into a bog in the rainy season. From early times, riders complained that horses went knee deep in mud on the only good trail. Wealthy people and even common folk appreciated the train and began to buy mansions or cottages down the peninsula once they could travel there easily. They mainly wanted to escape San Francisco's summer fog.[1]

Mayfield's second school, built in the 1860s.

In 1867, William Paul laid out Mayfield house lots on 60 acres, an endeavor successful enough that a year later W. Hawxhurst had more land surveyed and sold more lots for homes and businesses. Something about the place lent itself to hyperbole. An editor in the early days exaggerated when he called Mayfield the "uncrowned queen" of Santa Clara County. Mayfield was more a princess than a queen. About the time that Juana moved to town, Mayfield had five hundred residents, a big town by her standards.[2]

Mayfield had more kinship with San Jose, fifteen miles south, than with San Francisco, thirty-five miles north, until well-known San Franciscans of wealth started to buy properties in Juana's neighborhood. In 1865, George Gordon bought the whole Buelna Ranch, or what was left of it, for $250 and built a fine house and stables. The timber had been cleared and turned into charcoal in ovens around the property, so perhaps the owners sold the land so cheaply because they thought they had already used up its potential. Gordon himself went from one venture to another in San Francisco—iron houses that were supposed to resist fire, the first sugar refinery in California, real estate development. The Stanfords bought Gordon's place in 1876, enlarged the stables and the house, and got rid of the charcoal ovens. The year Juana died, the Stanford parcel was said to house the largest, best-equipped, and best-staffed trotting farm in the world.[3]

From Juana's hilltop house on the Briones Ranch, one traveled only about three miles to Mayfield, first downhill into a valley with springs that would have been good for doing laundry, then up a steeper hill and back down again, followed by a gentle ride over relatively flat land into town. Juana had a view of the bay from both places, but looking down from a hill felt different, a bit more majestic, than gazing out over the muddy terrain beyond town to a place where birds gathered by the thousands in sloughs.

Juana's grandson Tomás Dimas Mesa rode his horse out a few minutes from his Mayfield home, back toward the ranch, where he hunted easily for deer, rabbits, or quail for supper. About the time that his grandmother died in 1889, he had the habit of shooting with his muzzle-loading shotgun half-a-dozen ducks within minutes of lying in the tall grass and waiting for a flock. To take a boat out on the bay, one would need to transport the boat to the creek. In finding land more convenient than water, Tomás Dimas was like his ancestors. The horse was right outside his door. Whether he decided to go west into the hills or east toward the bay, game still flourished in the 1880s, and he no longer had to fear bears, as Chester Lyman did when he surveyed near Juana's house in 1848.[4]

The distance and the hilly terrain between Mayfield and the ranch would have reminded Juana of the trip during her young married years from the rural setting of the Ojo de Agua to the busier, more mercantile setting of Yerba Buena, where there were few people and no schools. Juana had managed well without formal education, but times were changing. A German innovation, kindergarten, inspired Jane Stanford in 1886 to open two local kindergartens, one north and one south of San Francisquito Creek. She especially wanted the schools for children of workers on the Stanford estate. For the kindergarten in Mayfield, she leased a house where she installed equipment and hired a teacher for children ages four to eight, and this at a time when the concept of such early education was novel and progressive. Within a decade, when Jane was busy helping her husband found Stanford University, the Women's Christian Temperance Union took over the school.[5]

Anglos originated Mayfield and ran most of the businesses, but the town shared a few Hispanic traditions, one a love of music. Virtually every visitor in the early days mentioned Californios' music. Thomes, the sailor who wrote about purchasing milk from Juana in Yerba Buena, often men-

Mayfield, ca. 1890, was a rural town with house yards along a dirt road. The long, low building in the distance is a lumber storage shed near the train station.

tioned how special the music of guitar and harp was everywhere you went in California in the 1840s. There was one story about music in Mayfield that must have been understood as a joke at one time. The humor was that the musicians called themselves the University Band, in which Juana's grandson, Tomás Dimas Mesa, played the trombone.

Once the United States took over, the long-lasting parties featuring dance that helped define Californio society either disappeared or got hidden, rather the way the Indians had once hidden their ways. Music that had been common in homes and on plazas in the Hispanic period became more organized. Every issue of Mayfield's 1870 newspaper told where to go to hear a band or watch a minstrel show.

Leland Stanford had once met with Mayfield leaders in the 1890s about shutting down saloons to promote sobriety among faculty and students. Mayfield had started with a business that sold liquor, and two breweries and a saloon were among its first enterprises. Proprietors refused to forfeit their livelihoods for a university still in the dream stage. Mayfield had been a going concern for nearly forty years by then and expected to continue so. Residents must have laughed over their beers at Stanford's audacity, but the fun subsided when Senator Stanford, former governor, wealthy almost beyond belief and accustomed to getting what he wanted, circumvented Mayfield by establishing alcohol-free Palo Alto. Mayfield capitulated and adopted a similar ban in 1905, but by then professors and students had congregated in Palo Alto. If there was a queen then, it was Palo Alto, not Mayfield.[6]

Another of Juana's grandsons, Alvino Mesa, made his living in several different jobs, one of which was bartender, in which capacity he gave an interview where he told how his grandmother gave medical treatment to bandits and outlaws, and subsequently buried their treasure. He was five years old when Juana died and thus received the lore of earlier generations in that compelling mode of overhearing stories or of hearing them as they are told to children. The reporter who wrote about Al, "the big Spaniard," said people went to his saloon to hear his "yarns." Like his grandmother, he could tell stories in ways people remembered.[7] Alvino never was known to have been a horseman, although he was a member of the United States Army when horses were standard, but "Spaniards" of Juana's generation were often described in terms of their fantastic skill with horses. Perhaps it was because Anglos heard stories of those wonders and decided to go for that honor in their own way. Many rich Anglos of Juana's locale in her elder years loved horses not as an occupation, but as an expensive hobby. The 1888 obituary of Henry Seale made much of him as "one of California's oldest turfmen" who raised "fast horses," but made no mention of his roundups with the Mirandas that predated his sport of breeding racing stock.

On land Martin Murphy purchased from Juana, he and his grandson, Martin Joseph Taaffe, bred racehorses. Also on Juana's former ranch, Betty Byrne de Zahara owned Westwind Hungarian Horse Farm, famed as the trainers of prize-winning Escargot. John Phippen, who lived in Mayfield, managed Stanford's trotting farm, said to be the world's finest. The year Juana died, Stanford had 775 horses meticulously cared for by 150 workers, about half of them Chinese. Stanford so cherished his breeding stallion Electioneer that he commissioned a statue of the horse that still stands in a prominent position near the entrance to Stanford University stables. Breeding horses must have seemed a contradiction in terms to Hispanic people, who stressed training and who thought of horses as capable of reproducing without human intervention.[8]

Hispanic society was largely out of fashion during Juana's last years. The so-called Mission Revival period that imagined elegance in housing and society began during the last decade of Juana's life but did not go national until 1893, when the World Columbian Exposition in Chicago showed a larger audience the beauty of stucco, red tile roofs, carved wooden balconies, and Spanish artifacts. Still, there was interest in the history, and Hispanic people were not averse to embellishing their own backgrounds. The frequent descriptive phrase that someone was of "pure Castilian descent" may have never, or hardly ever, been true of any Californio, most of whom were of mixed ancestry, Spanish, Indian, and African American.[9]

Carey McWilliams, a historian working in the 1940s, wrote that after 1880 there was little evidence of Spanish culture in California and that in general people who did not speak English retreated to southern counties. He could have found exceptions in Juana and her descendants, who did not retreat but instead stayed and prospered in business and continued as notable citizens among Anglos, many of whom belittled anyone outside their own narrow cultural parameters. She and her children and grandchildren remained confident and prominent, and Juana's descendants spoke admiringly to the press of their Hispanic grandmother at the same time that they maintained friendly relations with Anglos.[10]

Cross-cultural marriages, almost always between Hispanic women and Anglo men, smoothed the waters of understanding. Hispanics who married Anglos stayed connected to other Hispanics through relatives and religion. Rafael Soto, grantee of the Rancho Rinconada del Arroyo de San Francisquito, married María Antonia Mesa, related by marriage to Juana. María Antonia's daughter María Louisa Soto married seafarers, first the English sailor John Coppinger and after his death the Irish captain John Greer. The Mesas, Sotos, and Juana were connected significantly through the godparent bond. The Greers, Juana's daughters and other relatives, and Juana herself link up in the baptismal records at the Church of the Nativity in Menlo Park, just across San Francisquito Creek from Palo Alto, and at St. Matthew's Church in San Mateo, farther north on El Camino Road. Juana's sister Guadalupe Briones de Miramontes and her family appear regularly in St. Matthew parish records, but few Mesas or Mirandas do, except for the wedding of Ramón Mesa and Refugio Miranda, at which Lucas Greer and María Soto testified to the absence of impediments to the marriage.

The Greers had prominence for many years in Mayfield and Palo Alto. The family lived in a large, two-story wooden house, a mansion even by today's standards. In contrast, Juana and her offspring lived in various cottages in Mayfield and on the Briones Ranch, but, all told, the family owned several thousand acres. They could be called the landed gentry, but, more exactly, they were businesspeople, making their holdings pay. Probate records from when Narcisa died in 1879 and again when her youngest brother Dolores died in 1904 show that both owned lots in the town of Santa Clara. In delinquent tax records of 1919, Refugio, Tony, and Dolores are listed with considerable Mayfield land. One family-owned lot in Mayfield was about the size of the Ojo de Agua de Figueroa, one hundred feet square, on Lincoln, the main business street that was renamed California Avenue when Mayfield voted to become part of Palo Alto. None of Juana's family members owned or even seemed to want extravagant houses like those of Secundino Robles and Captain Greer. Juana's ranch house was big in a useful, workaday sense.[11]

People who had known Juana or knew people who had known her kept memory of her alive long after she died, but that memory pertained to her accomplishments, not to her physical appearance. A photograph said to be of her was donated in 2007 by family descendants to archives at Point Reyes, an image of an imposing woman who fits the descriptions of her personality that have survived.

Thomes called her a "buxom dark-faced lady," and very likely her complexion was darker than Thomes was used to in Boston, but the term *buxom* occurred too often as a description by men of women to trust. One may surmise that she was not slim, but with the amount of work she accomplished, it is highly unlikely that she was fat.

About her elder years, two recollections by a grandson and one in a court case during her lifetime mention that her physical condition deteriorated when she was in her late seventies. Juana was seventy-seven when her daughter Narcisa Miranda y Briones de García died a widow in 1879. In the absence of a will, Narcisa's younger brother José Julian Miranda explained how it was that he represented the estate. He said in a deposition taken by the family lawyer, Joseph Wallis, that Narcisa's elder brother, Tomás, did not wish to act; that another brother, Dolores, was insane; and that their mother was "aged and infirm and incompetent to act." José did not have to excuse Narcisa's three sisters because men were always presumed to handle official matters under the American system, although Juana herself apparently did not follow that practice, which is probably why José thought he had to mention her inability to handle the probate case.

In a letter to a historian in 1937, grandson Tomás Dimas Mesa, who was born in Juana's house on the Purísima Ranch, wrote that "[i]n her later days she was slightly stooped and walked with a long staff; but when she was angry she straightened to her full height, her eyes flashed, and she bore the dignity of a Spanish doña." A writer in the 1970s claimed that Juana had moved off the ranch and into town because her daughters, Refugio and

Manuela, lived in Mayfield and wanted to care for a mother "crippled with rheumatism."[12]

Although Juana's body showed signs of aging, her mind stayed alert. When some priests and Catholic lay people began a process to acquire church approval to canonize Padre Magín de Catala, the eighty-two-year-old Juana was one of the many persons who testified. Her daughters Refugio and Manuela were at her side. Juana spoke in favor of the case for Catala's deserving this honor. His belief in exorcism allied him with a strain of thought in some Indian philosophy. He could sense the presence of the devil, would advise his people when and where they must be on guard, and, when necessary, he would drive the devil away.

More frequently, people remembered his prophesies, as Juana did. One occasion was especially vivid in her memory. In telling about a particular Sunday in church at Santa Clara Mission, she incorrectly recalled either her age or the year. If it was 1817, she would have been fifteen, not eighteen or nineteen, as she said. Father announced at mass that all should pray for a person who would soon suffer an accident. A few days later, as Juana traveled with her father to Mission San Juan Bautista, they saw someone who had fallen to the ground. On stopping to help, they found the dead body of Antonio Soto, which they took as verification of the padre's prophesy. Juana also mentioned Catala's energetic style of preaching, a sidelight that helped to explain his audience's attentiveness.

The priest who interviewed Juana wrote at the top of the first page that hers was perhaps the most reliable of all the testimonies taken—high praise indeed, considering that the priests recorded fifty-two depositions. Juana's feelings about Catala were so strong that she cried as she described how he dressed poorly and went barefoot, how with a staff in his hand, which other sources tell us he used because of severe rheumatism, he appeared like a shepherd tending his flock as he cared for the sick and needy. His asceticism, which was part of the Franciscan credo, contributed to people's belief in his sanctity.

Juana's description of events and her interpretation of them are well expressed and more detailed than most, but a few of the other testimonials also have estimable qualities, which suggests that the interviewer thought that Juana's could be judged as best of all in part because it conveyed a compelling element of intensity and conviction that was obvious in her presence but did not fully translate into writing. Much evidence suggests that memories of Juana have been so often preserved because of her "personal magnetism," a phrase that biographer Walter Isaacson used in describing Benjamin Franklin.

Based on what we know about Juana and what people have said about her, it seems possible that when she cried in speaking of Father Catala, she was crying not only for her deep and abiding affection for him, but also crying for the demise of a time of mutual understanding within the church and among her people. In Juana's ninth decade of life, none of the priests who tended nearby parishes had Hispanic names.

During the thirty years that Catala served at Mission Santa Clara, he baptized the Indian Gorgonio, one of Juana's children in 1827, and many of her relatives' children, especially her brother Felipe's and her sister Epiciaca's. Even Gregorio Briones and his wife, whose lives centered longer in Bolinas than in any other single location, lived near Mission Santa Clara in 1825 and 1831, and two of their children were baptized there.

Catala died in 1830, three years before Gorgonio was named in records in connection with the Rancho la Purísima Concepción. A "page" accompanied Catala everywhere he went, and that assistant was almost certainly Gorgonio. Gorgonio's receipt of the first and largest land grant to an Indian of Mission Santa Clara had to be repayment for some outstanding service, even though he was not named in any leadership capacity in mission records. In testimony, Felix Buelna, a descendant of Juana's maternal aunt, mentioned an Indian page whose name is obscured by partly illegible handwriting, but appears to be "Gorgonio." Buelna testified in the Catala sainthood hearings that "[the page] was his [Catala's] faithful servant" and that Gorgonio told Felix that he had seen with his own eyes the priest embracing the altar crucifix high above the ground, although no ladder was visible or other means by which the priest could have reached it.[13]

When Juana left the ranch and moved to Mayfield, she could get to church more readily, and she would be returning to the mode of life she knew in her childhood and young womanhood in Yerba Buena. Mayfield, like Yerba Buena, was a promising town. Almost from the beginning, Mayfield had a blacksmith shop, a general store, and a cobbler's shop, businesses rather like the enterprises Juana oversaw at her Yerba Buena property. Many thought that Mayfield would become the economic heartbeat of the Santa Clara Valley, the fruit basket of California. The climate and soil attracted newcomers, and the railroad opened up doors to a wider world, providing for shipping grain and timber.

The short-lived *Mayfield Enterprise*, 1870-71, had an article in Spanish in each edition—one, for example, about "la crisis monetaria," explaining that a new and prosperous epoch was on the way. Juana is never mentioned by name in the paper's issues, but several ads remind a reader of aspects of her life—her medical career, her legal forays, and the produce of her ranch.

Juana's neighborhood in Mayfield in 1887.

"Medico Espanol, Senor M. S. Alvarez," announced in a brief notice in Spanish that he had just opened an office in town. Perhaps he, or someone like him, was the one who recommended to Juana that she set up a tent in her yard so that her grandson with tuberculosis could sleep in fresh air. Two of Juana's granddaughters and a grandson died of that nineteenth-century scourge.

Juana's attorney Joseph Wallis explained, also in business-card format in the *Mayfield Enterprise,* that his services were available as attorney and counselor at law. An ad for Kilgore & Co. reads, "having purchased all the fruit grown on Mayfield Farm, will run a wagon through the county to sell." Mayfield Farm was the Wallis home. Food delivered to one's door in a wagon drawn by a horse was still common thirty years later, when Birge Clark, later a notable local architect, was still a boy. Sarah Armstrong Montgomery Green Wallis's activity in the women's suffrage movement is mentioned in nearly every issue of the Mayfield newspaper, noting the time and place of meetings and some information about the speaker. One can well imagine that had Juana come of a different heritage, she would have attended those suffrage meetings. One of Juana's connections with Sarah was the Murphys, or perhaps the Murphys knew Juana through Sarah, who had been a member of the Stephens-Murphy party with her husband, Allen Montgomery, who deserted her when the party arrived in California.[14]

One of the remarkable things about Juana's family and their presence in the town of Mayfield was the large amount of property they amassed there while still holding various portions of the ranch, selling them off a little at a time. From probate records, land purchases, newspaper articles, oral histories, city directories, and unpaid tax lists, it has been determined that the following addresses belonged to Juana and her descendants in Mayfield: 230, 302, 320, and 345 Sheridan Avenue; 219 Washington Avenue; 680 California Avenue; and the corner of Grant and Second. Juana's house at the corner of Washington and Second was still standing in 1957 when historian Jacob Bowman published his magazine article about her.

Refugio, who inherited the largest single parcel of the Purísima Ranch, including Juana's house, retained ownership of that house until she was sixty-five years old. The porch and three rooms of Juana's ranch house still look very much as they did when the Nott family took photographs in the early 1900s. Around the same time that Joseph Mesa, the grandson who managed a bank, wrote promotional material about land near Mayfield for the Southern Pacific Railroad, he worked as a real estate agent for other family members, including some of the Miramontes clan in Half Moon Bay. About land that had been part of the Purísima Ranch, he wrote that it had previously been owned by a few, but had now been cut into small tracts that were selling fast and within the reach "of any industrious person of small means."

Born after Juana died, Joseph paid attention to the market and kept track of the family land as Juana had done, each of them in a way compatible with changing times. He wrote of various agricultural opportunities: vegetable gardens; strawberry patches; onion seed gardens; dairies; orchards of pears, apples, and figs; loganberries; blackberries; corn; and poultry, one farm with more than 120 turkeys and chickens too numerous to count. The Taaffe tract (the new name for the part of the ranch that Murphy had purchased from Juana), Arastradero Road, and Nott's farm all figure in his description.[15]

One appealing aspect of Juana's life was her choice of places with inherently positive characteristics. Oddly, that sensitivity extended even to her burial site. She was buried in Holy Cross Cemetery in Menlo Park, which was landscaped by Irish horticulturist Michael Lynch, hired by some of the richest of the California rich. In the 1970s, there were two wooden crosses, for "Tom" and for Mary Mesa, on the plot where eleven family members were buried. Today, although there are no tombstones on those graves, one now honors Juana, placed there in 2007 by the western history organization Y Clampus Vitus. Juana is also recalled in the vicinity of her residence in

Santa Clara County by Juana Briones School and Juana Briones Park in Palo Alto, and a state historic plaque placed in 2007 at the site of part of her ranch. San Francisco has honored Juana with a state historic plaque in Washington Square and a mural in the lobby of the Women's Building.[16]

A small but beguiling piece of evidence that surfaced after Juana died suggests that her progeny learned from her about holding your ground even when the dominant society disparages and marginalizes you. The Mayfield voting register of 1908 lists 221 voters, of which 12, about 5 percent, had Hispanic names. Half of them were Mesa men (women had no voting rights in California in 1908), another was a Miramontes cousin, and there were three Sotos, who might have been near relatives (Epiciaca's children were named Soto and frequented the Purísima Ranch, and Juana's son José Julián married María Soto in 1868). All but one of the Hispanic persons registered to vote in Mayfield nineteen years after Juana died were her descendants or connected to her by family ties.[17]

When Juana Briones y Tapia de Miranda died on December 3, 1889, it was not the end of an era. She was of many eras. She inherited a way of life and bestowed another. If one word had to be chosen to express the essence of her life, it should be *continuity*. She brought from the past and gave to the future, preserving and bestowing qualities both unique and universal. Every generation interprets Juana's life differently. She is worth remembering for many and varied reasons. Patricia Limerick summarizes "New Western History" as continuity, convergence, conquest, and complexity. Juana's biography could be written with each of those words as titles for sections, with the possible addition of a fifth, *controversy*, which historians who distrust evidence from oral-based culture are bound to insert into the conceptual framework.

Juana's street in Mayfield had changed from dirt to pavement by the time, nearly seventy years after she died, that historian Jacob Bowman wrote that Juana was the "pre-eminent woman of Hispanic California." She was more accurately the preeminent Hispanic woman of nineteenth-century California, which Bowman meant when he wrote that "[n]o other Spanish or Mexican woman . . . reached her position and maintained it through life." She died thirty years before Harry C. Peterson, who lived not far from her Mayfield home, wrote that "she became the best known and the best beloved woman in California."[18]

Notes

ABBREVIATIONS USED IN THE NOTES AND BIBLIOGRAPHY

AAM	Archives of the Archdiocese of Monterey
AASF	Archives of the Archdiocese of San Francisco
BHM	Bolinas History Museum
BL	Bancroft Library, University of California, Berkeley
CH	*California History*
CHS	California Historical Society
CHSQ	*California Historical Society Quarterly*
CMSA	California Mission Studies Association
CSA	California State Archives
HL	Huntington Library
HSJ	History/San Jose Archives
HSSCQ	*Historical Society of Southern California Quarterly*
JAH	*Journal of American History*
JW	*Journal of the West*
LAHM	Los Altos History Museum
LCA	*Los Californianos Antepasados*
PAHA	Palo Alto Historical Association
PHR	*Pacific Historical Review*
SCCHJ	*Santa Cruz County History Journal*
SCP	Society of California Pioneers
SCUA	Santa Clara University Archives
SMCHS	San Mateo County Historical Society
SUSC	Stanford University Special Collections
UCSC	University of California, Santa Cruz
WHQ	*Western Historical Quarterly*

CHAPTER I. STROLLING THROUGH MAYFIELD

1. *Mayfield Enterprise,* March through July 1870; *Mayfield Weekly Republican,* Nov. 25, 1905, grandson Joseph Mesa appointed to Board of Trade; *Mayfield News,* 1911–16.

2. Tapia genealogy courtesy of Briones y Tapia descendent Lorraine Ruiz de Frain and Mike Ford, Tapia descendant.

3. Milliken, *Time of Little Choice,* 259; State of California Land Records, case nos. 310 ND and 401 ND (Northern District), CSA; J. Brown, *Early Days of San Francisco,* 127.

4. Weber, *Spanish Frontier,* 1, 265; Bolton, *Fray Juan Crespi,* xix; Guest, *Fermín Francisco de Lasuen,,* 204.

5. J. Sanchez, *Spanish Bluecoats,* 32; Bancroft, *History of California,* 1:115.

6. W. Bean, *California,* 15; Sebastian Vizcaino, translated letter, May 23, 1603, in Beebe and Senkewicz, eds., *Lands of Promise and Despair,* 44; Cleland, *From Wilderness to Empire,* 46; Eldredge, *History of California,* 1:135; Engelhardt, *Mission San Carlos,* 3.

7. See Crespi, *A Description of Distant Roads;* Boneu, *Gaspar de Portolá,* 325.

8. Hough and Hough, *Spain's California Patriots,* pt. 2, pp. 1–4; Boneu, *Gaspar de Portolá,* 320, 325, 333; Engelhardt, *Mission San Carlos,* 19.

9. Engelhardt, *Mission San Luis Obispo,* 18–19; see also the Web site at http://www.californiamission.com/cahistory/sanluis, accessed Jan. 25, 2005.

10. Crespi, *A Description of Distant Roads,* xix; Boneu, *Gaspar de Portolá,* 308; Engelhardt, *Mission San Carlos,* 19.

11. Guerrero, *The Anza Trail,* 186; Mariano Vallejo, speech of July 4, 1878, as quoted in Davis, *Seventy-five Years,* 358.

12. W. Mason, *Census of 1790,* 65; Castañeda, "Presidarias y Pobladoras," 145.

13. Beilharz, *Felipe de Neve,* 115; Bouvier, *Women and the Conquest of California,* 64; Ford, *Dawn and the Dons,* 78.

14. Eldredge, *History of California,* 1:359; *History of Santa Clara County,* 20.

15. Limerick, *Something in the Soil,* 113.

16. National Park Service, at http://www.nps.gov/juba; Los Californianos sponsors the annual gathering.

17. *Tall Tree: Streets of Palo Alto,* PAHA, 4, 46.

18. Ibid., 51.

19. *Tall Tree: Mayfield,* PAHA, 2.

20. "Duhaut-Cilly's Account," 158.

CHAPTER 2. LIMITED CHOICES

1. Guerrero, *The Anza Trail,* 174; Culleton, *Indians and Pioneers of Old Monterey,* 128.

2. Haas, *Conquests and Historical Identities in California,* 24; sources for genealogy throughout are from mission baptismal, marriage, and death records,

AAM and AASF; Northrop, *Spanish-Mexican Families;* Mutnick, *Some Alta California Pioneers;* Harry Crosby, "The Little-Known Pioneers of Spanish Alta California 1769-1774," presentation given at the Presidio of San Francisco, June 27, 2003; Hough and Hough, *Spain's California Patriots,* pt. 2, 1-4; land, probate, and court records; Ballard, "History of the Stanford Campus."

3. Serra, *Writings of Junipero Serra,* 1:239; see also Piña, *Catalanes y Mallorquines,* 11, 116; Engelhardt, *Mission San Luis Obispo,* 192.

4. Older, *California Missions,* 74; Robert Hoover, "Geophysical Surveys at Mission San Antonio," in Krieger, ed., *The Mission and the Community,* 6; N. Sanchez, *Spanish Arcadia,* 59.

5. Crouch, Garr, and Mundigo, *Spanish City Planning,* 267.

6. Hurtado, *Indian Survival on the California Frontier,* 1; Bouvier, *Women and the Conquest of California,* 74; Weber, *Spanish Frontier,* 25.

7. Heizer and Elsasser, *The Natural World of the California Indians,* 7; Sandos, *Converting California,* 17.

8. Handwritten note on back of map of the presidio in 1820, BL.

9. See L. Thompson, *To the American Indian;* Fallon, *Journal,* 51; J. Mason, *Early Marin,* 123.

10. Heizer and Elsasser, *The Natural World of the California Indians,* 204.

11. Margolin, *The Way We Lived,* 14.

12. W. Robinson, *Land in California,* 30; Cleland, *Cattle on a Thousand Hills,* 29.

13. Monroy, *Thrown among Strangers,* 11; Phillips, *Indians and Indian Agents,* 78-79.

14. Sprietsma, *Mission San Antonio,* 13; Merriam, *Studies of California Indians,* 21.

15. Steven W. Hackel, "Land, Labor, and Production," in Gutiérrez and Orsi, eds., *Contested Eden,* 126; Morrall, *Half Moon Bay Memories,* 11.

16. G. James, *In and Out of the Old Missions,* 75-76.

17. Campbell, "The First Californios," 582.

18. Eldredge, *Beginnings of San Francisco,* 1:39, 44; Milliken, *Time of Little Choice,* 41; Palou, *Historical Memoirs,* 4:40.

19. Mutnick, *Some Alta California Pioneers,* 708-9; Langellier and Rosen, *El Presidio de San Francisco,* 30; Palou, *Historical Memoirs,* vii, xix; Eldredge, *Beginnings of San Francisco,* 1:150.

20. Eldredge, *History of California,* 1:188.

21. Langellier and Rosen, *El Presidio de San Francisco,* 30.

22. National Park Service Web site at http://www.nps.gov/juba, accessed July 7, 2003.

23. Denis, *Spanish Alta California,* 277; Bancroft, *History of California,* 1:311, 348-49; Skowronek, *Identifying the First Pueblo de San José,* 4-5.

24. Amador and Asisara, *Californio Voices,* 201; W. Mason, "Adobe Interiors in Spanish California," 243.

25. Greening, "A Musical Day of Times Past," 10.

26. Mary Null Boule, *Mission San Antonio,* 14–15; Brusa, *Salinan Indians of California,* 38–39.

27. Langdon-Davies, *Carlos,* 13; Sandos, *Converting California,* 38; F. Smith, *Mission of San Antonio,* 85–86.

28. Roslyn M. Frank, Susan Ayres, Monique Laxalt, Shelly Lowenberg, and Nancy Vosburg, "Etxeko-Andrea: The Missing Link? Women in Basque Culture," in Keller, ed., *Views of Women's Lives,* 148–49; Francis Guest, *Fermin Francisco de Lasuen,* 3; Jean François de la Perouse, in Margolin, ed., *The Way We Lived,* 83; Bouvier, *Women and the Conquest of California,* 156–57.

29. Brown in Boneu, *Gaspar de Portolá,* 11.

30. Piña, *Catalanes y Mallorquines,* 116.

31. Rolle, *California,* 70; Bancroft, *History of California,* 2:7.

32. Tibesar's introduction to Serra, *Writings of Junipero Serra,* 1:xxv.

33. Summers, "California Mission Music"; National Park Service, *Noticias de Anza,* no. 22 (Oct. 10, 2003), 4.

34. Sandos, *Converting California,* 140–41.

35. McCarthy, *History of Mission San Jose,* 125, 275.

CHAPTER 3. BORN AND BRED IN BRANCIFORTE

1. Pepper, *Bolinas,* 176; Briones Letter, 1863, BHM; Monte Linsley, "Real Local Pioneer," *Palo Alto Times,* Dec. 20, 1947.

2. Kimbro, "Restoration Research," 50; Jones, *Los Paisanos,* 214; W. Robinson, *Land in California,* 39; A. Brown, *Sawpits in the Redwoods,* 27; Bernucci, "History of the Villa de Branciforte," 5.

3. Collins, "The Miramontes Family"; Schuetz-Miller, *Building and Builders,* 82; Castañeda, "Presidarias y Pobladoras," 166.

4. Florian Guest, "Municipal Government in Spanish California," 307, 313; Denis, *Spanish Alta California,* 403; Schwartz, *From West to East,* 45.

5. J. Sanchez, *Spanish Bluecoats,* 100.

6. Schwartz, *From West to East,* 45.

7. Bernucci, "History of the Villa de Branciforte," 28; Rowland, *Santa Cruz,* 35.

8. Stevens Collection, ms., report of Royal Exchequer, 2d Naval Dept., USCS, 4.

9. J. Sanchez, *Spanish Bluecoats,* 78–80, 94–95.

10. Letter, translated in Langellier and Rosen, *El Presidio de San Francisco,* 79.

11. The age seven reference is from the the Alexander Taylor Collection, AASF.

12. The Borica letter, 1787, was translated by Starr Gurcke, "Some Early Spanish Documents," 46.

13. Langellier and Rosen, *El Presidio de San Francisco*, n. 78; Denis, *Spanish Alta California*, 401; Bancroft, *History of California*, 1:565; Garr, "Power and Priorities," 370.

14. Miranda, "Hispano-Mexican Childrearing Practices."

15. DeVoto, *Journals of Lewis and Clark*, xv.

16. Beilharz, *Felipe de Neve*, 41.

17. Sanchez, *Spanish Arcadia*, 135.

18. Excerpts from Stevens Collecion and Branciforte Archives translated by Starr Gurcke, "Some Early Spanish Documents"; Bancroft, *History of California*, 2:300.

19. Letter translated by Starr Gurcke, May 1799, no. 236–37, Prestatehood Documents, Provincial State Papers, CSA.

20. Government order no. 32, Dec. 3, 1807, in Williams, "Santa Cruz," 43.

21. Bancroft, *History of California*, 1:567.

22. Bernucci, "History of the Villa de Branciforte," 11.

23. Rowland, "Circuit Rider," 34.

24. Lorenzo Asisara, "The Killing of Fr. Andres Quintana at Mission Santa Cruz," in Beebe and Senkewicz, eds., *Lands of Promise and Despair*, 285; Monroy, *Thrown among Strangers*, 91; Geiger, *Franciscan Missionaries in Hispanic California*, 206.

25. Bancroft, *History of California*, 2:196.

26. Florian Guest, "Municipal Government in Spanish California," 323; Rowland, *Santa Cruz*, 35.

27. McCarthy, *History of Mission San Jose*, 143; Bryant, *What I Saw in California*, chap. 15, book accessed online May 14, 2006; Thomes, "California Life," 12.

28. Tracy, *Sausalito*, 3; Thomes, *On Land and Sea*, 239; Eldredge, *Beginnings of San Francisco*, 2:504; J. Hittell, *History of San Francisco*, 78.

29. A. Brown, *Sawpits in the Redwoods*, 2.

30. Torchiana, *Story of the Mission Santa Cruz*, 188.

31. T. Hittell, *History of California*, 73; Jose Velasquez, "Between Baja and Alta California," in Beebe and Senkewicz, eds., *Lands of Promise and Despair*, 247; Hurtado, "Indians of California," 373.

32. Reader, "History of the Villa de Branciforte," 18; Johnston, "Jose Eusebio Boronda Adobe," 3; Lund and Gullard, *History of Palo Alto*, 38.

33. Miranda, "Hispano-Mexican Childrearing Practices," 311.

34. Miller, *Juan Alvarado*, 7; Boule, *Salinan Tribe*, 21.

35. Oral histories from Margolin, ed., *The Way We Lived*, 47–48; Haas, *Conquests and Historical Identities in California*, 116.

36. Bouvier, *Women and the Conquest of California*, 85, 158; Langellier and Rosen, *El Presidio de San Francisco*, 48.

CHAPTER 4. HEADING NORTH

1. Provincial State Papers, 9:185, CSA; Florian Guest, "Municipal Government in Spanish California," 316.

2. Marie Duggan, "Franciscan Income and Expenditures at Missions San Jose and Santa Clara," in Krieger, ed., *The Mission and the Community*, 41–42.

3. Voss, "Archaeology of el Presidio de San Francisco," 112; Pritchard, "Joint Tenants of the Frontier," 25–26; Archibald, *Economic Aspects of California Missions*, 1, 27.

4. Wagner, "The Last Spanish Exploration of the Northwest Coast," 315; Milliken, *Time of Little Choice*, 177.

5. Weber, *Spanish Frontier*, 309.

6. Kimbro, "Restoration Research," 50; Guest, "Establishment of the Villa of Branciforte," 33; Whitehead, "Alta California's Four Fortresses," 71.

7. Bancroft, *History of California*, 1:603; J. Sanchez, *Spanish Bluecoats*, 74.

8. Brewer, *Up and Down California*, 24.

9. Engelhardt, *San Diego Mission*, 198; Langellier and Rosen, *El Presidio de San Francisco*, 51.

10. Langellier and Rosen, *El Presidio de San Francisco*, 139 n.; Davis, *Seventy-five Years*, 10; Steve Richardson, "Bears, Wolves, and Coyotes," in Barker, ed., *San Francisco Memoirs*, 65.

11. Castañeda, "Presidarias y Pobladoras," 152; Fava, *Los Altos Hills*, 28.

12. Shinn, "Californiana."

13. N. Sanchez, *Spanish Arcadia*, 48; quotation from Sawyer, *History of Santa Clara County*, 38.

14. Bancroft, *History of California*, 2:128; Langellier and Rosen, *El Presidio de San Francisco*, 60; Bowman, "Adobe Houses," 57; tour of site given to the author by Barbara Voss, Aug. 15, 2003.

15. Schuetz-Miller, *Building and Builders*, 175; Voss, *Tennessee Hollow Watershed*, 7.1–7.5; Bowman, "Adobe Houses," 57; Sprietsma, *Mission San Antonio de Padua*, 29.

16. See Crespi, *A Description of Distant Roads*.

17. Eldredge, *Beginnings of San Francisco*, 1:188; McCarthy, *History of Mission San Jose*, 272.

18. Vallejo as quoted in Davis, *Seventy-five Years*, 358.

19. Barbara Corff, conversation with the author, May 10, 2001; tour of the site by Voss, Aug. 15, 2003; Edward Vischer Papers, BL, handwritten note on back of 1820 map of presidio, as quoted in Voss, "Archaeology of el Presidio de San Francisco," 208.

20. W. Phelps, *Alta California*, 84.

21. Eldredge, *Beginnings of San Francisco*, 1:615; N. Sanchez, *Spanish Arcadia*, 373.

22. U.S. government reports: Barnes, *Circular no. 4*, and Lord, *Posts and Stations of Troops;* see also Langellier and Rosen, *El Presidio de San Francisco*, 67.

23. Native Daughters of the Golden West, form, San Francisco office; Nilda Rego, "Martinez Man Holds Up History," *Contra Costa Gazette*, Feb. 2, 1992; Castañeda, "Presidarias y Pobladoras," 210.

24. Web site of the Museum of the City of San Francisco, http://www .sfmuseum.org, subject: San Francisco Earthquake History 1769–1879, accessed Mar. 12, 2003.

25. Bancroft, *California Pioneer Register*, 249; Davis, *Seventy-five Years*, 7; Collins, "The Miramontes Family"; Downey, *The Cruise of the Portsmouth*.

26. Bancroft, *History of California*, 3:241; Bouvier, *Women and the Conquest of California*, 79.

27. Deed, Feb. 20, 1906, vol. 289, no. 446, Probate Records, Santa Clara County Hall of Records.

28. Pierce, *Martin Murphy Family Saga*, 107; Haas, *Conquests and Historical Identities in California*, 119.

29. N. Sanchez, *Spanish Arcadia*, 227; Schwartz, *From West to East*, 63.

30. Pico, *Cosas de California*, 19; Bouvier, *Women and the Conquest of California*, 85–86; Culleton, *Indians and Pioneers of Old Monterey*, 152; Johnston, "José Eusebio Boronda," 3.

31. Mutnick, *Some Alta California Pioneers*, 708–9; W. Mason, *Census of 1790*; Garate, *Juan Bautista de Anza*, 24; see also Bancroft, *California Pioneer Register*, and Manocchio, "Tending Communities, Crossing Cultures," 30.

32. McCarthy, *History of Mission San Jose*, 59; see Mission Dolores baptisms, such as the ones for Oct. 20, 1783, and Mission San Luis Obispo baptisms, for Jan. 13, Oct. 19, and Dec. 2, 1788.

CHAPTER 5. A PLACE OF ONE'S OWN

1. N. Sanchez, *Spanish Arcadia*, 277; Davis, *Seventy-five Years*, 183; Monroy, *Thrown among Strangers*, 147.

2. Pico, *Cosas de California*, 20; Wrightington, "Times Gone By in Alta California," 46.

3. Hackel, "Land, Labor, and Production," in Gutiérrez and Orsi, eds., *Contested Eden*, 132.

4. Milliken, *Mission Dolores*, 24; Bancroft, *History of California*, 2:496.

5. J. Mason, *Last Stage for Bolinas*, 3.

6. *History of Marin County*, 109; Lightfoot, *Indians, Missionaries, and Merchants*, 127; Paddison, *A World Transformed*, 168.

7. Payne, *Santa Clara County*, 35–37; Provincial State Papers, 11:371, CSA; Culleton, *Indians and Pioneers*, 139; Harlow, *California Conquered*, 15; Voss, "Archaeology of el Presidio de San Francisco," 112; Sherman, *Memoirs*, 1:36; Pritchard, "Joint Tenants of the Frontier"; C. Brown, "Statement of Recollections."

8. Bancroft, *History of California*, 3:169.

9. Ibid., 3:191; W. Phelps, *Alta California*, 113; Cook, *Conflict*, 273.

10. Data on deaths from AASF; Bojorquez marriage information comes from Rudecinda Lo Buglio, Women's Heritage Museum application for a state historic marker for Juana Briones, 1997.

11. Miranda, "Gente de Razón Marriage Patterns."

12. Twinam, *Public Lives, Private Secrets*, 62; Pepper, *Bolinas*, 24; Schuetz-Miller, *Building and Builders*, xi, 71; conversation with Marin County archivist Jocelyn Moss at Bolinas cemetery rededication, May 26, 2003; copy of Gregorio's will in Pepper, *Bolinas*, 176.

13. Gonzalez, "Searching for the Feathered Serpent," 148; Pepper, *Bolinas*, 9; Hurtado, "Indians of California," 374, 380; Bouvier, *Women and the Conquest of California*, 46–47, 169; Langellier and Rosen, *El Presidio de San Francisco*, 144; Weber, *Spanish Frontier*, 331; Cook, *Conflict*, 22.

14. Lund and Gullard, *History of Palo Alto*, 26; C. Lyman, *Around the Horn*, 249; Arbuckle, *History of San Jose*, 203.

15. Rowland, *Santa Cruz*, 4; Miller, *Captain Richardson*, 90.

16. State of California Land Records, Miranda Grant, case no. 401 ND, exp. 63, San Francisco County, CSA.

17. Glenn Farris, supervisor of the State Archaeological Collections Research Facility, California Department of Parks and Recreation, letter to the author, Oct. 5, 2004; San Luis Obispo early mission records were lost; estimated marriage year in Northrop, *Spanish-Mexican Families*, 89; W. Mason, *Census of 1790*, 78.

18. Sandos, *Converting California*, 21.

19. Gordon Morris Bakken, "The Courts, the Legal Profession, and the Development of Law in Early California," in Burns and Orsi, eds., *Taming the Elephant*, 85; State of California Land Records, Miranda Grant, case no. 401 ND, CSA.

20. Donna Schuele, "Women, Law, and Government in California, 1850–1890," in Burns and Orsi, eds., *Taming the Elephant*, 174; J. Mason, *Early Marin*, 141.

21. Eldredge, *Beginnings of San Francisco*, 2:525.

22. Heizer and Elsasser, *The Natural World of the California Indians*, 57; Terry Pimsleur, conversation with the author, Apr. 18, 2005.

23. Letter of application, 1833, in State of California Land Records, Miranda Grant, case no. 401 ND, Heirs of Apolinario Miranda, CSA.

24. Bouvier, *Women and the Conquest of California*, 75; Weber, *Spanish Frontier*, 327; Gonzalez, "Searching for the Feathered Serpent," 90; Bancroft, *History of California*, 3:318.

25. Haas, *Conquests and Historical Identities*, 36–37, 115–16; Camarillo, *Chicanos in a Changing Society*, 5; Consuelo Alba-Speyer, "Mexican Ballads Boast Substance, Passion," *San Jose Mercury News*, May 16, 2002.

26. Farris and Beebe, *Report of a Visit to Fort Ross*, prologue to Vallejo report, iv; also see Lightfoot, *Indians, Missionaries, and Merchants;* Crouch,

Garr, and Mundigo, *Spanish City Planning*, 201, 269; Bouvier, *Women and the Conquest of California*, 79; Rolle, *California*, 120.

27. Tays, "Mariano Guadalupe Vallejo and Sonoma."

28. Engelhardt, *San Francisco or Mission Dolores*, 199.

29. Sandos, *Converting California*, 3, 45, 50, 69; Osio, *History of Alta California*, 185; Monroy, *Thrown among Strangers*, 123.

30. C. Brown, "Statement of Recollections," 2; Bancroft, *History of California*, 2:751; Schuetz-Miller, *Building and Builders*, 127.

31. Monroy, *Thrown among Strangers*, 154; Langellier and Rosen, *El Presidio de San Francisco*, 125; Bancroft, *History of California*, 2:395; Thomes, *On Land and Sea*, 125.

CHAPTER 6. YERBA BUENA

1. Alexander and Heig, *San Francisco*, 41; Pierce, *Martin Murphy Family Saga*, 75; Muriel Knapp, conversation with the author, summer 1997.

2. William Clark, CD 245, BL.

3. Pepper, *Bolinas*, 54.

4. Dwinelle, *Colonial History of the City of San Francisco*, accounts of Juan Fuller, 75; Payne, *Santa Clara County*, 26.

5. Frederick William Beechey, "Narrative of a Voyage to the Pacific," in Paddison, ed., *A World Transformed*, 168; Eldredge, *Beginnings of San Francisco*, 2:499; Norris and Webb, *Geology of California*, 394.

6. A. Robinson, *Life in California*, 283; Bancroft, *History of California*, 3:137; J. Hittell, *History of San Francisco*, 83; Bowman, "Juana Briones de Miranda," 231; Hubbard, "Cities within the City."

7. C. Brown, "Statement of Recollections," 3; Bancroft, *History of California*, 3:709.

8. A. Robinson, *Life in California*, 37–38; Miller, *Captain Richardson*, 49–51; Dwinelle, *Colonial History of the City of San Francisco*, 36, addenda; Bancroft, *History of California*, 3:704.

9. Dwinelle, *Colonial History of the City of San Francisco*, 57; G. James, *In and Out of the Old Missions*, 276.

10. G. Lyman, *John Marsh*, 209–10; Soule, Gihon, and Nisbet, *Annals of San Francisco*, 158; Sherman, *Memoirs*, 67.

11. Thomes, *On Land and Sea*, 187.

12. Robert Miller, *Captain Richardson*, 49.

13. Davis, *Seventy-five Years*, 156; Eldredge, *Beginnings of San Francisco*, 2:505; Rolle, *California*, 123.

14. Older, *California Missions*, 280; J. Mason, *Last Stage for Bolinas*, 3; Thomes, *On Land and Sea*, 187.

15. William Taylor, "Life and Death at City Hospital," in Barker, ed., *San Francisco Memoirs*, 213; Eldredge, *Beginnings of San Francisco*, 2:615.

16. Documents, Early San Francisco, C-A 370, box 1, folder 54, BL.

17. Gonzalez, "Searching for the Feathered Serpent," 56–57; Alexander and Heig, *San Francisco*, 30.

18. Chávez-Garcia, *Negotiating Conquest*, 28–29.

19. Documents, Early San Francisco, C-A 370, box 1, folder 65, BL; Osio, *History of Alta California*, 158.

20. W. Mason, "Adobe Interiors in Spanish California," 235; W. Phelps, *Alta California*, 348; Adelbert von Chamisso, 1816, in Paddison, ed., *A World Transformed*, 135; Goodwin, *Establishment of State Government*, 6; Probate Records, Santa Clara County, 1221, register D, 172; Rolle, *California*, 104.

21. Phelps, *Alta California*, 119.

22. Bancroft, *History of California*, 4:668; Voss, "Archaeology of el Presidio de San Francisco," 222; A. Robinson, *Life in California*, 283; Carmen Miramontes, ms. no. 757, SMCHS.

23. Bowman, "Juana Briones de Miranda," 241.

24. Documentos, la historia de California, V, 267–269, Dec. 1838, BL; Hague and Langum, *Thomas O. Larkin*, 13.

25. Documents, Early San Francisco, C-A 370, box 1, folder 54, BL; Rowland, *Santa Cruz*, 101.

26. Anonymous, "Memorabilia."

27. Phil Frank, president of the BHM, oral communication to the author, Feb. 20, 2001; Pepper, *Bolinas*, 170–71 (Pepper incorrectly writes that Gregorio left the land to two sisters); Edna F. Kimbro, "Spanish-Era Settlement of the Mesa, 1795–1822," in Burton-Carvajal, ed., *Monterey Mesa*, 20.

CHAPTER 7. UNDER MEXICO

1. Sam P. May, letter, June 6, 1911, SCP.

2. White, *It's Your Misfortune*, 238.

3. Rae quoted in Bancroft, *History of California*, 4:668; Guire Cleary, "Mission Dolores," in Burns, ed., *Catholic San Francisco*, 53.

4. Alexander and Heig, *San Francisco*, 30; Davis, *Seventy-five Years*, 151–52; Hynding, *From Frontier to Suburb*, 47.

5. Davis, *Seventy-five Years*, 236; Bancroft, *History of California*, 4:362–63.

6. State of California Land Records, Land Commission, case no. 269 ND, Pilarcitos, CSA; Arbuckle, *History of San Jose*, 203; Alexander and Heig, *San Francisco*, 35; Rowland, *Santa Cruz*, 101; Ballard, "History of Stanford," 127.

7. Bancroft, *History of California*, 4:134, 4:233, and 2:628; see also Hunt, *John Bidwell*.

8. Spanish Documents, no. 54, Guerrero, BL; Bancroft, *History of California*, 4:685.

9. Departmental State Papers, San Jose, 6:23, 28, 29, 33–34; Documents, Early San Francisco, C-A 370, box 1, folder 65, BL.

10. Documents, Early San Francisco, folder 151, BL.

11. Langum, *Law and Community,* 235.

12. Davis, *Seventy-five Years,* 196.

13. This summary from many sources is not chronological. Many of Ridley's enterprises overlapped. His name is indexed in most books about early San Francisco.

14. Halleck, Peachy, Billings Papers, folder 150, box 3, and folder 430, box 4, BL; Engelhardt, *San Francisco or Mission Dolores,* 357; Shutes, "Henry Wager Halleck."

15. Documents, Early San Francisco, folder 53, BL; Bancroft, *History of California,* 4:685.

16. Mission San José, Jan. 10, 1840, AASF.

17. J. Mason, *Last Stage for Bolinas,* 5; Bowman, "Index of Spanish-Mexican Land" 21, 350.

18. Kirsten Kvam, curator at Point Reyes, National Park Service, e-mail to the author, Mar. 30, 2007.

19. Bancroft, *History of California,* 3:702; Engelhardt, *San Francisco or Mission Dolores,* 270.

CHAPTER 8. SAN FRANCISCO

1. The Bancroft Library houses state papers that contain court documents about the Miranda-Briones marriage: see Departmental State Papers, San Jose, vol. 6; Documents, Early San Francisco, C-A 370, box 1, folder 54, and box 2, folders 65, 81, 104, 136, BL.

2. Chávez-Garcia, *Negotiating Conquest,* 28.

3. See Geiger, *Franciscan Missionaries;* Langum, *Law and Community,* 235.

4. Fava, *Los Altos Hills,* 36; García Diego y Moreno, *Writings of Francisco García Diego y Moreno,* entry no. 147, July 14, 1844.

5. Levy and Drye, "Legacy of Francisco Sanchez"; Miller, *Juan Alvarado,* 85; Geiger, *Franciscan Missionaries,* vii.

6. Foucrier, "Sailors, Carpenters, Vineyardists," 141.

7. Davis, *Seventy-five Years,* 151.

8. Mission Dolores deaths, May, July, September 1847, AASF.

9. Bowman, "Juana Briones de Miranda"; Thomes, *On Land and Sea,* 187.

10. Thomes, *On Land and Sea,* 120, 191, 287.

11. Ibid., 194–96; Ackerman, "Statement"; Hubbard, "Cities within the City," 210.

12. Edward Morphy, "San Francisco's Thoroughfares," *San Francisco Chronicle,* Apr. 11, 1920.

13. Davis, *Seventy-five Years,* 256; Haas, *Conquests and Historical Identities in California,* 49.

14. Sherman, *Memoirs,* 1:33.

15. Davis, *Seventy-five Years*, 7, 376; J. Brown, *Early Days of San Francisco*, 32.

16. Munro-Fraser, *History of Contra Costa County*, 331, 329; Miller, *Captain Richardson*, 87; Ballard, "History of the Stanford Campus"; State of California Land Records, exp. 116 and 230, CSA; maps, SUSC; Alan Brown, historian, personal communication with the author, January 15, 2007.

17. J. Hittell, *History of San Francisco*, 83.

18. Greenwood, *The California Outlaw*, 12; Monroy, *Thrown among Strangers*, 214; see also Michael Gonzalez, "My Brother's Keeper," in Owens, ed., *Riches for All*, 122.

19. Davis, *Seventy-five Years*, 378; Hussey, "New Light upon Talbot H. Green"; Sarah Wallis, Regnery Papers, PAHA.

20. Peterson, "The Story of Stanford University"; Harry C. Peterson, "The Remarkable Story of Juana Briones," *San Francisco Call and Post*, Feb. 7, 1919.

21. Archives, SCP.

22. C. Lyman, *Around the Horn*, 248; Cleary, "Mission Dolores," in Burns, ed., *Catholic San Francisco*, 20–22; see Briones, "A Glimpse of Domestic Life in 1828," in Shinn, "Californiana."

23. Ulrich, *A Midwife's Tale*, 80.

24. J. Brown, *Early Days of San Francisco*, 27.

25. Eldredge, *Beginnings of San Francisco*, 2:518; J. Brown, "Early Days," in Barker, ed., *San Francisco Memoirs*, 70; Bryant, *What I Saw in California*, chap. 26.

26. Rawls and Orsi, *A Golden State*, 5.

27. See Tutorow, *Leland Stanford*.

28. Garner, *Letters from California 1846–1847*, 148; Biggs, *Conquer and Colonize*, 56, 119, 134.

29. Pierce, *Martin Murphy Family Saga*, 59; Hunt, *California in the Making*, 121; Willey, *Thirty Years in California*, 38; Paul, *California Gold*, 81; Sylvia Sun Minnick, "Never Far from Home," in Owens, ed., *Riches for All*, 146; *History of Santa Clara County*, 75.

30. Osio, *History of Alta California*, 185.

31. Stellman, *Sam Brannan*, 51; White, *It's Your Misfortune*, 163; G. Lyman, *John Marsh*, 320.

32. Lisbeth Haas, "War in California 1846–1848," in Gutiérrez and Orsi, eds., *Contested Eden*, 340.

33. Miller, *Captain Richardson*, 157; McGrath, "Taming the Elephant," 36–37.

34. James Ayers, "A Heterogeneous Population," in Barker, ed., *San Francisco Memoirs*, 197.

35. Royce, *California*, 217.

36. Tracy, *Sausalito*, 157–58.

37. Benecia Historical Museum Web site at http://www.beniciahistorical-museum.org, accessed Oct, 28, 2004.

38. Fava, *Los Altos Hills*, 37.

39. Bowman, "Juana Briones de Miranda," 232; Ambrose, *Nothing Like It in the World*, 185; Rolle, *California*, 228; E. Thompson, *Forest at the Presidio*, 1.

CHAPTER 9. "THIS WOMAN WHO CURED ME"

1. Documents, Early San Francisco, C-A 370, box 2, folder 136, March 5, 1846, BL.

2. Riptides scrapbook, Nov. 18, 1949, CHS; Davis, *Seventy-five Years*, 10.

3. E. James, *Notable American Women;* Florian Guest compares Civil War to mission Indian deaths in "Cultural Perspectives on California Mission Life"; Peterson, "The Remarkable Story of Juana Briones."

4. Peterson, "The Story of Stanford University"; biography file, SUSC.

5. Phelps, *Alta California*, 271.

6. Hoff and Smith, *Mapping Epidemics*, 16; Cook, *Conflict*, 19, 210; Holliday, *The World Rushed In*, 115.

7. Abbey, *California*, 163; C. Lyman, *Around the Horn*, 248; see also Ulrich, *A Midwife's Tale*.

8. Bancroft, *History of California*, 3:357–58; Antonia Castañeda, "Engendering," in Gutiérrez and Orsi, eds., *Contested Eden*, 216; Hurtado, *Indian Survival*, 46; Gillis and Magliari, *John Bidwell and California*, 99.

9. Weber, *Spanish Frontier*, 28; William Preston, "Serpent in the Garden," in Gutiérrez and Orsi, eds., *Contested Eden*, 263.

10. Tyson, *Diary of a Physician*, 1, 3, 80.

11. *Tall Tree: Mayfield*, 1; Santa Clara County Court Records, 1 to 266, HSJ.

12. "Old Settler of Mayfield Dead," *Palo Alto Times*, Dec. 21, 1920; Older, "Life of Old Pioneer in Mayfield"; Holtzclaw, "The Robles Family in California," 43; Santa Clara County Court Records, court case no. 219, Feb. 10, 1851, HSJ; Lund, *History of Palo Alto*, 30.

13. Peterson, "The Remarkable Story of Juana Briones."

14. Peterson, "Remarkable Story of Juana Briones"; Perrone, Stockel, and Kruege, *Medicine Women;* Coronel, *Tales of Mexican California*, 44.

15. Amador and Asisara, *Californio Voices*, 57.

16. Monroy, *Thrown among Strangers*, 30–31; Heinsen, *Mission San Antonio de Padua Herbs;* Milliken, *A Time of Little Choice*, 172–73; Sandos, *Converting California*, 116; James Sandos, "Between Crucifix and Lance: Indian-White Relations in California, 1769–1848," in Gutiérrez and Orsi, eds., *Contested Eden*, 200.

17. Cleland, *From Wilderness to Empire*, 56; Engelhardt, *Mission San Luis Obispo*, 49; Heizer and Elsasser, *The Natural World of the California Indians*, 129; Heinsen, *Mission San Antonio de Padua Herbs*.

18. Heinsen, *Mission San Antonio de Padua Herbs;* Perrone, Stockel, and Kruege, *Medicine Women*, 90.

19. Pierce, *Martin Murphy Family Saga*, 75.

20. McCarthy, *History of Mission San Jose*, 87–88; Farris, "Fr. Luis Gil y Taboada"; Michael Hardwick, volunteer at Purísima Mission, provided copy of Mission Account book, e-mail to the author, May 15, 2002.

21. Gabriela Cibrian, testimony, Catala Papers, AASF; Davis, *Seventy-five Years*, 42.

22. Untitled ms. 757, SMCHS.

23. Castañeda, "Presidarias y Pobladoras," 210, one doctor for all four presidios in 1844; *Contra Costa Gazette*, Jan. 3, 1968; *Contra Costa Times*, Feb. 2, 1992.

24. J. Mason, *Last Stage for Bolinas*, 5; Dauernheim, ms., 1979, BHM; Phil Frank, journalist and historian at BHM, conversation with the author, Feb. 20, 2001.

25. Bancroft, *History of California*, 2:441; 3:169; Warren, "Medical Quacks."

26. Anonymous, handwritten notes about Juana Briones, BHM; Pepper, *Bolinas*, 33.

27. C. Brown, "Statement of Recollections," 2; J. Mason, *Last Stage for Bolinas*, 18–19.

28. Castañeda, "Presidarias y Pobladoras," 219; Sprietsma, *Mission San Antonio*, 13; Guadalupe Vallejo, "Ranch and Mission Days," in Lewis and De Nevi, eds., *Sketches of Early California*, 24; Fava, *Los Altos Hills*, 34.

29. M. Gates, *Rancho Pastoria de las Borregas*, 17.

30. Pierce, *Martin Murphy Family Saga*, 75; Peterson, "The Story of Stanford University," chap. 23.

31. Pokriots, "Josefa Buelna's Memories of Spanish Santa Cruz," 140; Osio, *History of Alta California*, 215.

32. Geiger, *Franciscan Missionaries*, 54, 79, 189; Culleton, *Indians and Pioneers of Old Monterey*, 116; Bouvier, *Women and the Conquest of California*, 68.

33. Greenan, oral history, 1970, PAHA.

CHAPTER 10. "THE TROUBLESOME SERVICE OF THE MISSION"

1. Rojas, "Who Were the Vaqueros?" 37; Lightfoot, *Indians, Missionaries, and Merchants*, 229.

2. Sandos, *Converting California*, 5.

3. L. Thompson, *To the American Indian*, xxii, 24, 93–108, 239.

4. Macleod, *American Indian Frontier*, 18; Fray Martín quoted in Engelhardt, *San Miguel*, 20; L. Thompson, *To the American Indian*; Hurtado, *Indian Survival*, 17.

5. Edward Castillo, "The Language of Race Hatred," in L. Bean, ed., *Ohlone*, 283; Milliken, *A Time of Little Choice*, 21, 130.

6. Hurtado, *Intimate Frontiers*, 88.

7. Old Spanish Archives, July 21, 1839, Book 9, 425–26, Monterey County Courthouse Recorder's Office; this and future references to Rancho la Purísima Concepción are from State of California Land Records, case no. 130 ND, exp. 119, CSA.

8. Milliken, *A Time of Little Choice*, 104; Culleton, *Indians and Pioneers of Old Monterey*, 130; Silliman, *Lost Laborers in Colonial California*, 73–74.

9. From all the following by Milliken: *Founding of Mission Dolores*, 14; *Indians Listed*; *A Time of Little Choice*.

10. Doyce B. Nunis Jr., "Alta California's Trojan Horse," in Gutiérrez and Orsi, eds., *Contested Eden*, 310; Hartnell, "General Inspector"; Bancroft, *History of California*, 4:56; Coronel, *Tales of Mexican California*, 21.

11. Alan Brown, "European Contact of 1772," in L. Bean, ed., *Ohlone*, 36.

12. Guerrero, *Anza Trail*, 208; Haas, *Conquests and Historical Identities*, 3, 15, 18.

13. Milliken, telephone conversation with the author, Feb. 14, 2005; Bouvier, *Women and the Conquest of California*, 120.

14. Milliken, *A Time of Little Choice*, 124–25; Bancroft, *History of California*, 1:722–23; Geiger, *Franciscan Missionaries*, 42.

15. Papers Relative to the Secularization of Mission Santa Clara, Apr. 15, 1833, CSA.

16. Shoup, *Inigo of Rancho Posolmi*, 99, 104–5; L. Garcia, *Santa Clara*, 14.

17. Old Spanish Archives, 9:435–36, Monterey County Courthouse Recorder's Office.

18. Nunis, "Alta California's Trojan Horse," in Gutiérrez and Orsi, eds., *Contested Eden*, 312.

19. McCarthy, *History of Mission San Jose*, 143; Phillips, *Indians and Indian Agents*, 28–29, and *Indians and Intruders in Central California*, 116; Cook, *Conflict*, 228; Davis, *Seventy-five Years*, 237.

20. Harlow, *California Conquered*, 295; Shoup, *Inigo of Rancho Posolmi*, 89; Mofras, *Travels on the Pacific Coast*, 1:254.

21. Old Spanish Archives, Monterey County Courthouse, Recorder's Office.

22. Fava, *Los Altos Hills*, 28; Rowland, "Circuit Rider."

23. Kroeber, *Handbook of the Indians of California*, 462; J. Mason, *Early Marin*, 123.

24. A. Brown, *Reconstructing Early Historical Landscapes*, 10; G. James, *In and Out of the Old Missions*, 222.

25. Monroy, *Thrown among Strangers*, 186–88; Rawls, *Indians of California*, 64; G. James, *In and Out of the Old Missions*, 293.

26. Elizabeth Jameson, "Where Have All the Young Men Gone?" in Owens, ed., *Riches for All*, 205.

27. Magliari, "Free Soil, Unfree Labor," 355; Hurtado, *Indian Survival*, 1, 14, 129.

28. Weeks, "Reminiscences," 92, BL.

CHAPTER 11. "HORSES, CATTLE, AND EVERYTHING TO DO WITH A RANCH"

1. Monroy, *Thrown among Strangers,* 122; Cleland, *From Wilderness to Empire,* 62; Bancroft, *History of California,* 3:318.

2. Santa Clara Mission Informes, 1777–1838, SCUA; Webb, *Indian Life at the Old Missions,* 57–58.

3. Davis, *Seventy-Five Years,* 233; Shoup, *Inigo of Rancho Posolmi,* 100.

4. Brown, "European Contact of 1772," in L. Bean, ed., *Ohlone,* 37.

5. Monroy, *Thrown among Strangers,* 154–55, 173, 176; Hackel, "Land, Labor, and Production," in Gutiérrez and Orsi, eds., *Contested Eden,* 130; see also Dallas, "The Hide and Tallow Trade"; White, *It's Your Misfortune,* 49.

6. Pueblo Papers Summaries, 4:149–50, 2:512, 5:717, HSJ.

7. Silliman, *Lost Laborers in Colonial California,* 24.

8. Phelps, *Alta California,* 293; Rolle, *California,* 266.

9. Bancroft, *History of California,* 4:406; Rolle, *California,* 127–28; G. Lyman, *John Marsh,* 251; Hague and Langum, *Thomas O. Larkin,* 13, 88.

10. Shoup, *Inigo of Rancho Posolmi,* 105; Hansen, *Search for Authority in California,* 17; Carlos Salomon, "Pio Pico at Mission San Luis Rey, 1835–40: A Study in Mission Administration," in Krieger, ed. *The Mission and the Community,* 89.

11. J. Mason, *Early Marin,* 123–27.

12. Corri Jimenez, e-mail to author, May 21, 2007; Alan Brown, historian, oral communication with the author, Mar. 13, 2006, and *Sawpits in the Redwoods,* 27 n.; Schuetz-Miller, *Building and Builders,* 127.

13. Lund and Gullard, *Life on the San Andreas Fault,* 32–34; A. Brown, *Sawpits in the Redwoods,* 5.

14. Weeks, "Reminiscences," 119; Burgess, "Lumbering in Hispanic California," 239.

15. San Francisco Documents, no. 136, BL; Leidesdorff file, SCP; Davis, *Seventy-five Years,* 376.

16. Dwinelle, *Colonial History of the City of San Francisco,* 57; Garr, "Planning, Politics, and Plunder."

17. Harlow, *California Conquered,* 289.

18. C. Lyman, *Around the Horn,* 248; Pierce, *Martin Murphy Family Saga,* 92; Gonzalez, "Searching for the Feathered Serpent," 103.

19. Hunt, *John Bidwell,* 149; Sucheng Chan, "A People of Exceptional Character," in Starr and Orsi, eds., *Rooted in Barbarous Soil,* 50.

20. G. James, *In and Out of the Old Missions,* 78; Ned Martin and Jody Martin, lecture with artifacts, SCP, Sept. 2, 2004.

21. Probate Court Records, Santa Clara County, Aug. 23, 1855, HSJ; P. Gates, *Land and Law in California,* 17; M. Gates, *Rancho Pastoria,* 17.

22. State of California Land Records, exp. 119, translation.

23. Older, "Adobes of the Peninsula."

24. Charles Nott, letter, Nov., Regnery Papers, PAHA; Linsley, "Real Local Pioneer," *Palo Alto Times*, Dec. 20, 1947.

25. Bowman, "Juana Briones de Miranda," 237; Fava collection, LAHM; see also Lyon, *Some More Pioneer Women of Santa Clara County*.

26. Burch, "Dona Maria of Two Adobes."

27. Jeffrey Burns, "Why Celebrate?" in Burns, ed., *Catholic San Francisco*, 2.

28. Engelhardt, *San Francisco or Mission Dolores*, 357.

29. Kennett, *Sherman*, 29; Hart, *Old Forts of the Far West*, 88; Shirley Ann Wilson Moore, "Do You Think I'll Lug Trunks?" in Owens, ed., *Riches for All*; M. Gates, *Rancho Pastoria*, 17.

30. James A. Sandos, "Because He Is a Liar and a Thief," in Starr and Orsi, eds., *Rooted in Barbarous Soil*, 103.

31. Starr, *Americans and the California Dream*, 67.

32. Taylor, *Eldorado*, 118; Kennett, *Sherman*, 47; Chan, "A People of Exceptional Character," in Starr and Orsi, eds., *Rooted in Barbarous Soil*, 50–56; W. Robinson, *Land in California*, 100.

33. Bowman, "Juana Briones de Miranda," Bowman communicated with Juana's grandson by mail, 238.

CHAPTER 12. FIRST GOLD, THEN LAND

1. Paul, *California Gold*, 171, 243; John Henry Brown, "A Yankee Trick," in Barker, ed., *San Francisco Memoirs*, 143.

2. Craven, *Coming of the Civil War*, 97–99, 110; Haas, *Conquests and Historical Identities*, 58; Magliari, "Free Soil, Unfree Labor."

3. White, *It's Your Misfortune*, 147.

4. Fallon, *Journal*, 78.

5. Simonds, *Starr King in California*, 65, 70–71; Peterson, "U.S. Sanitary Commission," 325–26.

6. Kennedy, *Contest for California in 1861*, 83–86; Cleland, *From Wilderness to Empire*, 199; Limerick, *Legacy of Conquest*, 46.

7. Bancroft, *History of California*, 4:236.

8. Langum, *Law and Community*, 268; Biggs, *Conquer and Colonize*, 29, 50, 56.

9. West, "Reconstructing Race," 8; White, *It's Your Misfortune*, 238; Monroy, *Thrown among Strangers*, 202.

10. Sherburne Cook, "Migration and Urbanization of the Indians in California," in Heizer and Whipple, eds., *California Indians*, 467; S. Cook, *Conflict between the California Indian and White Civilization*, 320; Monroy, *Thrown among Strangers*, 189; Clappe, *Shirley Letters*, 11.

11. James Rawls, introduction to Rawls and Orsi, eds., *A Golden State*, 5–7; Malcolm J. Rohrbough, "We Will Make Our fortunes, No Doubt of It," in Owens, ed., *Riches for All*, 56.

12. Rolle, *California*, 191.

13. Shipek, *Autobiography of Delfina Cuero*, 26; Lightfoot, *Indians, Missionaries, and Merchants*, 87, 193, 220–30; Arrigoni, "The First Decades of a New Era," 24–27.

14. Strong, "La Purísima Concepción"; Fava collection, *California Today* article, August 6, 1972, LAHM.

15. Andrew Galvan, e-mail to author, Dec. 22, 2004; Lisa M. Krieger, "Bringing Back a Lost Language," *San Jose Mercury News*, Dec. 21, 2004.

16. State of California Land Records, Purísima Ranch documents, case nos. 119 and 130 ND, CSA; Hoffman, *Reports of Land Cases*, 111.

17. Buelna ranch, map collection, SUSC; State of California Land Records, exp. 230, Feb. 23, 1841, CSA.

18. Taylor, *Eldorado*, 187; Joseph Mesa, "Orchard and Small Fruits Flourish," *Stanford Daily*, 1905, PAHA; Lisa Krieger, "Goodbye Ranch Era," *San Jose Mercury News*, Aug. 30, 2005.

19. Purísima, Map Drawer, SCUA.

20. Davis, *Seventy-five Years*, 325; W. Robinson, *Land in California*, 106; Eifler, "Taming the Wilderness Within," 200; Rolle, *California*, 238; White, *It's Your Misfortune*, 238; Gillis and Magliari, *John Bidwell*, 131.

21. Pierce, *Martin Murphy Family Saga*, 88, 141; Fava, *Los Altos Hills*, 49.

22. Ballard, "History of the Stanford Campus," chap. 3 notes; Hunt, oral history, PAHA.

23. Cleland, *Cattle on a Thousand Hills*, 157; Santa Clara County Tax Records, HSJ.

24. Scott, "Mayfield."

25. Original and translation of letter from Juana to Pablo, BHM; J. Mason, *Last Stage for Bolinas*, 59, 61; Paul, *California Gold*, 264, 268; Frank, Rand, and Agnoli, *Bolinas and Stinson Beach*, 53.

26. Lightfoot, *Indians, Missionaries, and Merchants*, 87; Monajo Elsworth, Palo Alto resident of Miranda Green, personal communication with the author, Mar. 31, 2004; M. Gates, *Rancho Pastoria*, 14; Suggs, *Archaeology of San Francisco*, 126; Eldredge, *Beginnings of San Francisco*, 2:514.

CHAPTER 13. THE LAWYER'S OFFICE

1. Older, "Adobes of the Peninsula."

2. *Ah* usage, Judy Yung, e-mail to the author, Aug. 16, 2005.

3. Murphy Family Papers, SCUA, collection of letters, receipts, interviews, land documents.

4. Pierce, *Martin Murphy Family Saga*, 112; Cleland, *From Wilderness to Empire*, 183; Hoexter, *From Canton to California*, 86.

5. *Mayfield Enterprise*, July 16, 1870; Tsu, "Independent of the Unskilled Chinaman," 476.

6. Hardwick, *Changes in Landscape*, 3; Rolle, *California*, 276; M. Kat Anderson, Michael G. Barbour, and Valerie Whitworth, "A World of Balance and Plenty," in Gutiérrez and Orsi, eds., *Contested Eden*, 15, 16; Cleland, *Cattle*, 232.

7. Payne, *Santa Clara County*, 69; Hunt, oral history, PAHA; Griffin and Young, *A Regional Geography*, 110; Pierce, *Martin Murphy Family Saga*, 75.

8. Randy Jensen, "Growing a Giant Pumpkin," *Palo Alto Daily News*, Oct. 10, 2004; M. Gates, *Rancho Pastoria*, 19; Mission Informes, 1777–1838, translations by Veronica Lococo and others unnamed, SCUA; McCarthy, *History of Mission San José*, 134.

9. Doten, *The Journals*, 1:380; Hittell quoted in Rolle, *California*, 276.

10. Lawrence James Jelinek, "Property of Every Kind: Ranching and Farming during the Gold-Rush Era," in Rawls and Orsi, eds., *A Golden State*, 237; Payne, *Santa Clara County*, 78–88.

11. Rose Briones, oral history, Marin County Library, California Room.

12. Fava, research collection 715.5, on subject of Rose Marie Hoffman Taaffe, LAHM; Fava, *Los Altos Hills*, 47; N. Sanchez, *Spanish Arcadia*, 67.

13. *Stanford Daily*, Nov. 25, 1905.

14. Sullivan, *Martin Murphy Jr.*, 6.

15. McKevitt, *University of Santa Clara*, 25, 28, 40; McKevitt, "Hispanic Californians and Catholic Higher Education," 328; Pierce, *Martin Murphy Family Saga*, 110.

16. Murphy Family Papers, oral transcription, Sullivan, file 60, SCUA; Garcia, *Santa Clara*, 49.

17. Fava, *Los Altos Hills*, 49; Murphy Family Papers, 995-032 F10, SCUA.

18. P. Gates, *Land and Law in California*, 17; Bureau of Land Management, case no. 137550, February 2, 1863.

19. Golobic, "Mayfield"; Strong, "Purísima Concepción"; J. Mason, *Early Marin*, 141; Lund and Gullard, *History of Palo Alto*, 30.

20. State of California Land Records, case no. 130 ND, CSA; Strong, "La Purísima Concepción," 2–3.

21. Santa Clara County Court Records, 266.

22. Murphy Family Papers, Nov. 17, 1870, SCUA.

23. Tracy, *Sausalito*, 12; Sandos, "Because He Is a Liar and a Thief," in Starr and Orsi, eds., *Rooted in Barbarous Soil*, 89; N. Sanchez, *Spanish Arcadia*, 136; Probate Court Records, Santa Clara County, Aug. 23, 1855, HSJ; *Tall Tree: Mayfield*, 1; Munro-Fraser, *Bolinas 1834–1880*, 23.

24. Ballard, "History of the Stanford Campus," chap. 3; Lund and Gullard, *History of Palo Alto*, 30.

25. As quoted in Pubolos, "Fathers of the Pueblo," 2.

26. Halleck Papers, HL; Patricia Loomis, "Halleck, a Genius at Building," *San Jose Mercury News*, Dec. 4, 1980; P. Gates, *Land and Law in California*, 140; Marszalek, *Commander of All Lincoln's Armies*, 30; Ambrose, *Halleck*, 3.

27. Halleck, Peachy, and Billings Papers, C-B 421, BL.

28. Hoffman, *Reports of Land Cases*, 112; State of California Land Records, case no. 130 ND, June 3, 1852, 7, CSA; Nott letter, Regnery Papers, PAHA.

29. Halleck Papers, Huntington Library; State of California Land Records, Miranda Grant, case no. 401 ND, CSA.

30. Ambrose, *Halleck*, 3; Dwinelle, *Colonial History of the City of San Francisco*, 54–55.

31. San Jose Hall of Records, District Court of the 3rd Judicial District of California for County of Santa Clara, see case information collected in Strong, "La Purísima Concepción."

32. Santa Clara County Book of Deeds 21, 583–84, Oct. 25, 1871.

33. Murphy Family Papers, SCUA.

34. Halleck, Peachy, and Billings Papers, C-B 421, May 9, 1853, BL.

35. Nativity Church marriage records, February 12, 1890.

36. *Palo Alto Times*, obituary, Dec. 21, 1920.

37. *Stanford Daily*, Feb. 9, 1937; Ridge, *Joaquin Murieta*, 19; G. Lyman, *John Marsh*, 326, 335; Brewer, *Up and Down California*, 154; Fava, *Los Altos Hills*, 38; Linsley, "Real Local Pioneer," *Palo Alto Times*, Dec. 20, 1947.

38. *Palo Alto Times*, Feb. 16, 1918.

39. Tax receipt, Murphy Family Papers, SCUA.

40. Rowland scrapbook, newspaper clipping, 223, UCSC.

CHAPTER 14. CARING FOR A GRANDSON, REMEMBERING A PRIEST

1. Kathy Bodovitz, "Palo Alto: Getting Started," in Gullixxon and Howton, eds., *Palo Alto*, 8; Beilharz, *Felipe de Neve*, 100; Willey, *Thirty Years in California*, 35–36; Fava, *Los Altos Hills*, 39; *Tall Tree: Mayfield*, 2.

2. *Tall Tree: Mayfield*, 1, 14–15; Sanborn Insurance Map, 1884, PAHA.

3. Ballard, "History of the Stanford Campus," 9–10; Shumate, *The California of George Gordon*, 100–119; Tutorow, *Leland Stanford*, 178.

4. Linsley, "Real Local Pioneer," *Palo Alto Times*, Dec. 20, 1947; C. Lyman, *Around the Horn*, 249.

5. *Tall Tree: Mayfield*, 20.

6. Thomes, *On Land and Sea*, 115, 271; American Association of University Women, *Gone Tomorrow?*

7. *Stanford Daily*, Feb. 9, 1937.

8. Henry Seale obituary, *Redwood City News*, Sept. 22, 1888; Byrne, oral history, LAHM 715.3; Tutorow, *Leland Stanford*, 178; Lund and Gullard, *History of Palo Alto*, 82.

9. D. Weber, *Spanish Frontier*, 343; Pepper, *Bolinas*, 8.

10. McWilliams, *North from Mexico*, 93.

11. *Tall Tree: Streets of Palo Alto*, 30; Probate Records, Santa Clara County

Hall of Records, 1221, register D, 172; Santa Clara County Book of Deeds, vol. 286, p. 73.

12. Thomes, *On Land and Sea,* 187; Bowman, "Juana Briones de Miranda"; Fava, *Los Altos Hills,* 39.

13. Catala testimony, AASF; Isaacson, *Benjamin Franklin,* 37; Bancroft, *History of California,* 2:600.

14. Winslow, *Palo Alto,* 23; B. Clark, ms., 3, PAHA; Sarah Wallis ms., Regnery Papers, PAHA; G. D. Greenan, oral history, March 6, 1970, PAHA.

15. Mesa files, PAHA.

16. Michael Svanevik and Shirley Burgett, "Royal Livestock," *Palo Alto Daily News,* Apr. 11, 2005; Fava, *Los Altos Hills,* 39.

17. Registered Voters, PAHA.

18. Limerick, *Something in the Soil,* 18; Bowman, "Juana Briones de Miranda"; Peterson, "Story of Stanford University," chap. 23.

BIBLIOGRAPHY

ARCHIVAL SOURCES

Ackerman, John D. Statement. Ms., 1901, CHS.

Alexander Taylor Collection. AASF, BL transcript.

Anonymous. Handwritten notes about Juana Briones, BHM.

Ballard, Roy Page. "History of the Stanford Campus." Ms. 127, 1994, SUSC.

Barnes, Joseph K. *Circular no. 4.* Washington, D.C.: U.S. War Department, Surgeon General's Office, 1870.

Bowman, J. N. "Index of Spanish-Mexican Private Land Grants." Ms., 2 vols. 1958, BL.

Briones, Rose. Oral history interview. Ms., July 29, 1977, Marin County Library, California Room.

Brown, Charles. "Statement of Recollections of Early Events in California." Ms., 1878, BL.

Buelna ranch. Map collection, SUSC.

Bureau of Land Management. Case no. 137550, February 2, 1863. Washington, D.C.

Byrne, Betty. Oral history. Ms., 1960, LAHM.

Catala, Magín de. Parishioners' testimony regarding sainthood, AASF.

Clark, Birge. Ms., PAHA.

Clark, William Squire. CD 245, BL.

Coronel, Antonio Franco. Oral history, 1877, BL.

Dauernheim, Ruth. Ms., 1979, BHM.

Departmental State Papers. San Jose.

Documentos, la historia de California. BL.

Documents, Early San Francisco. BL.

Farris, Glenn. "Fr. Luis Gil y Taboada: Misionero-enfermero of the California Missions." Feb. 19, 2000, revised Oct. 21, 2003, CMSA.

Fava, Florence. Research collection, LAHM.

Golobic, Robert C. "Mayfield: Its Development and the Annexation." Ms., 1957, PAHA.

Greenan, G. D. Oral history typescript, 1970, PAHA.

Halleck, William Henry. Papers, Huntington Library.

Halleck, Peachy, and Billings Papers. BL.

Hartnell, W. E. P. "General Inspector of Missions in Alta California in 1839–40: Diary and Blotters." Translated by Starr Gurcke. Ms., 1839–40, UCSC.

Hubbard, Anita Day. "Cities within the City." Newspaper file, Aug.–Nov. 1924, vol. 2, p. 210, CHS.

Hunt, Tom. Oral history typescript, Mar. 3, 2005, Juana Briones Heritage Foundation, PAHA.

Johnston, Robert B. "Jose Eusebio Boronda Adobe." Ms., 1998, Monterey County Historical Society.

Kimbro, Edna E., with Mary Ellen Ryan, Robert H. Jackson, Randall T. Milliken, and Norman Neuerburg. "Restoration Research: Santa Cruz Mission Adobe." Ms., undated, McPherson Center Archives, Santa Cruz, Calif.

Leidesdorff, William. File, SCP.

Lord, Lt. J. H. *Posts and Stations of Troops.* Government report, Jan. 1. Washington, D.C.: U.S. War Department, 1871.

May, Sam P. Letter, June 6, 1911, SCP.

Mesa files. PAHA.

Miramontes, Carmen. Ms. no. 757, SMCHS.

Mission Informes. 1777–1838, transcript, translations by Veronica Lococo and others unnamed, SCU.

Murphy Family Papers. SCUA.

Nott, Charles Palmer. Excerpts from letters. Regnery Papers, PAHA.

Old Spanish Archives. Monterey County Courthouse Recorder's Office, Salinas, Calif.

Older, Cora Fremont. "Life of Old Pioneer in Mayfield." *Palo Altan,* Feb. 8, 1918, PAHA.

———. "Adobes of the Peninsula." *Palo Alto Times,* Feb. 16, 1918, PAHA.

Papers Relative to the Secularization of Mission Santa Clara. Apr. 15, 1833, CSA, Sacramento.

Peterson, Harry C. "The Story of Stanford University." Ms., 1919, SUSC.

Probate Court Records, Santa Clara County. HSJ.

Probate Records. Santa Clara County Hall of Records, San Jose.

Provincial State Papers. BL.

Provincial State Papers. CSA, Sacramento.

Pueblo Papers Summaries. HSJ.

Purísima. Map Drawer, SCUA.

Registered voters. PAHA.

Riptides scrapbook. Nov. 18, 1949, CHS.

Rowland, Leon. Scrapbook and file note card collection, no. 145, UCSC.

San José Marriage Index. HSJ.

Sanborn Insurance Map. 1884, PAHA.

Santa Clara County Book of Deeds. Santa Clara County Hall of Records, San Jose.

Santa Clara County Court Records. Court case nos. 1 to 266. HSJ.

Santa Clara County Tax Records. HSJ.

Santa Clara Mission Informes. 1777–1838, SCUA.

Scott, T. B. "Mayfield." Ms., 1911, PAHA.

Spanish Documents. BL.

State of California Land Records. Case nos. 116, 119, 230, 269, 310, 401 ND (Northern District). CSA, Sacramento.

Stevens Collection. UCSC.

Strong, Jeanne Waters. "La Purísima Concepción: A History of Part of Juana Briones' Land." Ms., 1993, San Jose State University Library, California Room.

Sullivan, Sister Gabrielle. Oral history interview with Dan Murphy, Murphy Family Papers, SCUA.

Tall Tree. Booklet series, 1959–present, PAHA.

Thomes, William H. "California Life." Ms. C-D 319, 1884, BL.

Untitled ms. No. 757, SMCHS.

Vischer, Edward. Papers, BL.

Wallis, Sarah. Regnery Papers, PAHA.

Weeks, James. "Reminiscences." Ms., 1877, BL.

Williams, C. D. "Santa Cruz: A Peep into the Past." Comments on and translations of government documents, published from July 1876 to Aug. 1877, BL.

NEWSPAPERS

Contra Costa Gazette
Contra Costa Times
Mayfield Enterprise
Mayfield News
Mayfield Weekly Republican
Palo Alto Daily News
Palo Alto Times
Redwood City News
San Francisco Call and Post
San Francisco Chronicle
San Jose Mercury News
Stanford Daily

SECONDARY SOURCES

Abbey, James. *California: A Trip across the Plains*. New Albany, Ind.: Kent and Norman, 1850.

Alexander, James Beach, and James Lee Heig. *San Francisco*. San Francisco: Scottwall, 2002.

Amador, José María, and Lorenzo Asisara. *Californio Voices: The Oral Memoirs*. Translated and edited by Gregorio Torres. Denton: University of North Texas Press, 2005.

Ambrose, Stephen. *Halleck: Lincoln's Chief of Staff*. Baton Rouge: Louisiana State University Press, 1962.

———. *Nothing Like It in the World: The Men Who Built the Transcontinental Railroad*. New York: Simon and Schuster, 2000.

American Association of University Women. *Gone Tomorrow?* (booklet). Palo Alto, Calif.: American Association of University Women, 1986.

Anonymous. "Memorabilia." *CHSQ* (June 1946).

Arbuckle, Clyde. *History of San Jose*. San Jose, Calif.: Smith and McKay, 1985.

Archibald, Robert. *Economic Aspects of California Missions*. Washington, D.C: Academy of American Franciscan History, 1970.

Arrigoni, Aimee. "The First Decades of a New Era: The Native Americans of the East Bay after the Gold Rush." In *Bay Miwok* (conference papers). Martinez, Calif.: Contra Costa County Historical Society, 2003.

Bancroft, Hubert Howe. *California Pioneer Register and Index, 1542–1848*. 1884. Reprint. Baltimore: Regional, 1964.

———. *History of California*. 7 vols. San Francisco: San Francisco History Company, 1886.

Barker, Malcolm, ed. *San Francisco Memoirs 1835–1851*. San Francisco: Londonborn, 1994.

Bean, Lowell John, ed. *The Ohlone, Past and Present: Native Americans of the San Francisco Bay Region*. Menlo Park, Calif: Ballena Press, 1994.

Bean, Walton E. *California: An Interpretive History*. New York: McGraw-Hill, 1973.

Beebe, Rose Marie, and Robert M. Senkewicz, eds. *Lands of Promise and Despair*. Santa Clara and Berkeley: Santa Clara University and Heyday Books, 2001.

Beilharz, Edwin A. *Felipe de Neve: First Governor of California*. San Francisco: CHS, 1971.

Bernucci, Peg. "The History of the Villa de Branciforte." Master's thesis, San Jose State College, 1969.

Biggs, Donald C. *Conquer and Colonize: Stevenson's Regiment and California*. San Rafael, Calif.: Presidio Press, 1977.

Bolton, Herbert Eugene. *Fray Juan Crespi: Missionary Explorer*. 1927. Reprint. New York: AMS Press, 1971.

Boneu, F. *Gaspar de Portolá: Explorer and Founder of California.* Translated by Alan K. Brown. Madrid: Lerida, 1983.

Boule, Mary Null. *California's Heritage Mission San Antonio de Padua.* Vashon, Wash.: Merryant Publishers, 1988.

———. *Salinan Tribe.* Booklet no. 18 in the series California Native Indian Tribes. Vashon, Wash.: Merryant, 1992.

Bouvier, Virginia Marie. *Women and the Conquest of California, 1542–1840.* Tucson: University of Arizona Press, 2001.

Bowman, J. N. "Adobe Houses in the San Francisco Bay Counties." In *Geologic Guidebook of the San Francisco Bay Counties.* Sacramento: State of California Division of Mines, 1951.

———. "Juana Briones de Miranda." *HSSCQ* (Sept. 1957).

Brewer, William H. *Up and Down California in 1860–1864.* Berkeley and Los Angeles: University of California Press, 1966.

Brown, Alan K., trans. *Reconstructing Early Historical Landscapes in the Northern Santa Clara Valley.* Research Manuscript Series no. 11. Santa Clara, Calif.: Santa Clara University, 2005.

———. *Sawpits in the Redwoods.* Redwood City, Calif.: San Mateo County Historical Association, 1966.

Brown, John Henry. *Early Days of San Francisco, California.* 1886. Reprint. Oakland, Calif.: Biobooks, 1949.

Bryant, Edwin. *What I Saw in California.* Available at: http://www.author ama.com/what-i-saw-in-california-1.html. Accessed Sept. 18, 2006.

Burch, Glenn. "Dona Maria of Two Adobes." *CMSA Newsletter* (July 1993).

Burgess, Sherwood. "Lumbering in Hispanic California." *CHSQ* (winter 1962).

Burns, Jeffrey M., ed. *Catholic San Francisco: Sesquicentennial Essays.* Menlo Park, Calif.: Archdiocese of San Francisco, 2005.

Burns, John F., and Richard J. Orsi, eds. *Taming the Elephant: Politics, Government, and Law in Pioneer California.* Berkeley and Los Angeles: University of California Press, 2003.

Burton-Carvajal, Julianne, ed. *Monterey Mesa: Oldest Neighborhood in California.* Monterey: City of Monterey, 2002.

Camarillo, Albert. *Chicanos in a Changing Society: From Mexican Pueblos to American Barrios.* Cambridge, Mass.: Harvard University Press, 1979.

Campbell, Leon. "The First Californios: Presidial Society in Spanish California, 1769–1822." *JW* (Oct. 1972).

Castañeda, Antonia I. "Presidarias y Pobladoras: Spanish-Mexican Women in Frontier Monterey, Alta California, 1770–1821." Ph.D. diss., Stanford University, 1990.

Chaffin, Tom. *Pathfinder: John Charles Fremont and the Course of American Empire.* New York: Hill and Wang, 2002.

Chávez-Garcia, Miroslava. *Negotiating Conquest: Gender and Power in California, 1770s to 1880s.* Tucson: University of Arizona Press, 2004.

Clappe, Louise. *The Shirley Letters.* San Francisco: T. C. Russell, 1922.

Cleland, Robert Glass. *Cattle on a Thousand Hills: Southern California 1850–1870.* San Marino, Calif.: Huntington Library, 1941.

————. *From Wilderness to Empire: A History of California, 1542–1900.* New York: Knopf, 1944.

Collins, Helen. "The Miramontes Family." *Los Fundadores* (Jan.–Mar. 2004).

Cook, Sherburne F. *Conflict between the California Indian and White Civilization.* Berkeley and Los Angeles: University of California Press, 1976.

Coronel, Antonio Franco. *Tales of Mexican California.* Translated by Diane de Avalle-Arce. Santa Barbara, Calif.: Bellerophon, 1994.

Craven, Avery. *Coming of the Civil War.* Chicago: University of Chicago Press, 1957.

Crespi, Juan. *A Description of Distant Roads: Original Journals of the First Expedition into California, 1769–1770.* Edited and translated by Alan K. Brown. San Diego: San Diego State University Press, 2001.

Crouch, Dora, Daniel Garr, and Axel Mundigo. *Spanish City Planning in North America.* Cambridge, Mass.: MIT Press, 1982.

Culleton, James. *Indians and Pioneers of Old Monterey.* Fresno, Calif.: Academy of California Church History, 1950.

Dallas, Sherman F. "The Hide and Tallow Trade in Alta California." Ph.D. diss., Indiana University, 1955.

Dana, Richard Henry, Jr. *Two Years before the Mast, with Journals and Letters.* 2 vols. Los Angeles: Ward Ritchie Press, 1964.

Davis, Clark, and David Igler, eds. *The Human Tradition in California.* Lanham, Md.: Rowman and Littlefield, 2002.

Davis, William Heath. *Seventy-five Years in California.* San Francisco: Howell, 1929.

De Neve, Don, and Noel Moholy. *Junipero Serra: The Illustrated Story.* San Francisco: Harper and Row, 1985.

Denis, Alberta Johnston. *Spanish Alta California.* New York: Macmillan, 1927.

DeVoto, Bernard, ed. *The Journals of Lewis and Clark.* Boston: Houghton Mifflin, 1953.

Doten, Alfred. *The Journals, 1849–1903.* 3 vols. Edited by Walter Van Tilburg Clark. Reno: University of Nevada Press, 1973.

Downey, Joseph T. *The Cruise of the Portsmouth: A Doctor's View.* Edited by Howard R. Lamar. New Haven, Conn.: Yale University Press, 1958.

"Duhaut-Cilly's Account of California in the Years 1827–1828." Translated by Charles F. Carter. *HSSCQ* (June 1929).

Dwinelle, John W. *The Colonial History of the City of San Francisco.* 1863. Reprint. San Diego: Frye and Smith, 1924.

Eifler, Mark A. "Taming the Wilderness Within." *CH* (winter 2000).

Eldredge, Zoeth Skinner. *The Beginnings of San Francisco.* 2 vols. San Francisco: Eldredge, 1912.

———. *History of California.* Vol. 1. New York: Century History, 1915.

Engelhardt, Zephyrin. *Mission San Antonio de Padua.* Santa Barbara, Calif.: Schauer, 1929.

———. *Mission San Carlos Borromeo.* 1934. Reprint. Ramona, Calif.: Ballena Press, 1973.

———. *Mission San Luis Obispo.* 2d ed. Santa Barbara, Calif.: Genns, 1963.

———. *San Diego Mission.* San Francisco: Barry, 1920.

———. *San Francisco or Mission Dolores.* Chicago: Franciscan Herald Press, 1924.

———. *San Miguel, Archangel: The Mission on the Highway.* Ramona, Calif: Acoma Books, 1971.

Fallon, Thomas. *Journal of a California Cavalier.* Edited by Thomas McEnery. San Jose, Calif.: Inishfallen Enterprises, 1978.

Farris, Glenn, and Rose-Marie Beebe, trans. *Report of a Visit to Fort Ross and Bodega Bay in April 1833 by Mariano Vallejo.* With notes. Occasional Paper no. 4. Santa Clara, Calif.: CMSA, 2000.

Fava, Florence. *Los Altos Hills.* Woodside, Calif.: Gilbert Richards, 1979.

Ford, Tirey. *Dawn and the Dons: The Romance of Monterey.* San Francisco: Robertson, 1926.

Foucrier, Annick. "Sailors, Carpenters, Vineyardists." *SCCHJ,* no. 3 (1997).

Frank, Phil, Kendrick Rand, and Tamae Agnoli. *Bolinas and Stinson Beach.* San Francisco: Arcadia, 2004.

Garate, Donald T. *Juan Bautista de Anza: Basque Explorer in the New World 1693–1740.* Reno: University of Nevada Press, 2003.

Garcia, Lorie. *Santa Clara: From Mission to Municipality.* Research Manuscript Series no. 8. Santa Clara, Calif.: Santa Clara University, 1997.

García Diego y Moreno, Francisco. *The Writings of Francisco Garcia Diego y Moreno, Obispo de Ambas Californias.* Translated and edited by Francis J. Weber. Mission Hills, Calif: Archdiocese of Los Angeles, 1976.

Garner, William Robert. *Letters from California 1846–1847.* Edited by Donald Munro Craig. Berkeley and Los Angeles: University of California Press, 1970.

Garr, Daniel J. "Planning, Politics, and Plunder." *SCHSQ* (winter 1972).

———. "Power and Priorities: Church-State Boundary Disputes in Spanish California." *CH* (winter 1978–79).

Gates, Mary J. *Rancho Pastoria de las Borregas.* San Jose, Calif.: Cottle and Murgotten, 1895.

Gates, Paul W. *Land and Law in California.* Iowa City: Iowa University Press, 1991.

Geiger, Maynard. *Franciscan Missionaries in Hispanic California 1769–1848: A Biographical Dictionary.* San Marino, Calif.: Huntington Library, 1969.

Gillis, Michael J., and Michael F. Magliari. *John Bidwell and California: The Life and Writings of a Pioneer.* Spokane, Wash.: Clark, 2003.

Gonzalez, Michael J. "Searching for the Feathered Serpent: Exploring the Origins of Mexican Culture in Los Angeles, 1830–1850." Ph.D. diss., University of California at Berkeley, 1992.

Goodwin, Cardinal. *The Establishment of State Government in California, 1846–1850.* New York: Macmillan, 1914.

Greening, Eric. "A Musical Day of Times Past at the Old Mission San Antonio de Padua." New World Baroque Orchestra program notes, Apr. 28, 2002.

Greenwood, Robert. *The California Outlaw.* Los Gatos, Calif.: Talisman Press, 1960.

Griffin, Paul F., and Robert N. Young. *A Regional Geography: California, the New Empire State.* San Francisco: Fearon, 1957.

Guerrero, Vladimir. *The Anza Trail and the Settling of California.* Santa Clara and Berkeley, Calif.: Santa Clara University and Heyday Books, 2006.

Guest, Florian. "Cultural Perspectives on California Mission Life." *HSSCQ* (spring 1983).

———. "The Establishment of the Villa de Branciforte." *CHSQ* (spring 1962).

———. "Municipal Government in Spanish California." *CHSQ* (winter 1967).

Guest, Francis F. *Fermín Francisco de Lasuen, 1736–1803: A Biography.* Washington, D.C: Academy of American Franciscan History, 1973.

Gullard, Pamela, and Nancy Lund. *History of Palo Alto: The Early Years.* San Francisco: Scottwall, 1989.

Gullett, Gayle. *Becoming Citizens: The Emergence and Development of the California Women's Movement, 1880–1911.* Chicago: Univ. of Illinois Press, 2000.

Gullixxon, Paul, and Elizabeth Howton, eds. *Palo Alto: The First Hundred Years.* Palo Alto, Calif.: Palo Alto Weekly, 1994.

Gurcke, Starr, trans. "Some Early Spanish Documents: Excerpts from the W. B. Stevens Collection and the Branciforte Archives." In *Branciforte,* special issue of *SCCHJ,* no. 3 (1997).

Gutiérrez, Ramón A., and Richard J. Orsi, eds. *Contested Eden: California before the Gold Rush.* Berkeley and Los Angeles: CHS and University of California Press, 1997.

Haas, Lisbeth. *Conquests and Historical Identities in California, 1769–1936.* Berkeley and Los Angeles: University of California Press, 1991.

Hague, Harlan, and David J. Langum. *Thomas O. Larkin: A Life of Patriotism and Profit in Old California.* Norman: University of Oklahoma Press, 1990.

Hansen, Woodrow J. *The Search for Authority in California.* Oakland, Calif.: Biobooks, 1960.

Hardwick, Michael R. *Changes in Landscape: The Beginnings of Horticulture in the California Missions.* 2d ed. Orange, Calif.: Paragon Agency, 2005.

Harlow, Neal. *California Conquered: War and Peace of the Pacific 1846–1850.* Berkeley and Los Angeles: University of California Press, 1982.

Hart, Herbert M. *Old Forts of the Far West.* Seattle: Superior, 1965.

Heinsen, Val. *Mission San Antonio de Padua Herbs.* Booklet no. 15. N.p.: n.p., n.d.

Heizer, Robert F., ed. *The Destruction of California Indians.* Santa Barbara, Calif.: Peregrine Smith, 1974.

Heizer, Robert F., and Albert B. Elsasser. *The Natural World of the California Indians.* Berkeley and Los Angeles: University of California Press, 1980.

Heizer, Robert F., and Mary Anne Whipple, eds. *The California Indians: A Source Book.* 2d ed. Berkeley and Los Angeles: University of California Press, 1971.

History of Marin County. San Francisco: Alley, Bowen, 1880.

History of Santa Clara County. San Francisco: Alley, Bowen, 1881.

Hittell, John. *History of San Francisco and Incidentally of California.* San Francisco: Bancroft, 1878.

Hittell, Theodore. *History of California.* Vol. 1. San Francisco: Stone, 1898.

Hoexter, Corinne K. *From Canton to California.* New York: Four Winds Press, 1976.

Hoff, Brent H., and Carter Smith III. *Mapping Epidemics: A Historical Atlas of Disease.* New York: Four Winds Press, 1976.

Hoffman, Ogden. *Reports of Land Cases Determined in the United States District Court for the Northern District of California.* San Francisco: Nuna Hubert, 1862.

Holliday, J. S. *The World Rushed In.* New York: Simon and Schuster, 1981.

Holtzclaw, Jeanne. "The Robles Family in California." *Santa Clara County Historical and Genealogical Society Quarterly* (Oct. 6, 1979).

Hough, Granville W., and N. C. Hough. *Spain's California Patriots in Its 1779–1783 War with England.* Laguna Hills, Calif.: Hough Press, 1998.

Hunt, Rockwell D. *California in the Making.* Caldwell, Idaho: Caxton, 1953.

————. *John Bidwell.* Caldwell, Idaho: Caxton, 1942.

Hurtado, Albert L. "Indians of California." *CH* (fall 1992).

————. *Indian Survival on the California Frontier.* New Haven, Conn.: Yale University Press, 1988.

————. *Intimate Frontiers: Sex, Gender, and Culture in Old California.* Albuquerque: University of New Mexico Press, 1999.

Hussey, John Adam. "New Light upon Talbot H. Green." *CHSQ* (Mar. 1949).

Hynding, Alan. *From Frontier to Suburb: The Story of the San Mateo Peninsula.* Belmont, Calif.: Star, 1982.

Isaacson, Walter. *Benjamin Franklin: An American Life.* New York: Simon and Schuster, 2003.

James, Edward T., ed. *Notable American Women, 1607–1950.* Cambridge, Mass.: Belknap Press of Harvard University Press, 1971.

James, George Wharton. *In and Out of the Old Missions.* Boston: Little, Brown, 1910.

Jensen, Rosa McKay. "Romance of the Ranchos." *Peninsula Life* (Dec. 1948).

Jones, Oakah L., Jr. *Los Paisanos: Spanish Settlers on the Northern Frontier.* Norman: University of Oklahoma Press, 1979.

Keller, Frances Richardson, ed. *Views of Women's Lives in Western Tradition.* Lewiston, N.Y.: Edwin Mellen Press, 1990.

Kennedy, Elijah. *The Contest for California in 1861.* Boston: Houghton Mifflin, 1912.

Kennett, Lee B. *Sherman: A Soldier's Life.* New York: HarperCollins, 2001.

Krieger, Dan, ed. *The Mission and the Community.* CMSA proceedings. Santa Clara, Calif.: CMSA, 2004.

Kroeber, A. L. *Handbook of the Indians of California.* New York: Dover, 1976.

Langdon-Davies, John. *Carlos: The King Who Would Not Die.* Englewood Cliffs, N.J.: Prentice-Hall, 1962.

Langellier, John Phillip, and Daniel Rosen. *El Presidio de San Francisco: A History under Spain and Mexico, 1776–1846.* Spokane, Wash.: Arthur Clark, 1996.

Langum, David J. *Law and Community on the Mexican California Frontier 1821–1846.* Norman: University of Oklahoma Press, 1987. 2d ed., San Diego: *LCA,* 2006.

Levy, Joan, and Shirley Drye. "Legacy of Francisco Sanchez." *La Peninsula* 32, no. 2 (fall–winter 2000).

Lewis, Oscar, and Donald De Nevi, eds. *Sketches of Early California: A Collection of Personal Adventures.* San Francisco: Chronicle, 1971.

Lightfoot, Kent. *Indians, Missionaries, and Merchants.* Berkeley and Los Angeles: University of California Press, 2004.

Limerick, Patricia Nelson. *The Legacy of Conquest: The Unbroken Past of the American West.* New York: Norton, 1988.

——. *Something in the Soil.* New York: Norton, 2000.

Lund, Nancy, and Pamela Gullard. *History of Palo Alto: The Early Years.* San Francisco: Scotwall, 1989.

——. *Life on the San Andreas Fault: A History of Portola Valley.* San Francisco: Scotwall, 2003.

Lyman, Chester S. *Around the Horn to the Sandwich Islands and California 1845–1850.* New Haven, Conn.: Yale University Press, 1924.

Lyman, George D. *John Marsh, Pioneer.* New York: Scribner, 1933.

Lyon, Mary Lou. *Some More Pioneer Women of Santa Clara County.* Vol. 2. Cupertino, Calif.: Grandma Lyon Enterprises, 1999.

Macleod, William Christie. *The American Indian Frontier.* New York: Knopf, 1928.

Magliari, Michael. "Free Soil, Unfree Labor: Cave Johnson Couts and the Binding of Indian Workers in California, 1850–1867." *PHR* (Aug. 2004).

Manocchio, Regina Teresa. "Tending Communities, Crossing Cultures: Midwives in Nineteenth-Century California." Master's thesis, Yale University School of Nursing, 1998.

Margolin, Malcolm, ed. *The Way We Lived: California Indian Reminiscences.* Berkeley, Calif.: Heyday Books, 1981.

Marszalek, John F. *Commander of All Lincoln's Armies: A Life of General Henry W. Halleck.* Cambridge, Mass.: Harvard University Press, 2004.

Mason, Jack. *Early Marin.* Inverness, Calif.: North Shore Books, Marin County Historical Society, 1971.

———. *Last Stage for Bolinas.* Inverness, Calif.: North Shore Books, 1973.

Mason, William. "Adobe Interiors in Spanish California." *HSSCQ* (fall 1998).

———. *Census of 1790.* Menlo Park, Calif.: Ballena, 1998.

McCarthy, Francis Florence. *History of Mission San Jose California 1797–1835.* Fresno, Calif.: Academy Library Guild, 1958.

McGrath, Roger. "Taming the Elephant." *CH* (fall 2003).

McKevitt, Gerald. "Hispanic Californians and Catholic Higher Education." *CH* (winter 1990–91).

———. *University of Santa Clara.* Stanford, Calif.: Stanford University Press, 1979.

McWilliams, Carey. *North from Mexico: Spanish Speaking People of the United States.* Philadelphia: Lippincott, 1949.

Merriam, C. Hart. *Studies of California Indians.* Edited by the staff of the Department of Anthropology, University of California at Berkeley. Berkeley: University of California, 1955.

Miller, Robert Ryal. *Captain Richardson: Mariner, Ranchero, and Founder of San Francisco.* Berkeley, Calif.: La Loma Press, 1995.

———. *Juan Alvarado, Governor of California 1836–1842.* Norman: University of Oklahoma Press, 1998.

Milliken, Randall. *Founding of Mission Dolores and the End of Tribal Life* (booklet). Santa Clara, Calif: California Mission Studies Association, Feb. 1996.

———. *Indians Listed in Mission Santa Clara Baptismal Register 1777 to 1849.* Database. San Jose: Santa Clara County Transportation Agency, 1995.

———. *A Time of Little Choice: The Disintegration of Tribal Culture in the San Francisco Bay Area, 1769–1810.* Menlo Park, Calif.: Ballena Press, 1995.

Miranda, Gloria. "Gente de Razón Marriage Patterns." *HSSCQ* (spring 1981).

———. "Hispano-Mexican Childrearing Practices in Pre-American Santa Barbara." *HSSCQ* (winter 1983).

Mofras, Duflot de. *Travels on the Pacific Coast.* 2 vols. Translated and edited by Marguerite Wilbur. Santa Ana, Calif.: Fine Arts Press, 1937.

Monroy, Douglas. *Thrown among Strangers: The Making of Mexican Culture in Frontier California.* Berkeley and Los Angeles: University of California Press, 1990.

Morrall, June. *Half Moon Bay Memories.* Half Moon Bay, Calif.: Moonbeam Press, 1978.

Munro-Fraser, J. P. *Bolinas 1834–1880* (booklet). 1880. Reprint. Bolinas, Calif.: Bolinas Museum, 1990.

———. *History of Contra Costa County.* 1882. Reprint. Oakland, Calif.: Brooks-Sterling, 1974.

Mutnick, Dorothy. *Some Alta California Pioneers.* 3 vols. Lafayette, Calif.: Past Time, 1982.

Norris, Robert M., and Robert W. Webb. *Geology of California.* 2d ed. New York: John Wiley and Sons, 1990.

Northrop, Marie. *Spanish-Mexican Families of Early California: 1769–1850.* 2 vols. Burbank: Southern California Genealogical Society, 1987.

Older, Cora Fremont. *California Missions and Their Romances.* New York: Coward-McCann, 1938.

Osio, Antonio María. *The History of Alta California: A Memoir.* Translated by Rose Marie Beebe and Robert M. Senkewicz. Madison: University of Wisconsin Press, 1996.

Owens, Kenneth, ed. *Riches for All: The California Gold Rush and the World.* Lincoln: University of Nebraska Press, 2002.

Paddison, Joshua, ed. *A World Transformed: Firsthand Accounts of California before the Gold Rush.* Berkeley, Calif.: Heyday Books, 1999.

Palou, Francisco. *Historical Memoirs of New California.* 4 vols. Edited and translated by Herbert Eugene Bolton. Berkeley: Univ. of California, 1926.

Paul, Rodman W. *California Gold: The Beginning of Mining in the Far West.* Cambridge, Mass.: Harvard University Press, 1947.

Payne, Stephen M. *Santa Clara County: Harvest of Change.* Northridge, Calif.: Windsor, 1987.

Pepper, Marin W. *Bolinas: A Narrative of the Days of the Dons.* New York: Vantage, 1965.

Perrone, Bobette, H. Henrietta Stockel, and Victoria Kruege. *Medicine Women, Curanderas, and Women Doctors.* Norman: University of Oklahoma Press, 1989.

Peterson, Harry C. "The Remarkable Story of Juana Briones." *San Francisco Call and Post,* Feb. 7, 1919.

Peterson, Richard H. "U.S. Sanitary Commission." *CH* (winter 1993–94).

Phelps, Robert. "On Comic Opera Revolutions: Maneuver Theory and the Art of War in Mexican California, 1821–45." *CH* (fall 2006).

Phelps, William Dane. *Alta California 1840–1842: The Journal and Observations of Master of the Ship "Alert."* Edited by Briton Cooper Busch. Glendale, Calif.: Clark, 1983.

Phillips, George Harwood. *Indians and Indian Agents: The Origins of the Reservation System in California, 1849–1852.* Norman: University of Oklahoma Press, 1997.

———. *Indians and Intruders in Central California, 1769–1849.* Norman: University of Oklahoma Press, 1993.

Pico, María Inocenta de Avila. *Cosas de California.* Translated by Rudecinda Lo Buglio. San Diego: *LCA,* 2002.

Pierce, Marjorie. *The Martin Murphy Family Saga.* Cupertino: California History Center, 2000.

Piña, Román. *Catalanes y Mallorquines en la fundación de California.* Barcelona, Spain: Editorial Laia, 1988.

Pokriots, Marion. "Josefa Buelna's Memories of Spanish Santa Cruz." *SCCHJ,* no. 3 (1997).

Pritchard, Diane Spencer. "Joint Tenants of the Frontier: Russian/Hispanic Interactions in Alta California, 1812–1841." *Californians* (Mar.–Apr. 1992).

Pubols, Louise. "Fathers of the Pueblo." Lecture. Available at the Autry Museum Web site, http://www.autry-museum.org. Accessed Oct. 30, 2001.

Rawls, James J. *Indians of California: The Changing Image.* Norman: University of Oklahoma Press, 1984.

Rawls, James J., and Richard Orsi, eds. *A Golden State: Mining and Economic Development in Gold Rush California.* Berkeley and Los Angeles: University of California Press, 1998–99.

Reader, Phil. "History of the Villa de Branciforte." *SCCHJ,* no. 3 (1997).

Ridge, John Rollin. *The Life and Adventures of Joaquin Murieta, the Celebrated California Bandit.* Norman: University of Oklahoma Press, 1955.

Robinson, Alfred. *Life in California.* 1846. Reprint. San Francisco: Doxey, 1891.

Robinson, W. W. *Land in California: The Story of Mission Lands, Ranchos, Squatters, Mining Claims, Railroad Grants, Land Scrip, Homesteads.* 1949. Reprint. Berkeley and Los Angeles: University of California Press, 1979.

Rojas, Arnold R. "Who Were the Vaqueros?" *Californians* (Nov.–Dec. 1992).

Rolle, Andrew. *California: A History.* Arlington Heights, Ill.: Davidson, 1987.

Rowland, Leon F. "Circuit Rider." *SCCHJ,* no. 3 (1997).

———. *Santa Cruz: The Early Years.* Santa Cruz, Calif.: Paper Vision Press, 1980.

Rowland, Leon, and Starr Gurcke, eds. *Branciforte.* Special issue of *SCCHJ,* no. 3 (1997).

Royce, Josiah, *California: From the Conquest in 1846 to the Second Vigilance Committee in San Francisco.* Boston: Houghton Mifflin, 1897.

Sanchez, Joseph P. *Spanish Bluecoats: The Catalonian Volunteers in North-western New Spain 1767–1810.* Albuquerque: University of New Mexico Press, 1990.

Sanchez, Nellie Van de Grift. *Spanish Arcadia.* San Francisco: Powell, 1929.

Sandos, James A. *Converting California: Indians and Franciscans in the Missions.* New Haven, Conn.: Yale University Press, 2004.

———. "Identity through Music: Indian Choristers at Mission San Gabriel, 1771–1791." Paper presented at the conference "Alta California: People in Motion, Identities in Formation, 1769–1850." Huntington Library, Sept. 29, 2006.

Sawyer, Eugene T. *History of Santa Clara County.* Los Angeles: Historic Record Company, 1922.

Schuetz-Miller, Mardith K. *Building and Builders in Hispanic California 1769–1850.* Tucson, Ariz.: Southwestern Mission Research Center, 1994.

Schwartz, Stephen. *From West to East: California and the Making of the American Mind.* New York: Free Press, 1998.

Serra, Junipero. *Writings of Junipero Serra.* 4 vols. Edited by Antonine Tibesar. Washington, D.C.: Academy of American Franciscan History, 1955.

Sherman, William Tecumseh. *Memoirs.* Vol. 1 of 2. New York: Appleton, 1875.

Shinn, Charles Howard. "Californiana." *Century Magazine* (Jan. 1883; Jan. 1891).

Shipek, Florence. *The Autobiography of Delfina Cuero, a Diegueno Indian.* Los Angeles: Dawson, 1968.

Shoup, Laurence, with Randall Milliken and Alan K. Brown. *Inigo of Rancho Posolmi: The Life and Times of a Mission Indian and His Land.* Novato, Calif.: Ballena Press, 1999.

Shumate, Albert. *The California of George Gordon and the 1849 Sea Voyages.* Glendale, Calif.: Clark, 1976.

Shutes, Milton H. "Henry Wager Halleck: Lincoln's Chief-of-Staff." *CHSQ* (Sept. 1937).

Silliman, Stephen W. *Lost Laborers in Colonial California.* Tucson: University of Arizona Press, 2004.

Simonds, William Day. *Starr King in California.* San Francisco: P. Elder, 1917.

Skowronek, Russell K. *Identifying the First Pueblo de San Jose de Guadalupe: Some Archaeological, Historical, and Geographical Considerations.* CMSA Occasional Paper no. 2. Santa Clara, Calif.: CMSA, Feb. 1999.

Smith, Frances Rand. *Mission of San Antonio de Padua.* Stanford, Calif.: Stanford University Press, 1932.

Soule, Frank, John H. Gihon, and James Nisbet. *Annals of San Francisco.* New York: Appleton, 1855.

Sprietsma, Leo. *Mission San Antonio de Padua, Part One: The Mission Period 1771–1835.* Jolon, Calif.: Mission San Antonio, 1988.

Stanger, Frank M. *Sawmills in the Redwoods: Logging on the San Francisco Peninsula, 1849–1967.* Redwood City, Calif.: San Mateo County Historical Association, 1967.

Starr, Kevin. *Americans and the California Dream 1850–1915.* Santa Barbara, Calif., and Salt Lake City, Utah: Smith, 1981.

Starr, Kevin, and Richard J. Orsi, eds. *Rooted in Barbarous Soil: People, Culture, and Community in Gold Rush California.* Berkeley and Los Angeles: University of California Press, 2000.

Stellman, Louis J. *Sam Brannan: Builder of San Francisco.* New York: Exposition, 1953.

Suggs, Robert C. *The Archaeology of San Francisco.* New York: Crowell, 1965.

Sullivan, Gabrielle. *Martin Murphy Jr: California Pioneer 1844–1884.* Stockton, Calif.: Center for Western Historical Studies, University of the Pacific, 1974.

Summers, William John. "California Mission Music." Available at the CMSA Web site, http://www.ca-missions.org. Updated Feb. 9, 2002.

Taylor, Bayard. *Eldorado: Adventures in the Path of Empire.* 1850. Reprint. Santa Clara, Calif.: Santa Clara University, Heyday Books, 2000.

Tays, George. "Mariano Guadalupe Vallejo and Sonoma." *CHSQ* (Sept. 1937).

Thomes, William H. *On Land and Sea.* 1884. Reprint. Upper Saddle River, N.J.: Literature House, 1970.

Thompson, Erwin N. *Forest at the Presidio: A Cultural Resource.* Architectural Resources Report. Golden, Colo.: Architectural Resources, 1994.

Thompson, Lucy. *To the American Indian: Reminiscences of a Yurok Woman.* 1916. Reprint, edited by Peter Palmquist. Berkeley, Calif.: Heyday Books, 1991.

Torchiana, Henry Albert. *Story of the Mission Santa Cruz.* San Francisco: Elder, 1933.

Tracy, Jack. *Sausalito: Moments in Time.* Edited by Wayne Bonnett. Sausalito, Calif.: Wingate, 1983.

Tsu, Cecilia. "'Independent of the Unskilled Chinaman': Race, Labor, and Family Farming in California's Santa Clara Valley." *WHQ* (winter 2006).

Tutorow, Norman E. *Leland Stanford: Man of Many Careers.* Menlo Park, Calif.: Pacific Coast, 1971.

Twinam, Ann. *Public Lives, Private Secrets: Gender, Honor, Sexuality, and Illegitimacy in Colonial Spanish America.* Stanford, Calif.: Stanford University Press, 1999.

Tyson, James L. *Diary of a Physician in California.* 1850. Reprint. Oakland, Calif.: Biobooks, 1955.

Ulrich, Laurel Thatcher. *A Midwife's Tale: The Life of Martha Ballard, Based on Her Diary, 1785–1812.* New York: Random House, 1990.

Voss, Barbara Lois. "Archaeology of el Presidio de San Francisco: Culture Contact, Gender, and Ethnicity in a Spanish-Colonial Military Community." Ph.D. diss., University of California at Berkeley, 2002.

————. *Tennessee Hollow Watershed Archaeology Project.* Preliminary Report. Washington, D.C., and San Francisco: U.S. National Park Service, Presidio of San Francisco, Oct. 2004.

Wagner, Henry Raup. "The Last Spanish Exploration of the Northwest Coast and the Attempt to Colonize Bodega Bay." *CHSQ* (winter 1932).

Wall, Rosalind Sharpe. *When the Coast Was Wild and Lonely: Early Settlers of the Sur.* Pacific Grove, Calif.: Boxwood, 1987.

Warren, Viola Lockhart. "Medical Quacks and Heroes of Early California." *HSSCQ* (June 1959).

Webb, Edith. *Indian Life at the Old Missions.* Los Angeles: W. F. Lewis, 1952.

Weber, David J. *The Spanish Frontier in North America.* New Haven, Conn.: Yale University Press, 1992.

West, Elliott. "Reconstructing Race." *WHQ* (spring 2003).

White, Richard. *It's Your Misfortune and None of My Own: A New History of the American West.* Norman: University of Oklahoma Press, 1991.

Whitehead, Richard S. "Alta California's Four Fortresses." *HSSCQ* (spring 1983).

Willey, D. D. *Thirty Years in California.* San Francisco: Bancroft, 1879.

Williams, Jack S. "Vidas Perdidas: Forgotten Lives of the Women of the San Diego Presidio: Archaeological, Cultural, and Historical Perspectives on Alta California." Paper presented at the CMSA conference, San Diego, 2003.

Winslow, Ward. *Palo Alto: A Centennial History.* Palo Alto, Calif.: Palo Alto Historical Association, 1993.

Wrightington, Juana Machado Alipáz de. "Times Gone By in Alta California: Recollections of Machado." Translated by Raymond S. Brandes. *HSSCQ* (Sept. 1959).

ILLUSTRATION CREDITS

ABBEY, SHANNON

Juana's world. Map by Shannon Abbey.

THE BANCROFT LIBRARY,
UNIVERSITY OF CALIFORNIA, BERKELEY

Ojo de Agua de Figueroa map.
The Presidio of San Francisco and Polin Spring. Drawing by Edward Vischer.
The Pueblo of San Jose and nearby fields.
Yerba Buena Cove. Drawing by Daniel Wadsworth Coit.

BERTHIAUME, DENNY

San Francisco, ca. 1850. Lithograph by Louis Le Breton.

BOLINAS MUSEUM

Gregorio Briones.
Pablo Briones.
Chinese chest. Photograph by Elia Haworth.

CORBIS

Mission Dolores, ca. 1860. © Corbis.

DENNIS, REID W.

Juana's house at North Beach. Painting by Frederick Tobin.

MIRAMONTES, ERNIE

The Miramontes family.

NATIONAL ARCHIVES AND RECORDS ADMINISTRATION, COLLEGE PARK, MARYLAND

Map of Rancho la Purísima Concepción. California Private Land Claims, Board of Land Commissioners, Copies of Diseños, Number 119, from the Records of the Bureau of Land Management, Record Group 49.

PALO ALTO HISTORICAL ASSOCIATION

Encajonado, Juana's ranch house.
Juana's neighborhood in Mayfield in 1887.
Mayfield circa 1890.
Mayfield's second school.
Harvesting redwoods.
El Palo Alto in 1875.
Pile of stones at Juana's house, ca. 1890.

POINT REYES NATIONAL SEASHORE MUSEUM

Juana Briones.

SAN FRANCISCO HISTORY CENTER, SAN FRANCISCO PUBLIC LIBRARY

La Playa de Juana Briones.

SANTA CLARA UNIVERSITY ARCHIVES

A military bounty land warrant. Murphy Family Papers.
Rancho la Purísima Concepción survey, ca. 1855.

UNIVERSITY OF SOUTHERN CALIFORNIA, SPECIAL COLLECTIONS

Mission San Antonio de Padua southeast of Monterey, ca. 1884.

VOSS, BARBARA L.

Sherds of table ceramics.

Index

ABOUT THE AUTHOR

Jeanne Farr McDonnell has attended Stephens College, Ohio State University, University of Brussels on a Fulbright Scholarship, Columbia University for an M.A. in American literature, an intensive journalism course at Stanford University over one semester, and many continuing studies classes at Stanford. She was born in Akron, Ohio, and lived in New York and Pennsylvania before settling in Palo Alto, California. After various jobs in the newspaper and publishing business, she entered the nonprofit sector, serving on the boards of nine organizations and acting as the executive director of three. As the founder and executive director of the Women's Heritage Museum, now the International Museum of Women in San Francisco, McDonnell first learned about Juana Briones, helped over several years to manage public and school tours of her house in Palo Alto, and worked to preserve that house.